The Culture of Giving in Myanmar

ALSO AVAILABLE FROM BLOOMSBURY

Buddhism, Education and Politics in Burma and Thailand,
Khammai Dhammasami
A Critique of Western Buddhism, Glenn Wallis
A Social History of the Ise Shrines, Mark Teeuwen and John Breen

The Culture of Giving in Myanmar

Buddhist Offerings, Reciprocity and Interdependence

Hiroko Kawanami

BLOOMSBURY ACADEMIC
LONDON • NEW YORK • OXFORD • NEW DELHI • SYDNEY

BLOOMSBURY ACADEMIC
Bloomsbury Publishing Plc
50 Bedford Square, London, WC1B 3DP, UK
1385 Broadway, New York, NY 10018, USA
29 Earlsfort Terrace, Dublin 2, Ireland

BLOOMSBURY, BLOOMSBURY ACADEMIC and the Diana logo are
trademarks of Bloomsbury Publishing Plc

First published in Great Britain 2020
This paperback edition published in 2021

Copyright © Hiroko Kawanami, 2020

Hiroko Kawanami has asserted her right under the Copyright, Designs and
Patents Act, 1988, to be identified as Author of this work.

For legal purposes the Acknowledgements on pp. ix–xi constitute an
extension of this copyright page.

All rights reserved. No part of this publication may be reproduced or
transmitted in any form or by any means, electronic or mechanical,
including photocopying, recording, or any information storage or retrieval
system, without prior permission in writing from the publishers.

Bloomsbury Publishing Plc does not have any control over, or responsibility for, any
third-party websites referred to or in this book. All internet addresses given in
this book were correct at the time of going to press. The author and publisher
regret any inconvenience caused if addresses have changed or sites have
ceased to exist, but can accept no responsibility for any such changes.

A catalogue record for this book is available from the British Library.

Library of Congress Control Number: 2020934704

ISBN: HB: 978-1-3501-2417-2
PB: 978-1-3502-6730-5
ePDF: 978-1-3501-2418-9
eBook: 978-1-3501-2419-6

Typeset by Integra Software Services Pvt. Ltd.

To find out more about our authors and books visit www.bloomsbury.com
and sign up for our newsletters.

To Hidemi Kawanami (1957–2019)

Contents

List of figures viii
Acknowledgements ix
Notes for transliteration xii

Introduction 1

1 The culture of giving 21

2 The laity 45

3 Buddhist monks 69

4 Buddhist nuns 95

5 Donor groups and social outreach 119

Towards a society of interdependence 145

Glossary 149
Notes 152
Bibliography 173
Index 180

Figures

All photos have been taken by the author.

1.1 On mother's day in January, children come together to pay respect, offer token gifts and express gratitude to the immense sacrifice she makes for the children 26

1.2 The ritual of *yezet-cha* (pouring water) points to the essence of life and its continuation into the next, confirming the meritorious deed done by the lay donors 42

2.1 *Shinbyu* is an initiation ceremony for boys from Buddhist families in Myanmar. They are taken around in a procession before becoming temporary novices in the village monastery 60

3.1 Many of the committed lay donors are women, who take a keen interest in offering food to the monks 74

3.2 The largest reclining Buddha in Myanmar in the outskirt of Monywa, which was constructed as a result of one monk's vision of the Buddha's spiritual power 78

3.3 Traditionally, Buddhists in Myanmar express their respect by taking off their sandals and prostrating themselves on the ground when welcoming a senior monk 82

4.1 Buddhist nuns offering *dāna* to a monk. They are enthusiastic supporters of the sangha, providing material support to and upholding the authority of monks 107

4.2 Nun-students pay ritual obeisance to their teacher. A close relationship with their teacher is what sustains the students throughout their monastic life 111

5.1 Twice a year, boats of the Malun Rice-offering Association arrive from Mandalay to offer rice bags to thousands of monks and nuns in Mingun, Minwun and Sagaing 128

Acknowledgements

This book is an outcome of my fascination with the Buddhist culture of giving (and receiving), and the attention and care Myanmar people pay one another despite so much hardship in their daily lives. Many things happen in fieldwork, both positive and negative, and sometimes there are chance meetings that take you to an unfamiliar field and difficult experiences, and at other times there are sudden openings that were unthinkable a few years ago. In fact, conducting research in an unpredictable and politically unstable country has taught me many things: about the importance of following the flow rather than imposing control and trusting my local friends and informants, who have helped me overcome many difficulties in the field. I have understood what impermanence means by observing the country over the decade and shared some experiences with Myanmar people who lived through major upheavals from Ne Win's last phase of socialism to student uprisings in the late 1980s to successive military regimes that followed in the 1990s to the opening up of Myanmar and her major political and economic transition. It has not been easy to live and conduct research in a sensitive and secretive environment, but what sustained me throughout the years is the continuous support given by the Myanmar people, family and friends, monastic members and local informants.

I have become acquainted with the Buddhist community in Myanmar and owe special thanks to the monastic members as well as lay Buddhists who have helped me in so many ways. I am especially indebted to the *thilashin* community and would like to acknowledge the names of many nun-teachers, who helped me in my earlier research, but are no longer with us: Daw Kulapati and Daw Sarawati (both of Thameikdaw Gyaung nunnery), Daw Ponnyami (Zeiyatheingi Gyaung), Daw Khinsana (Eimyo Gyaung), to name a few, and the renowned Kachin Buddhist nun, Daw Nyaneti (Myitkyina Thilashin Kyaung), a dear friend, who passed away in 2017.

On the other hand, monastic members I first knew as young male novices and teenage nuns have grown up to become established dhamma teachers and prominent Buddhist scholars. They have given me many kinds of help due to the depth of their knowledge in the scriptures and guided me through various phases of my enquiry. I am especially indebted to the respectable nun-teachers: Daw Zanaka Molini, Daw Kusalawati and Daw Pavanateri. Senior monks, in particular, have given me protection during the difficult times of political upheaval, and I am especially grateful to U Tiloka Insein Ywama Sayadaw, U Nandamala Pa-chok Sayadaw and U Nyanissara Sitagu Sayadaw for their continued guidance and support.

There are many more names I would like to mention since hundreds of lay Buddhists and their families have helped me conduct research over the past decades. I would like to express my heartfelt thanks to all of them as to mention a few would be unfair to the rest. Everyone I met in Myanmar, even strangers, have been generous with their time and information, and I have been invited to so many meals! I can say with certainty that without their support and kindness, I would have stopped working long time ago, ruled by fear and paralysed by anxiety. Much of the descriptions in this volume are based on my observations and many discussions that took place with monastic members and their lay donors who frequented the monastic community of Sagaing Hill. Daw Nang Myint Myint Lwin, Ma Myint Myint Thaung and Ko Shwe Lin from Mandalay have been my valuable friends who were always there to feed me and look after my wellbeing. I also have to mention Ko Win Tun who acted as my bodyguard and driver, and I apologize to his wife for taking up so much of his family time while he was helping me with research. I have visited many other families and friends and conducted interviews in several provincial towns mainly in Sagaing, Magwe and Mandalay Regions, and in local villages such as Nondwin where Manning Nash conducted fieldwork in the 1950s.

I have also learned a great deal from the previous generations of scholars in Burmese studies, who continued their research regardless in isolation and under the culture of fear. In the last few years, especially since Myanmar embarked on its democratic reforms, it feels almost like a new research field has opened with an influx of a new generation of scholars. It is a welcome sign to see many young and enthusiastic researchers coming from abroad as well as Myanmar scholars returning from self-imposed exile. As many new possibilities and avenues for research in Myanmar studies have opened, I hope more collaborations will take place with local Myanmar scholars for the next phase of Myanmar studies.

On the home front, I would like to express my thanks to the Department of Politics, Philosophy and Religion at Lancaster University for giving me the support over the years and allowing me to leave during my research leave to write up my manuscript. My PhD students have had to put up with (but with good faith) a supervisor who would disappear from time to time. The Institute of Global Ethnology and Anthropology at Minzu University of China in Beijing has been the most generous host, providing me the space and time to work on completing my manuscript in the spring of 2019. The National Library of Beijing was where I spent many days in its magnificent space for reading and writing, and I am grateful to Professor Haoqun Gong who has made this visit possible. On two occasions I gave a lecture on the theme of this book: *The Culture of Giving in Myanmar*. These were Séminaire 'Anthropologie comparée du bouddhisme' at the Centre Asie du Sud-Est in Paris organized by Dr Nicolas Sihlé and Dr Bénédicte Brac de la Perrière in March 2018, and an open lecture at the School of Social and Behavioral Sciences at Nanjing University organized by Professor Jianfang Chu in March 2019. I benefited enormously from both occasions from the lucid comments I received from students and staff, and enjoyed the lively discussions that followed. In addition, the anonymous reviewers who read this manuscript gave me useful comments and suggestions that have helped me pay attention to details and fine-tune the manuscript at the late stage of revision.

I would like to thank Lucy Carroll at Bloomsbury Academic who has given me the opportunity to publish this book and my language editor Daniel Maccanel whose editing skills have given the manuscript a little sparkle! I also have to mention my sister Motoko Kawanami and my niece Karuna for keeping my spirits up, and my husband U San Myint Aung who has been my rock. The book, however, is dedicated to my late brother Hidemi Kawanami who passed away soon after I completed the manuscript. May his spirit rest in peace!

Notes for transliteration

Burma was officially renamed 'Union of Myanmar' on 18 June 1989 by the State Law and Order Restoration Council (SLORC) and I have referred to the country and people as 'Myanmar' for most of my writing. However, following the convention used by historians, I refer to the country as 'Burma' especially when talking about the country before independence (1948) and more generally until the military takeover in 1962. In 1989, the government has changed the transcription of names of places, towns, rivers and ethnic groups to link them more closely to the pronunciation of Myanmar language, which I have followed in this book.

'Burma' during the British colonial times was designated into 'Lower Burma' and 'Upper Burma', and being accustomed to these terms of designation, I have struggled to find alternative terms to replace them. 'Upper Burma' where I conducted most of my fieldwork is composed of central and northern Burma, including Magway, Mandalay and Sagaing administrative regions, but the alternative term I used here, 'upper country' or 'upper regions in Myanmar', does not make clear whether the ethnic-controlled zones of Shan, Kachin or Chin states are included in the term or not. Thus to clarify, when I use the term, 'upper regions in Myanmar', it does not include the ethnically controlled zones in the north.

The way Myanmar language is transcribed can be quite inconsistent especially in the way people's names are transcribed, and scholars also are not always uniform in their transcription methods. The Myanmar government recommends the MLC Transcription System (MLCTS) for rendering Burmese into the Latin alphabet. However, this transcription system is based on the orthography of formal Burmese and not suited to transcribe colloquial Burmese, which has substantial difference in phonology from the formal language. In this book, I have used my teacher John Okell's method of conventional transcription with accented tones, following his book *A Guide to the Romanization of Burmese*. However, I have removed most tonal marks for simplicity's sake. For the Pali words, I have followed the romanized version of Pali terms in Theravada Buddhist texts rather than those of the Myanmar transcription, but have listed them both whenever necessary in the Glossary.

Introduction

From an Asian perspective, many people in the West appear to be unfamiliar with the subtleties of the social custom of gift-giving and its cultural benefits, with many seeing only its negative side of self-centred profiting. Giving to charity is widely seen as acceptable, but gifts are not generally used as a means of expanding one's network or lubricating social relations. Moreover, when it comes to receiving gifts, people can become reluctant or even suspicious, especially when givers are from outside their intimate circle of family and friends. Some may even presume that receiving gifts could result in future demands for favours, while others regard all gift transactions for the purpose of building relations as 'unethical'. This widespread reluctance to receive gifts in the West today may be a by-product of fierce competition and strong class divisions in capitalist societies, in which every person must continuously guard against his/her position being exploited, and thus is less capable of imagining – let alone fully participating in – building relationships of trust and mutual help that remain normative in more traditional societies.

Certainly, there can be a fine line between giving a gift in the expectation that some kind of favour from the recipient will follow, and a genuine gift offered out of kindness and simple good intention. But in many gift-giving societies, including Myanmar and Japan, there are implicit rules and social protocols that everyone is expected to follow if gift-giving is to operate as it should in society. In Japan, for example, social gifts are customarily and frequently given to business partners, doctors, solicitors, teachers and even matchmakers to express appreciation for their professional services.[1] Yet, such gift-giving is also a personal expression of gratitude, implying a social reciprocity that transcends what might otherwise be seen as impersonal transaction: part of the payment for a one-off professional service. It also assumes an ongoing social relationship sustained by many such reciprocal transactions of gratitude and goodwill. The 'gift' also reveals the deeper character of the giver (who is the customer/recipient of such services) by showing how he/she perceives the service-giver and gift-recipient as a person, rather than merely one who executes a professional role. The act of giving in these gift-giving societies can also be described as a kind of 'art', since the gift can impress as well as offend the recipient, and thus requires careful planning and consideration especially on the part of a giver.

As far as I am aware, little research has focused on the social and religious contexts in which gifts are given – that is, when, how and to whom – as opposed to the implications of what happens once the gift is given. In addition to social giving, offerings made in a religious context reveal another layer of gift-giving to add complexity to the practice. Religious gifts are normally placed in a different category from social gifts, as reflected by the separate term: 'donations', which is often applied to them, and those tend to be seen as 'purer' and more 'selfless' as far as the intention of the donor is concerned. However, this book aims to understand religious gifts not as altruistic as they may appear at first glance, and expand the scholarly discussion on gift-giving, based on an insight that both religious offerings and social gift-giving can form part of a single series of reciprocal transactions. Thus although it is often conceived of by scholars as a single and linear relationship, I will argue that religious transactions imply a continuum ranging from an ideal of the pure gift at one end to parasitic dependency at the other, and hope to identify the giver's motives in a continuing spectrum from the secular to the soteriological. In addition, a person's motives in offering religious donations and social gifts often converge, if the act of giving is performed in the spirit of wanting to 'do good'. Meanwhile, as religious donations in Myanmar today are increasingly offered in cash rather than in kind, it is worth asking whether this evolution is an effect, or indeed a cause, of fundamental changes in the nature of religious donations.

Buddhist monks and nuns who are full-time recipients have customarily played a pivotal role in Myanmar donors' acquisition of merit by receiving their gifts and donations. Although religious offerings also form part of a series of transactions that are ongoing in society, the most important role monastic members perform is to keep the wheel of generosity turning by receiving the people's goodwill. Having received as much as they need, monks and nuns normally give away surplus food or donated items to those lower down the monastic hierarchy, and in doing so transfer laypeople's original goodwill to people and places beyond the narrow contexts in which it was originally given. In this way, monastics' dual role as both recipients and re-distributors of accumulated wealth forms a bridge between the sangha and the laity, which is foundational to an interdependent Buddhist society.

Debates and issues surrounding 'the gift'

In the social sciences, reciprocity and gift-giving have formed an important area of debate since Mauss's celebrated book *The Gift* was translated into English in 1954.[2] Mauss understood that there is inevitably a degree of self-interest in the act of giving and shed considerable light not only on the nature of gift-exchange itself, but also on the social relations that were instigated by it – especially the giver's social leverage over the recipient. Mauss, however, was interested primarily in pre-capitalist societies, in which *prestation totale* took place: for example, in the case of *potlatch*, whereby an act of gift-exchange implied the total involvement of both the giver and the receiver. Subsequently, Mauss's work has been subjected to extensive criticism by Western scholars.[3] This book is, in part, a re-evaluation of his ideas and their usefulness in understanding the continuous transactions that take place in the particular context of Buddhist society in Myanmar.

As Mauss argued, the gift is never 'free'. This is not simply because the giver reaps a degree of influence over the recipient, but also because the latter takes on a 'moral burden' as a result of receiving the gift. In response, a strong urge to reciprocate is created (even if one is not able to reciprocate in material terms), as will be shown in the pages that follow, particularly in the case of Buddhist nuns in Chapter 4. Problematically, prior scholarly explorations of this topic have often conceived of a gift as a one-off and a one-to-one transaction.

And as we shall see in Chapter 5 and throughout the book, such a conception is, at best, a 'snapshot' of what goes on in social reality. Moreover, 'giving' or the act of offering in a Buddhist society is rarely conducted as an interaction between a single lay donor and a monastic recipient; it is usually conducted as a collective act by a married couple, a larger family and kin group, or at times a whole village – and sometimes, received by a whole monastic lineage or a Buddhist monastery rather than a lone monk or a nun. Thus, over-emphasizing individual transactions (or the individual components of all transactions) may be to fundamentally misconstrue the social contexts in which such relational dynamics take place, in a manner that may express Eurocentric bias towards the centrality of the individual as agent, and against the importance of the collective especially in a traditional Buddhist society.

One noteworthy exception to such bias is provided by anthropologist Michael Carrithers's research on Buddhist monks in Sri Lanka,[4] which sought to understand alms-giving as a form of gift-exchange by articulating the importance of 'personal relationships' between the sangha and its lay supporters, and shifting the focus of discussion from what is being offered to a single monk to the meritorious return for the particular donor. His work provided an important insight into the relational dynamics that form the crux of gift-giving transactions with the monastic community, which could be applied to the exploration of parallel activities taking place throughout society. However, that seemed to have gone against the grain of the anthropological consensus then. In the 1960s, for instance, Michael Ames claimed that 'non-reciprocity' was a prerequisite for the sacred, and that all reciprocal transactions are fundamentally 'profane';[5] and similarly, in the 1980s, Jonathan Parry stated that reciprocated gifts belong to the profane world, and unreciprocated ones to a 'quest for salvation from it'.[6] In Parry's view of 'ethicized religions, such as […] Theravada Buddhism',[7] once a gift is offered, it becomes alienated from the giver. He concluded that gifts made to a Buddhist monk should never be reciprocated, due to their ideal goal-orientation towards a future existence. A similar stance in favour of non-reciprocity has also been advocated by many Buddhist textual scholars.[8] Their viewpoint derives from the textual ideal of a holy monk, who is 'worthy' only due to his complete lack of interest in the religious offering (as distinct from denial or rejection). The anthropologist Joanna Cook,[9] drawing on prior work by Ian Strenski,[10] also stressed that a Buddhist monk should uphold a position of 'non-reciprocity', since personal relationships between monks and their lay donors were expressly de-emphasized by the Vinaya rules. However, she did not explore whether the monks' apparent lack of gratitude when receiving alms might be an outward public performance rather than an innate lack of compassion or of the will to reciprocate.

Here it is important to consider the contribution of Maurice Godelier, who enriched the discussion on the significance of gifts in social life by reassessing the works of Mauss and Levi-Strauss.[11] By focusing on sacred objects, Godelier critiqued both traditional and more recent gift-giving theories, arguing that they did not take into consideration the conferral of authoritative power associated with them when offered as gift. Seeking a 'precise' definition of the term 'gift', Alain Testart focused on the difference between two verbs, 'to give' and 'to make a gift',[12] highlighting the features of exchange implied in the verb 'to give' and recommending that it be replaced by other verbs such as 'to pay' or 'to transfer' to avoid misunderstandings. In his view, '"Giving" [...] is not making a gift; "to give" is not to make a donation'.[13] For Testart, a gift implied a gratuitous act, and 'giving' was always attended by some degree of moral obligation on the part of the recipient.[14] As such, the notion of 'reciprocity' was not to be confused with the fundamental features of the (religious) gift, and he suggested that the expression 'gift-exchange' was simply an oxymoron. Moreover, the relationship between a lay donor and his/her religious recipient, he explained, could never be described as 'reciprocal', due to its inherent inequality in their respective status.

A recent article by Nicolas Sihlé highlighted the need for a more culturally specific definition of reciprocity, especially in the context of Buddhist societies, on the grounds that this term is 'marked by substantial terminological vagueness with, for instance, recurring confusion between *reciprocity per se* and the expectation of *returns* (typically in terms of merit) for acts of giving'.[15] Meanwhile, Richard Gombrich alluded to 'merit' as a kind of 'spiritual currency', although it is intangible and cannot be saved or stored.[16] By the same token, a person cannot lose merit, nor can meritorious value become depleted in the way that money can, since if one conducts the wholesome deed of making an offering, it is assumed to result in the bettering of one's karmic position. Sihlé, exasperated by this discussion, indicated that it was not always clear whether the lay donor had received anything in return, given how difficult 'merit' as a concept was to quantify.[17] I address this point in Chapter 2, where I argue that, while neither tangible nor actually given in return for the religious offering made to the monastic recipient, 'merit' appears to operate subjectively: that is, as a sort of karmically uplifting reward that certainly does exist, even if only on the level of the lay donor's feelings. Therefore, the notion of 'reward' must be examined further here, if we are to be certain as to whether it can be something material or immaterial. Moreover, the value of exchanges is constantly changing, and the parties involved have to consider carefully what they will reciprocate with, to ensure that – in terms of both quantity and quality – the gift accords with the aim of a balanced exchange. Sihlé, following Testart, sought to clarify the terminologies of the 'gift' (religious) and 'patterns of transfers', describing them as more similar to an 'exchange' or 'reciprocal transaction'.[18] As part of this exploration, he asked an important question: 'To what extent can we speak of "reciprocity" in the face of actual Buddhist gifts?'[19]

Indeed, the combination of Buddhism and reciprocity in the term 'Buddhist reciprocity' may appear problematic, and especially strange to those scholars and others who perceive Buddhism as an 'other-worldly' religion in which a monastic who is a renouncer should not be expected to reciprocate. So, returning to Mauss, the main question posed by this book is whether religious offerings, especially in a Buddhist culture, can stay completely value-free and above social reciprocity.

Dān or *dāna*

Dāna, a Pali term pronounced as *dàna* in the Myanmar vernacular, normally refers to the religious practice of generous offering to members of the monastic community. *Dāna* or generosity is listed as the first *pāramī* or transcendental virtue and is regarded as an essential meritorious deed in both the Mahāyāna and Theravāda Buddhist traditions. However, most of the important anthropological discussions of gift-giving have been based on observation of

Indian Hindu society. In this respect, then, *dān* in Indian Hindu contexts and *dāna* in Southeast Asian Buddhist ones must be clearly distinguished from each other to avoid confusion.

Considering the absence of social stratification based on the caste system in Buddhist societies in Southeast Asia, it is problematic that the 'particular case' of Indian gift-giving was cited by Sihlé to discuss the relationship between a Buddhist monk and his lay donor.[20] Parry and Gloria Raheja, writing in the 1980s, both focused primarily on the 'unreciprocated' nature of the gift due to the fear of pollution transfer in Indian society. Parry, who worked with Brahman funerary priests in Benares, argued that an ideal *dān*, that is, a 'pure gift', should not result in social relations at all.[21] This tension was explained by Raheja as arising from an innate conflict between the role of a Brahman ascetic who aspired to renunciation and a social reality in which he had to accept *dān* despite regarding it as a 'poisonous' embodiment of the sin of the donor, capable of transferring that sin to him.[22] Nonetheless, in many parts of Hindu South Asia, the donor/recipient relationship is not as straightforward as is generally assumed, since *dān* could be offered 'not only to Brahmans, but also to Barbers, to Sweepers, to Doms and Dakauts, to anyone who happened to pass by a crossroads'.[23] Given the great heterogeneity of these recipient groups, their moral quality cannot be assumed to be uniformly high.[24] Having said that, Brahman priests remain the ideal models of religious recipients in Hindu India, and offering them *dān* is believed by local donors to be the most efficacious means of ensuring they receive future benefits in return.

The concepts of the 'non-reciprocated gift' and one-way flows of offerings may be meaningful in a society where social transactions are circumscribed by notions of purity vs. pollution and auspiciousness vs. inauspiciousness, and especially in one where religious ideology forms the basis of both social stratification and communal boundaries. In such a context, intra-caste transactions may be perceived as potentially threatening, as they can violate taboos and transfer pollution in either direction. In a Buddhist society such as Myanmar's, however, people have few if any such sensitivities around pollution or sin, not to the degree of those in Indian society. The Buddhist textual scholar Maria Heim, for instance, found no evidence of belief in poisonous transference by gifts either in contemporary anthropological or in premodern textual accounts of Buddhism, implying a clear distinction between Buddhist *dāna* and Hindu *dān*.[25] There is also no expectation on the part of Buddhist donors in Myanmar that monastic recipients will fulfil the function of consuming and digesting the former's pollution or sin. On the contrary, a Buddhist monk is a medium through whom a religious offering has its initially neutral symbolic value transformed into the positive one described as 'merit'. In addition, social stratification and notions of boundary transgression are weak in Southeast Asia, whose societies are fairly egalitarian and meritocratic compared to those of South Asia. Therefore, the social context in which gift-giving takes place should be accorded primary importance in any scholarly discussion of either its symbolic connotations or societal ramifications.

While the flow of gifts in Indian Hindu contexts is conceived of as a linear, unidirectional flow from lay devotees to Brahmin priests, in a Buddhist society such as Myanmar, it tends to be more circular, and facilitated by a multitude of reciprocal transactions; relationships are conducted in the expectation that a continuous flow of items will be given, received and passed around. *Dāna* also has to be understood as a pattern of transactions that have evolved between a monastery and its lay donors over a sometimes very lengthy period of time, and not simply a one-time, person-to-person transaction. For instance, in the case of alms collecting and giving, it comprises socio-religious transactions that a monastery has sustained with the local population for generations, creating a kind of mutual support system in the community. Therefore, in contrast to the 'Indian gift', which flows in a one-way linear direction, gift transactions in Myanmar encourage social reciprocity rather than their avoidance.

Nonetheless, there remains a wide gap between the practice and understanding of *dāna* that we can observe in a living Buddhist society, and the interpretation of it by scholars who draw on Buddhist texts or on other works from the context of ancient Indian Buddhism. Some scholars continue to reiterate that *dāna* should not be reciprocated due to the 'inherent dangers' of accepting it,[26] and should be a one-way offering if the lay donor is to reap any meritorious outcome.[27] Even Cook's fieldwork in Thailand led her to suggest that *dāna* accrues merit 'only if it is not reciprocated'.[28] I have argued elsewhere that *dāna* in actual religious transactions has to be understood not as 'soteriology, but sociology'.[29] Incidentally, it is normative for Buddhist monks (and nuns) to express their gratitude and to publicly recognize gifts offered to them by reciting blessing chants or by making public proclamation of the donors' meritorious acts in gratitude. In Tibetan Buddhism, one can observe ceremonial offerings of white scarves in which the recipient lamas reciprocate by placing them over the donors' heads by way of blessing them and showing their deep appreciation. Such examples highlight the fact that although many perpetuate a 'should-be' model, wherein the religious practitioners ought not to reciprocate, the observation of actual societal practices suggests otherwise.

Social dynamics of religious transactions

Scholars following the binary juxtaposition theory of Claude Levi-Strauss, and those who have worked in Buddhist societies – notably Spiro, Tambiah, Bunnag and Terwiel among many others – have tended to pair up the monk recipient and his lay donor to emphasize the system of structural complementarity. More specifically, many have depicted the act of *dāna* as a symmetrical interaction between a monk and his lay donor, linked by a system of ritual exchange, and the latter's objective as being to gain both religious merit and social status.[30] Usually, in their analyses, the two members of such a pair are positionally juxtaposed as if they are interlocked in a dichotomous recipient-donor relationship: with the lay donor expected to offer *dāna* to the morally superior monk, who reciprocates by offering ritual service and conferring merit. This relationship is also presented as an idealized model of transactions in the *Visuddhimagga* between the sangha and the laity, with the former positioned as a 'field of merit' into which lay donors 'plant' their goodwill offering and later 'reap' improved karmic states.[31] For this complementary system of worship to work, however, according to Tambiah, it requires 'an unblemished sangha and virtuous monks [...] and the distinction between monk and layman [... to be] preserved'.[32]

This idealized prototype does not leave much room for the reality of people's motives or social actions. It also places the monk on a superior moral pedestal, as if he were a living deity of some sort. In actuality, the sorts of relationships that monastic members maintain with their lay donors vary considerably, and the transactions among them are much more dynamic than such a model would seem to allow. As Sihlé recently pointed out, the nature of the religious recipient – whether a Brahman priest or a Buddhist monk – has thus been far insufficiently considered and poorly articulated by scholars.[33] In particular, he pointed out that not all monastics were free from the pressure to reciprocate and that Buddhist nuns in particular came under tremendous moral pressure to give some kind of 'return gift' to their donors. As such, these relationships would appear to be much more fluid and complex than the simple image of lay-monastic complementarity tends to suggest, and they stand in need of closer examination of the type that this book will provide.

The ideal model also says nothing about the relative socio-economic positions of its two complementary parties. In fact, far from enjoying uniformly superior positions, monastic recipients are often in a vulnerable state. Moreover, whether a Brahman priest or a Buddhist monk, religious recipients are obligated to receive whatever is given and from whoever is willing, and hence, the potentially dire consequences of accepting inappropriate offerings also need to be considered from the standpoint of monastic recipients. There are anecdotal stories of Buddhist monks being poisoned or otherwise harmed by alms food they had accepted from donors who had malicious intent. Beyond such physical dangers, religious recipients can also be threatened by negative human emotions – hatred, envy and jealousy – which can result in powerful curses against them, often without their prior knowledge.

The nature of transactions between the Buddhist monastic community and its lay supporters can also vary markedly over time, and it is thus useful to examine them longitudinally, as I have explained in an earlier monograph.[34] As briefly noted above, these transactions can range from a 'genuine gift' with no expectation of any material return at one end of the spectrum to, at the other, a 'parasitic unilateral dependency' exemplified by begging or even theft.[35] In between these opposing extremes are many kinds of 'balanced reciprocities' in which social conventions 'stipulate returns of commensurate worth or utility within a finite and a narrow period'.[36] In practice, a variety of relationships are observed between lay benefactors and monastic beneficiaries in Myanmar: including balanced ones in the relatively traditional settings of provincial towns or rural villages, where both parties know each other and value each other's roles, and more impersonal transactions in large cities such as Yangon, where they are gradually being drained of essential 'religious' meaning. The actual transactions we observe also reveal various degrees of commitment and patterns of lay-monastic engagement. A typical *dāna* offering to the monastic community, whereby a lay donor expects a 'karmically uplifting return', would represent the middle of the spectrum.[37] Nonetheless, as Chapter 3 will explain, some beneficiaries such as charismatic monks can control the flow of *dāna* offerings towards themselves, and even create a reverse flow of gifts that redistributes them downwards within the monastic hierarchy as well as outwards to the circles of lay supporters.

Therefore, reciprocal transactions with the monastic community should also be understood as an almost-tidal phenomenon of incomings and outgoings. And we can readily observe circular patterns, in which each transaction is linked in a long winding chain of one-to-one relationships. Some of these relationships have lasted for a long time, handed down from parents to children; some are more stable than others, and some lay donors have more power over their monastic recipients than others do. Many religious transactions in the past seem to be remembered in the locality and are reciprocated in the present to strengthen close alliances between the monastic community and its long-term regular donors. Donors will be shown to engage in various exchange patterns and relationships, at times competing with one another in regard to the quality of their offerings, especially to gain the attention of important *dhamma* teachers or charismatic monks, and at other times cooperating with other donors to raise funds for a large project led by an influential abbot; and these transactions and the resultant relationships can result in increased social prestige and feelings of self-worth on their part.

The politics of Buddhist reciprocity

Studies of religious offering and *dāna* activities in the fields of Buddhist studies and anthropology have not hitherto attempted to understand its actors, either lay or monastic, from a broad societal viewpoint that takes account of their subjectivity or the details of their transactions. Even macro-perspectives on

Buddhist culture have tended to adopt structuralist viewpoints that arguably over-emphasize oppositional power relationships in society. Specifically, such scholarship has portrayed the sangha as a religious institution in a complementary relation to the power of the state, in which the former is the recipient of state patronage, and the latter the protector of faith. Peter Jackson has updated this model somewhat, by showing how, at least in urban centres in Thailand, the sangha functioned through the twentieth century not just in this symbiotic way, but was itself a primary site of contention between different factions of the elite, each of which was striving to shape Thai society in a particular direction.[38] Ann Blackburn, meanwhile, has cogently argued that the symbiosis model of the state and the sangha does not give due consideration to monastic agency, as in reality monks seldom simply do what is expected of them, either by the sangha or by their countries' civil authorities. In fact, as Blackburn showed, the ways in which monks assert their agency – in relation to both 'traditional' and 'modernizing' norms – are intensely complex.[39]

This book utilizes a ground-up empirical approach to examine the positions of both laity and monastics in Myanmar through their religious offering activities, and to investigate how social influence, which can be generated at the local level, sometimes comes into conflict with political power. In Chapter 3, I touch on the recent outburst of monastic agency in Myanmar whereby Buddhist monks led a nationalist movement to promote and protect its tradition in the face of a perceived Muslim threat to Buddhism. In such a time of crisis, whether real or imagined, monks seldom idly conform to their traditional religious roles expected of them by the state, and instead assert an autonomous position with regards to the presumed future trajectory of the Buddha *sāsana* and the country. Over the years, many prominent monks have asserted their distinctive leadership by presenting visions of the country's future that has a wide appeal to their lay followers. As we will see in Chapter 5, their activities are no longer confined to the other-worldly, as they take interest in issues that concern the 'common good'. The *dāna* offerings by lay Buddhists are also shown to have social implications beyond one-dimensional giver–receiver transactions, and this book will describe how the religious and social offerings are interdependent as a single series of reciprocal transactions. Besides, some groups of donors that have regularly engaged in collective merit-making activities have generated wider social dynamics, inciting various types of political movements as a result.[40] And as a general matter, when people appreciate and act on, and through the reciprocal relationships arising from their offering activities, the social ramifications of their original donation activity appear to be much more profound than would otherwise be the case, often over-spilling its original 'religious' categorization. As a consequence, however, the reciprocal relations mentioned here can have two different trajectories: for an ongoing stability and order within the monastic hierarchy, if people conform to the traditional flow of *dāna* towards monastic recipients; or a wider movement for social change if led by a dynamic charismatic monk. As Myanmar's modern history has shown us, a monk of the latter type can become a kind of centripetal force, inculcating his lay devotees with both the desire and ability to instigate a movement for social change.

Social psychologists such as Daniel Batson have argued that people are generally pleased to have the opportunities to be truly altruistic,[41] and thus there are lay donors who clearly expect nothing in return, apart from the joy and fulfilment they reap from the act of offering itself. This conception of altruism no doubt makes sense in the context of monotheistic religions for which 'charity is its own reward, in the sense that the donor has the intention of saving his soul; God rewards alms-giving [and] Allah rewards zakat. No human hand need make a return'.[42] And perhaps we have to accept that 'altruism remains a central feature of our beliefs about religious giving, even if our actions suggest otherwise'.[43] Indeed, the practice of offering *dāna* simply as a means to express one's genuine wish to contribute to some monk's wellbeing cannot be denied. Nonetheless, I remain doubtful whether a 'pure gift' can truly exist in a religious tradition such as Buddhism, where there is no God to reward him/her or even to acknowledge the goodness of the gift-giving act of the donor, but only society in a Durkheimian sense.

Challenging normative ideas of Buddhist giving

As part of this book's re-examination of the notion of 'giving' using the case of contemporary Buddhist society in Myanmar, it will explore the many 'personal' and 'non-personal' relationships that exist between the monastic community and lay donors, and examine religious practices that accrue merit to the donors during rituals and ceremonies. *Dāna* can be offered as a personal gift or a collective one, but as we will see, most religious offerings in Myanmar society are performed as collective acts, by some groupings who rejoice in the belief that this will help bring them together again in the next life. At times, a child or a parent may take a vow or abstain from certain practices or even become a monastic for a certain number of days, in the hope that this will speed the recovery of a family member's health. Such acts are believed to generate merit that can be transferred to the ill person one is concerned about, despite the vow having been made by another. Some may argue that such joint practices go against the principle of karma whereby only the individual can take responsibility for whatever he or she has done or will do.

This brings us to the randomness of religious offering and of the meritorious consequences that one expects, not instantly, but in the near or distant future. Transaction models, as mere snapshots of what takes place between a donor and a monastic recipient, are inherently incapable of capturing this whole story. In fact, as this book will illustrate, most religious transactions in Myanmar are relatively minor expressions of long-term relationships in which many other reciprocal transactions also take place or have taken place already. Some such relationships may start off randomly, as a result of impulses or chance meetings, and persist despite the original donor's lack of knowledge of their eventual outcomes, including worldly aspects such as the young monastics' eventual level of academic success or fame. Of course, a donor's safest bet to reap merit would be on a bright monk affiliated with a reputable monastery, but even the most prestigious monastery connections cannot by themselves guarantee that a given monk will not drop out and eventually 'make it' as a Buddhist scholar. Investing in a long-term donor relationship with a nun, meanwhile, can be a complete gamble, since in the absence of an officially sanctioned ordained status, her spiritual qualities are anyone's guess. Thus, lay donors frequently enter regular relationships with monastic beneficiaries without any expectation of a meritorious return. Nevertheless, the joy of seeing someone develop and grow may also be counted as part of what they receive in return for the countless *dāna* offerings Myanmar Buddhists continue to make regardless.

Gendered perspectives on giving

My discussion of gift-giving and religious transactions also examines whether Buddhist women in Myanmar are generally more inclined towards playing an offering role as opposed to a receiving role. Morny Joy has edited two volumes focusing on women's involvement in gift-giving and reflected on the gender issues that have been overlooked in sociological discussions of gift transactions.[44] As Joy points out, women were rarely mentioned in Mauss's writings on the *gift*, while Levi-Strauss – who was Mauss's student – described how women themselves were exchanged as commodities/gifts in matrimonial settlements between tribes, irrespective of their own wishes.[45] In terms of *dāna* in Buddhist societies, women are definitely more prominent as lay donors and are actively engaged in their roles as givers of offerings to the monastic community. However, their giving tends to be directed towards male recipients, gurus or monks, who are the more socially acceptable recipients of their gifts. Laure Carbonnel, who looked at the gender-specificity of these roles in Myanmar Buddhism, described how women fed and nurtured the male monks, as part of a gender system that assigned Buddhist nuns and female donors to the same category as 'nurturing women'.[46] In fact, one often observes enthusiastic female followers hanging around prominent young monks, in a similar manner to the 'groupies' of male celebrities. Men, in contrast, tend to take the back seat to their wives, sisters and so forth, who act as families' principal donors – except when the thing being offered is 'service' as monks' personal attendants. This is despite the fact that men in Myanmar often assume the formal role of primary gift-giver on behalf of a family or a group unit in public occasions, such as in politics; and male householders commonly serve as the main donor who ceremoniously offers *dāna* to the sangha on special occasions. However, the regular act of offering alms and the daily care of monastic beneficiaries usually falls to their wives and kinswomen.

Buddhist nuns, just like monks, are entirely dependent on the generosity of their lay donors for daily sustenance. They, too, live by collecting weekly alms in the form of raw grains of rice and take part in many religious functions alongside the monks. And yet nuns do not fit into the neat, symmetrical juxtaposition between a monk beneficiary and his lay benefactors that scholars usually envisage, for precept nuns in particular come under a social obligation to reciprocate, as a result of their incomplete renunciant position. Moreover, they struggle to find regular donors who are committed enough to support them over the long term. That is, being on the threshold between this-worldly and other-worldly realms, Buddhist nuns are basically an anomaly who can present a threat – in an ideological sense – to the religious authority of monks.[47] In spite of or because of this, however, nuns are also frontline devotees who protect the sanctity of monks by performing many roles generally perceived as secular, such as cash handling and budgeting for ceremonies on their behalf. In practice, then, nuns in Myanmar exhibit an interesting mixture of secular and religious characteristics, not least when transacting with their lay donors. They are also renowned for their blessing chants whenever they receive *dāna*, and the focus of every transaction they engage in is the conferral of *mettā* (loving kindness) upon the lay donors, and therefore, the nuns perform an indispensable role as generators of generosity, securing a flow of offerings and goodwill between the sangha and society.

Fieldwork and research methodology

As far as research methodology is concerned, my early training was in the Department of Anthropology at London School of Economics and Political Science, where I studied as a postgraduate student. The department continues to uphold the legacy of Bronislaw Malinowski (1884–1942), who taught many notable anthropologists there and influenced those conducting empirical fieldwork. I have learned from his method of 'becoming native' by immersing myself in the field and conducting participant observation as well as learning the vernacular language. Nonetheless, the struggle I encountered during my first fieldwork in Myanmar (1986–1987) is described in my earlier monograph.[48] The difficulties included accessing information about a 'remote' isolated country to start with, overcoming red tapes and bureaucracy under the military regime as well as the general anxiety that came with stepping into an unknown territory. To add to the list, I became a Buddhist nun and was confined to a monastic lifestyle of observing Eight Precepts during my first fieldwork. Obviously, there was no internet or smartphones in the 1980s, which could have alleviated my sense of isolation, and the only means of communication with my supervisor was through writing letters. As a matter of habit, however, I have continued to write down my observations and everyday queries in my journal ever since, and this book has been written based on the re-readings of them and recent reflections over the past decades in the face of Myanmar's political reforms and a transition to a new era that started in 2012.

I have continued to visit the country almost every year, except for the three-year interval between 1989 and 1991. The way I interacted with or the way my informants treated me also changed over the decades according to my status change from a non-descript student not speaking the language to a full-time scholar with a command of the vernacular; from a Buddhist nun to a lay donor; from a single woman to a married woman, and so on, and accordingly different kinds of information were collected due to the changes in my standpoint. The major change in the relationship took place when I decided to buy a plot of land and donated it to one of the senior nuns who not only helped me during my initial fieldwork, but also saved my life when I had several bouts of dengue fever. My relationship with the country also changed when I married a local man and that affiliated me with his kin base and local networks, and as a result, I had unwittingly become an insider.

There are many books written about qualitative research methods and data collection, telling us how to formulate research design, find informants and conduct practice-based open-ended research.[49] There is also practical advice given to novice researchers as to how to prepare interview questions and conduct interviews; structured, semi-structured or in focus groups.[50] In my case, however, much of the meaningful information collected (in the vernacular language) came from open-ended conversations about any topic (however trivial) that interested me and I also encouraged my informants to take part in discussions as well as query my research project. Sometimes a casual conversation in a group situation developed into a lively argument into which everyone wanted to voice their opinions. I often probed local friends whenever I encountered an interesting ritual or a social transaction, which I wanted to know more about why people behaved in a certain way. However, much of the basis for an anthropological enquiry derives from being perceptive in observation and careful in listening, and even a small observation at times can open up a new channel of enquiry.

One of the important benefits I reaped from my earlier experience as a Buddhist nun was the relationships I had established with many Buddhist families, who previously were my lay donors and supporters. The relationships I maintained with them had snowballed over the years into hundreds of contacts and a network of informants spanning over three generations. I have been visiting them ever since in many provincial towns and rural villages mostly in the upper region of the country. As nuns like monks stand in a pivotal position in society, I was able to, also in my former position as a nun, get to know many groups of people and conduct research, without coming under the influence of any one family, or confined to one group of people. Generally speaking, it is difficult to maintain such a position of non-affiliation, especially as a foreign visitor who attracts a lot of attention. On the other hand, I could keep myself affiliated with the nuns' main scholarly lineage through my earlier affiliation with a prominent nunnery and also through my involvement with the activities of the nunnery school I founded in 1998. It is important for a researcher, who is basically an outsider, to consider how to affiliate oneself with a unit or a group and become a participant observer during fieldwork. In my case, I have become an insider due to my long-term association with my many informants, and yet managed to retain a position of non-affiliation as an outsider, ironically by way of affiliating myself with the nun's monastic community.

Organization of chapters

This introduction has provided an overview of anthropological theories regarding the gift and reciprocity in general, and Buddhist *dāna* offerings in particular. It also offers a critique of the prevailing one-dimensional view of such socio-religious transactions, which ignores the circular movements of donation offerings that so often occur in practice. Chapter 1 looks at the broad social context of Myanmar, a country where more than 80 per cent of the population is affiliated with the conservative tradition of Theravada Buddhism and explores why Myanmar has topped a global generosity list for the past four years. The primary value of generosity and how people live interdependently are among its main themes. Chapter 2 focuses on the Buddhist laity, and discusses their *dāna* offering activities in the context of the donor's karmic position and the resultant meritorious outcomes. It also examines the soteriological and ethical motives for laypeople's engagement with the monastic community and interrogates the difference between religious offering and social giving. Chapter 3 examines the fundamental workings of the Buddhist monastic community in Myanmar, and the factors that allow monks to assert wide social and political influence there. It also describes the extensive network of Buddhist monks and their lay supporters that extends into even the remotest villages in the country. Chapter 4 investigates the socio-religious position of Myanmar's Buddhist nuns, both as donors to the monastic community and as recipients of *dāna* offerings, focusing on their crucial bridging role between the sangha and laity. It also highlights the complexities of the role of monastic recipient especially being filled by female monastics and by those who are not fully ordained. Chapters 3 and 4 equally emphasize the regularity, high frequency and reciprocity of transactions between the monastic community and its lay donors; and argue against the widespread assumption that monastic members are always the recipients in such relationships. Especially in the cumulative process whereby particular monks acquire high levels of societal influence, the flow of goods and resources is centripetal as well as centrifugal, with the monk occupying a key commanding position in the operation.

Myanmar today is undergoing a radical phase of political reform, alongside constant readjustment to the influx of global information, advancement in communication technology (not least through social media) and rising materialism. It has always been a generous society influenced by Buddhist teachings, but the patterns of religious as well as social transactions are changing quickly in this new social and political milieu. My final chapter therefore focuses on the social and political roles of the many donor groups formed by school friends, neighbourhood associations and any sort of like-minded lay enthusiasts, both historically and currently, sharing the same interests and acting upon them. Some are newly formed women's groups, or have emerged from teachers' associations, and achieve their religious aims by pooling their resources and travelling together to donate to monasteries and nunneries of their choice; and some, indeed, become influential religious cliques in support of the monastic community. Last, the chapter examines how the arrival of foreign humanitarian aid and organizations since 2008 has affected socio-religious transactions involving Myanmar's Buddhist monastic community. It was during the Cyclone Nargis relief operations that Buddhist monks found that they could perform important intermediary roles, not only acting as monastic beneficiaries when it came to the receipt of large sums of donations, but also acting as monastic benefactors to the families of victims and playing active roles in transporting and distributing aid supplies. Because of their disciplined conduct, monastics came to be seen, during this episode, as moral and selfless leaders who could play beneficial roles in all kinds of social welfare activities. As a result, over the ensuing decade, social donations and religious offerings have begun to converge conceptually in Myanmar society, with donors gradually coming to see both types of giving as equally meritorious. Meanwhile, given that the country's 'third sector' remains both underdeveloped and over-regulated, the chapter poses a broader question of whether the monastic community could play a more active, albeit still a non-political role, in Myanmar's emergent 'civil society'.

1

The culture of giving

To clearly understand the nature of religious transactions and social reciprocity, it is first necessary to examine the specific local contexts in which people interact with one another and form relationships in their everyday lives. Accordingly, this chapter focuses on Myanmar society – a majority Buddhist country, where more than 80 per cent of the population, since the eleventh century, have been affiliated with the more conservative tradition of Theravada Buddhism. The country has undergone a major transition since opening its doors to the outside world and embarking on democratic reforms and economic development since 2012. Myanmar has also topped a global generosity list for the past few years, despite having at one time been listed by the World Bank as one of the poorest countries in the world in GNP terms, and more than 90 per cent of the population is now reported to engage in 'giving activities', offering donations to charity and to a large extent to the Buddhist monastic community.[1] Generally speaking, the country's people are known to be exceedingly hospitable and generous even towards strangers, and as an indication of this there are earthenware water jars placed at almost every street corners offered to quench the thirst of anyone who passes by. As John Holt recently observed, even a simple act of offering a glass of water to a visitor 'reflects the ubiquity of merit-making acts generated by the generosity that permeates social life in Myanmar'.[2] Or, as one European traveller commented to me, 'You can never outdo a Myanmar person with generosity. They never stop giving'. Both these observations resonated strongly with my own experience living in Myanmar for several years. I have learned even to be careful about uttering the vernacular expression *chai-de* ('I like it') to my local Myanmar friends, because the moment one shows any fondness for, say, an item of food or clothing, the next moment it is to my horror that my host has bought it for me.

While one cringes with embarrassment at being showered with gifts and hospitality by friends and strangers alike, such experience is eventually accompanied by the realization that their behaviour reflects a fundamental moral value in Myanmar people's cultural upbringing. In fact, it amounts to a defining social feature of how they relate to one another in their own society. By the same token, the discomfort we outsiders experience in Myanmar is likely to derive from our own upbringing and what we take for granted in our social relations in comparison, which in many cases emphasizes independence over dependence (interdependence) and the individual over the collective. Hence, being unaccustomed to receiving the levels and types of hospitality and care that Myanmar people commonly bestow upon one another, we may experience them as burdensome impositions, particularly due to a lack of sufficient cultural knowledge of how and when to reciprocate their generosity. At worst, one may even conclude that friendship in Myanmar is untenable, since the kindness and care shown by its people are too extreme to ever be reciprocated. Buddhist monks and nuns are of course enmeshed in this same generous social milieu; and being constantly on the receiving end of people's generous offerings, simply due to their monastic status, they can reasonably be expected to experience the cultural magnification of this vocational recipient position with some considerable social and perhaps moral discomfort.

Interdependent culture and rituals of gratitude

As noted in the Introduction, academic discussions of religious offerings have normally focused on one-dimensional transactions between a monk and his lay donor, rooted in an assumption of a one-way flow of goods and services from the laity to the monastic community. Hardly any research has extended the observation of this primary relationship into an understanding of wider Buddhist cultures, let alone of how deeply reciprocal transactions of giving and receiving – often, but not necessarily involving monastics – are implicated in the Buddhist faith. As far as religious offering is concerned, *dāna* in Myanmar presents itself in layers of multiple 'giving' and 'receiving', more akin to a circular movement of goods motivated by goodwill, passed on continuously in the moral sphere of merit to the next recipient who is expected to make good use of the received gift.[3] Despite some scholarly assumptions, monastic members also return the gratitude to their lay supporters in many different ways, and Buddhist nuns especially are expressive by way of conferring *mettā* (loving kindness) to them in blessing chants. On special occasions such as on their birthdays, senior monks and nuns invite their lay donors to large feasts and give out presents to express their gratitude. In the moral hierarchy of Myanmar culture, students show gratitude to their teachers by offering them token gifts in reciprocation for their tutelage and guidance, and filial piety of children towards their parents is also expressed in their common protocols of showing respect. Such frequent transactions of mutual care are not expressed in a unidirectional flow or as a one-time show, but reciprocal transactions are constant in their social and religious life, which build on and further cement their concern and affection for one another.

Hence, the Buddhist tradition in Myanmar is marked by the close relationship laypeople enjoy with the monastic community, affiliating themselves with the running of village monasteries and offering daily alms to them as well as listening to monks' sermons. Religious activities that are regarded to generate meritorious returns are understood to be in the key practices of *dāna* (offering donations), observing *sīla* (morality) and *bhāvanā* (meditation). The list of Ten Good Deeds is not only canonical, but it is also widely influential in Buddhist societies. In the Myanmar vernacular, the listed deeds are called 'Ten Bases of merit': *ponnya kariya withu se-ba*, or *dasa puñña kiriya vatthu* in Pali.[4] Rita Langer notes that these ten activities are a popular sermon topic in Sri Lanka, and often cited by monks to encourage the lay congregation to conduct meritorious deeds. In Myanmar, however, only the first three activities out of the ten feature commonly in Buddhist sermons.[5] To add some more details here, *ponnya kariya withu se-ba* include: *dāna*, *sīla*, *bhāvanā*, *apaciti* (showing reverence), *veyyāvacca* (conducting personal or social services), *pattānuppadāna* (transferring one's merit to others), *abbhānumodanā* (rejoicing in the merit gained by others), *dhamma savana* (listening to sermons), *dhamma desanā* (preaching and disseminating the *dhamma*) and *ditthuju kamma* (having faith in the power of Triple Gem: the Buddha, the Dhamma and the Sangha). Having faith and believing in the Buddha's words are commonly referred to as *thada tayà* in the vernacular. These deeds show that merit-making is not just an individual act, but merit can be transferred to others as well, and everyone shares in the joyous occasion of accumulating merit.[6] *Apasahyana*, which implies upholding a respectful attitude towards authoritative figures in the Buddhist tradition, is also counted as one of the meritorious deeds. Thus, serving the monks justifies people's active engagement with the monastic community and instils in devotees a deep sense of fulfilment in offering support to the sangha, also referred to as *thathana lokngan* or *sāsana* work.

Hence Buddhist monks are essential in people's daily worship; in return they conduct ritual for the community, offer moral advice and regular admonition. Nonetheless, the relations with the monastic community must be considered within their social and political contexts to understand their wider implications on society, since in Myanmar's culture, as noted above, offering donations is not just a soteriological exercise in making merit for the betterment of one's rebirth. Indeed, Buddhist cultures commonly hold that a giving disposition is one of the most important moral and social values, derived from a deep sense of wanting to help others in a spirit of compassion and interdependence.

Seasonal transactions and moral hierarchy

There are certain times of the year when lay Buddhists in Myanmar offer *dāna* and transact actively with the monastic community. These are *Thingyan* (Myanmar New Year and water festival) in mid-April; *thadingyut* (the light festival) in October, at the end of *wadwin* (the three months of rains retreat); and the robe-offering season of *kathina* during October and November. In contrast to the solemn three months of *wadwin* that coincide with the monsoon season, *thadingyut* starts the cycle of festivities associated with the cool dry season. The full-moon day in October is celebrated with candles, colourful lights and firecrackers to welcome the Buddha back from heaven where, according to the folk legend, he has been there to preach to his mother during rain retreats.[7] As at the Myanmar New Year, people customarily visit monasteries, and conduct *kadaw* and pay obeisance to their parents, elderly community members as well as to teachers to express gratitude for their supervision and care. *Thingyan* is also a time for Myanmar people to reflect, repent and perform additional meritorious deeds: for example, visiting old people's homes to offer special services, washing their hair and helping them to bathe and displaying respect for their ripe old age. It is also deemed an appropriate occasion for Buddhists to release captured birds into the wild and fish into rivers, as a kind of symbolic means of releasing themselves from past sins and starting the year anew. These ritual exchanges are believed to be good omens for the community, since they highlight the importance of its senior members nurturing the junior members, as well as the latter's acceptance – with gratitude – of their junior place in the moral hierarchy, which also confirms their interdependent existence.

Other types of moral transactions

In the recent years, I have witnessed the popularization of a special Buddhist ceremony aimed at showing respect to the mothers on *ameimya nei* (mother's day), which usually takes place in early or mid-January according to the lunar calendar. The focus is on recognizing the sacrifice mothers make for their children and it allows children to pay respect to them in a special ceremony. Such appreciation for motherhood contrasts sharply with her ambiguous treatment in the Buddhist literature since motherhood in Buddhism is viewed as secular rather than sacred, associated with reproduction, familial responsibilities and attachment.[8] As represented by a pregnant woman trapped in the Wheel of Life,[9] the mother is metaphorically seen to be eternally caught up in the cycle of *saṃsāra*. That is, she symbolizes the continuity of life and rebirth in one of the realms of existence, but she suffers even more because she cannot free herself from the deep love and attachment she has for her children and family.

Having said that, children in Myanmar pay respect to their parents, as they customarily do at the New Year in April, but their act of deference is normally directed towards the father, the figurehead of the household. And there has been no special occasion, until recently, that is, on which special respect is paid to the mother. Now, however, children on *ameimya nei* come together to offer their mother token gifts, while prostrating themselves in front of her to formally express their gratitude to the immense sacrifice she has made for them. Interestingly, the impetus to shine a spotlight on motherhood has come from Buddhist nuns, who – though they are celibate themselves – began performing this ritual in Buddhist nunneries to show their gratitude to their own mothers and soliciting their lay supporters as well to join in their show of appreciation. In recent years, this ritual to celebrate motherhood has spread, but still conducted in the confines of Buddhist nunneries.

Another important ceremony that has become widely popular in the last decade is *asariya puzaw pwe*, translated as a 'ceremony to pay respect to teachers', organized by alumni and students who invite their former teachers back to their old schools, or sometimes visit them at home if they are ill or too elderly. This ceremony is also called *saya kadaw pwe*, the same name given to the ritual of paying respect to teachers and mentors traditionally conducted during

Figure 1.1 *On mother's day in January, children come together to pay respect, offer token gifts and express gratitude to the immense sacrifice she makes for the children.*

thadingyut in October. In recent years, however, the ceremony honouring former teachers, becoming separated from the traditional celebration, has come to serve an additional function of supporting retired teachers by offering them cash gifts, collected by alumni who come together to supplement the state's meagre old-age pension for teachers.[10] These transactions are the result of long-term reciprocity based on the students' remembrance of the care bestowed on them as students in their earlier lives and they return the kindness of their teachers, albeit after many decades in their old age.

Another factor that adds to its social significance is that the majority of school teachers in Myanmar are unmarried single women who devote their whole life to teaching and guiding students, but in old age they often find themselves without any immediate family member to support or care for them. Especially in recent years, some alumni with the support of social media have started local alumni groups composed of old classmates to help their former female teachers, such as the Apyu-yaung Ngethangejin-mya (Pure Childhood Friends Group) in Sagaing town. This group was formed by former classmates from local primary schools and is sustained by a monthly membership of a few US dollars to support their retired teachers in old age.[11] As this example shows, the teacher-student relationship in Myanmar is an excellent illustration of how, in a Buddhist culture of interdependence, people sustain social relations as an ongoing bond and acknowledge the needs for mutual care especially when the state authorities do not provide any welfare support for citizens.

Deferential mode of transactions

We have seen how social relations in Myanmar are sustained by various modes of giving and receiving, and through them respectful deference is also passed on from the laity to monastic members, from students to teachers, from children to parents and from junior members to senior members, in an array of customs and religious practices. In order to outwardly express their respect, a child from a Buddhist family learns from an early age to do *ucha* (clasping their hands together) towards any senior person in the family or to a monastic member. Buddhists pay respect to the Five Pillars in Buddhism – the Buddha, the

Dhamma, the Sangha, parents and teachers – which collectively constitute the foundation of their Buddhist faith. Thus, each child is expected to care for one's parents and act respectfully to elderly members of the community, in addition to the Triple Gem. Such a deferential act of paying respect is performed as an obligatory protocol, similar to bowing or bending the knee to courtesy, which is more rigidly observed towards and within the monastic community. This act is called *kadaw*, another act of obeisance, performed when transactions take place between a junior and a senior member in acknowledgement of both respective positions in the moral social hierarchy. Literally meaning to 'pay respect', an ideal *kadaw* involves first raising both clasped hands to the forehead and then prostrating oneself with the hands and forehead almost touching the floor. The act obliges the person prostrating oneself on the floor to be humble and deferential in front of those to whom gratitude is owed. *Kadaw* is generally performed three times in front of parents, teachers, preceptors, monks and nuns, and in the same manner that one pays obeisance before a Buddha image.[12] When a public show of *kadaw* is directed at them, senior recipients do not remain impassive or aloof, but reciprocate by sending out verses of loving kindness to those who pay them the honour. Deferential transactions are frequent and appear to be heartfelt, which reaffirm their mutual bonds at a deeper psychological level. The recipient may be touched by the display of humility by someone who is junior and is made aware of the responsibility that comes with one's senior position, and it subsequently has a function of confirming the place each person occupies in relation to one another in a moral community.

The act of *kadaw* is also done as a kind of ritual petition when asking for forgiveness of wrongs committed, as the person prostrates oneself on the floor uttering the words *kadaw ba paya* (please forgive me 'Lord'). Similarly, another sub-type of *kadaw* is enacted as a standard formula within the *awkatha* chant, which is a devotional chant commonly recited to start a Buddhist ritual by invoking the monk to take up his ritual position. The chant starts by calling out three times the term *awkatha* or asking for *okāsa* in Pali, meaning 'permission'.[13] The formula lists three types of deeds done in the past – in one's thought, in one's words and in action, and contained in it is the request for forgiveness from the Triple Gem for any unwholesome deeds being committed. The whole congregation recites the following formula:

> Listen, listen, listen. Deeds done by the body, deeds done by the mouth, deeds done by the mind, one conducts three kinds of deeds. Having conducted an unwholesome deed, I pray so that I can offset the many kinds of crime I have committed. Once, twice, three times, I pay respect to the Triple Gem of the Buddha, the Dhamma, the Sangha. Through the senses of the body, the mouth and the mind, I clasp my hands together, worship and pay respect to our Lord Buddha …. Buddha, the Dhamma, and the Sangha.

The recitation solicits protection from misfortune and asks to be free from woeful states by praying to and invoking the powers of the Triple Gem. The officiating monk recites a formula saluting the special qualities of the Buddha, and by doing so he bestows his blessings on all the lay participants in the congregation.

> With the worship, offerings, respect and good deeds I perform, may we all be freed from being reborn into the four lower abodes, and freed from the three misfortunes, eight big hells, five enemies, four kinds of impairment, five formless hells. May we be able to follow the noble path and attain nirvana, our Lord Buddha.

As the passage focuses on 'confession' and then 'forgiveness', Khin Myo Chit notes, 'This reciprocal action is often called "erasing the slate," which is the same as "burying the hatchet" so that one can start life again with a clean "slate."'[14] In other words, such verbal exchanges of confession and forgiveness granted in a ceremonial context allow any wrongdoing of the participants to be acknowledged and then forgiven, not only by the monks, but also by the whole congregation. As a result, these passages are recited at every Buddhist ritual function as a means to expel tension brought upon by any wrongdoings in society and maintain a harmonious coexistence.

Day-to-day social transactions

A morning in a provincial Myanmar town starts with locals greeting each other with *noh-set te*, a social protocol of paying each other recognition. This can consist of as little as nodding to one another to a verbal expression of *nei kaung ya la?* 'How are you?' This is the simplest kind of transaction aimed at showing concern for the wellbeing of another person in the vernacular. In a small town or village where everyone knows or at least recognizes one another, people say hello and goodbye all the time, and also ask each other at any time of the day by saying, *tamin sabi la?* 'Have you eaten already?' Or *bà sa le?* 'What have you eaten?' These expressions may appear strange to those who live in a fast-moving society in the West where such simple acknowledgements of others' presence have little or no bearing on who has eaten or not. In contrast, Myanmar people even in cities mark their meeting and parting with one another via a common protocol signalled by phrases like *la no-set te* 'I came to say hello' or *twa no-set-te* 'I went to say good-bye'. They offer much more verbal acknowledgements of each other's presence during exchanges of pleasantries than what people from Europe or North America would probably accept as normal transaction. The closeness constantly shown in their day-to-day transactions is not only restricted to verbal exchanges, but Myanmar people visit each other frequently at auspicious as well as inauspicious times of illnesses, death, family disputes and in encountering trouble in life. They welcome neighbours and friends to come for a visit when anyone is gravely ill or has had an accident, and news spread quickly through word of mouth so that the community comes together to support the family. Gifts are also offered and exchanged on many social occasions such as rites of passages to confirm their reciprocal relationships. People can also be spontaneous in giving small presents to friends to confirm their love and care, but 'gifts' are not normally given to one's spouse or to family members since members are not bound by reciprocity. Nonetheless, when it comes to souvenirs or foodstuff from different places people visit, they always return with, not only to share with family and neighbours what is rare and unavailable in their locality, but also to remind their loved ones that they are remembered even when apart and such a gift is evidence of their close bond.

Meanwhile, the people's repeated acknowledgement of one another's presence, sustained through frequent verbal and reciprocal transactions, may make one who is not accustomed to it feel imposed upon – but at the same time compelled to accept all manner of gestures of goodwill, to avoid being considered impolite or even anti-social. That being said, the goodwill and generous dispositions can at times backfire for Myanmar people if those who impose the giving do not understand the recipients' likes/dislikes, specific needs or social position in the local community. Subsequently, the latter problem could arise if a gift being given appeared too expensive or inappropriate to the recipient's social standing and become a burden to the recipient and his/her family. This is one of the main reasons why boundaries are maintained in Myanmar society between social groups, and there are various protocols and customary norms that regulate or even limit reciprocity in society. Verbal marking of interpersonal encounters can also be less prominent when the interlocutors include those not affiliated with local fraternities or social acquaintances, revealing that their interdependent way of life does not always extend to those considered outside their social circles.

In their daily transactions, they commonly utilize the expression of *à-na-de*,[15] literally meaning 'I feel bad' or implying that 'I feel uncomfortable to *engage in a relationship with you*'. This phrase is used to express verbal reluctance about receiving someone else's favour or gift offering, and at times uttered to refuse engaging in any transaction with the person who is offering. It shows people's general sense of 'territory', since the expression marks the boundary between no-relation parties, so that neither will lose face nor become offended by the other's refusal to accept a gift or engage in a reciprocal relationship. Paradoxically, the expression is also used when one cannot say 'no', having been asked to do something important (or difficult) by the person whose patronage one is dependent on. There are other expressions of non-offensive refusals that are used and reveal how people mark their social boundaries and protect the integrity of their standing in relations to others. In general terms, the best excuse in refusing Myanmar person's generous offer, for instance, in taking you out for lunch, would be to say, 'I'm afraid I cannot accept your offer as I have to go to a *pongyi kyaung* (monastery)'. Any Myanmar person will accept such a situation without qualms since business with the monks is accepted as taking precedence over most other matters in a Buddhist culture like in Myanmar.

The transactions in rural communities, however, are less bound by social protocols since their residents are normally related by kinship or affinity, and their daily lives are sustained on mutual aid and countless reciprocal transactions. In other words, social transactions in these communities are not restricted by social rank, gender or age, and the notion of privacy is almost absent there, as people drop in on one another at any time of the day. In a village setting, the front reception area of a house is generally reserved for social exchange, and a pot of tea and pickled tea leaves are always on the table to welcome a visitor. If the visit is somewhat unusual – for example, by an *ede* (a guest) or someone from afar in the case of a foreign visitor – people are even happier to converse and welcome him/her. This reflects not only their curiosity about the world beyond their own daily confines, but also a general sense of duty embedded in Myanmar's culture that obliges them to treat a guest with hospitality.

As briefly noted above, it is believed that a generous act will, eventually, both enhance the giver's social reputation and bring meritorious reward. More specifically, as a result of one's generous disposition, the person in question would have helped and supported a host of people in the past, building up a store not only of merit but also of their gratitude. Thus, to be addressed as *thabaw kaùng de lu* (generous person) implies that he/she is valued by others and has a wide network of friends who are willing to reciprocate whatever goodwill they were shown in the past. Such a person seems to appreciate the value of giving rather than holding on to cash or material things, and 'giving away', if done well, since the person is usually considerate, enhances his/her public reputation.[16] Meanwhile, 'blind giving' is out of keeping with what is otherwise considered meaningful, whereas 'good giving' implies understanding what is relevant to and required by the recipient especially at a particular moment of need. Another relevant Myanmar concept to introduce at this point is *hpòn* (a kind of charismatic appeal) or *hpòn*-gan (special karma that attracts good fortune). A person equipped with *hpòn* has an 'emanating sort of influence', benefitting the person 'so that he would never be short of money or influential friends, and whatever he wished for was always granted'.[17] On the contrary, to be called *kasii-ne thi* (stingy) implies that the person is unpopular, and the saying that stinginess makes one *myiena-nge-thi* (small faced) reflects the small base of one's social influence and general support.

Popularity is obviously important to Myanmar people and towns' folks aspire to be invited to as many social functions and *ahlu* (religious feasts) so that their presence is constantly acknowledged and recognized. They also like their names to be 'called' in public and if a person is not 'called out' during events – for example, if no one says 'hello' or calls his/her name when at an invited feast – it implies not only his/her unpopularity, but that the person has been somehow disfavoured and placed outside the main loop of social reciprocity. Therefore, to 'be called' and 'called on', as well as constantly 'calling' on others, form the basis of their social identity and communal affiliation, as well as an essential display of mutual concern and recognition in Myanmar society.

Myanmar's new social and economic environment

Myanmar's dramatic transformation and development in the last decade, especially in its large cities of Yangon or Mandalay and its many emerging semi-urban centres, are expected to continue over the foreseeable future. However, despite highly visible large-scale infrastructure projects, major advancement in telecommunications and reforms of her political system, the country's socio-cultural fabric appears fundamentally unchanged. Certainly, Myanmar remains predominantly traditional, with the majority of the population still living in rural agricultural communities and provincial towns of less than half a million people. In these communities, social life revolves around local ties and kinship, and people continue to rely on close networks of acquaintances they have known for generations.[18] And yet, even in a prototypical agricultural village in upper country like Nondwin, where Manning Nash conducted fieldwork more than half a century ago,[19] stark changes have been manifest in village demography especially in the last decade. As of 2017, the number of households in Nondwin remained not substantially less as in the last three decades, between 90 and about 110, but these now consist mainly of the elderly and retired, as the younger generations have gone to work in factories in South Korea and Malaysia, and others moved to Yangon or Naypidaw to find work. Life in Myanmar is rife with socio-economic problems, including corruption, legal irregularities, an underdeveloped economy; and a gap between the rich and poor, and between the urban and rural communities, continues to widen at a speed. The country is still regarded as relatively poor, and as of 2019, the average monthly income in the largest city Yangon is about $300 USD. High inflation means that even middle-class families, earning an average of $1,000 USD per month, struggle to pay for their children's education or private medical expenses, and can hardly make any savings.

The nature of transactions with the Buddhist monastic community is, like the wider society, changing as well. Bright young boys from rural communities were traditionally sent to study in large monasteries in Yangon, Mandalay or Sagaing, and came back to their native villages after completing their monastic education. Today, monks from rural communities may come back to perform ceremonial roles on important occasions and fulfil their sense of communal obligation, but they rarely stay there and return to their urban monasteries to further their monastic careers. The nature of alms transactions people used to engage with local monks is also changing in large cities from a regular relationship of giving and receiving to more sporadic ones. In urban monasteries, it is also observed that a gap is widening between monastic beneficiaries who are regarded as 'good value' and others deemed 'ordinary', whether monks or nuns. That is, new urban elites with disposable income increasingly favour prestigious monastery schools to offer donations, and popular preachers and monk scholars are invited to conduct religious ceremonies for them. The social milieu in Myanmar is also increasingly affected by the information disseminated by the social media, and global materialism is impacting people's attitudes even towards their monastic beneficiaries.

However, as Holt recently observed, the democratic reforms in Myanmar have not dented the traditional Buddhist notion of what he calls the 'ideology of merit', which continues to provide lay donors with a sense of the value for their good deed actions.[20] Gift-giving continues to be a fundamental part of Myanmar Buddhist life, and every action and interaction is based on the notion of reciprocity. Traditional and regular alms transactions are still conducted in many areas in the old town of Yangon and in satellite towns around it, but for the more mobile (and busy) majority of the urban population relationships with the monastic community have become more temporal and fluid. Meanwhile, wealthy urban donors form donor clubs and associate themselves with prestigious monasteries or celebrity monks, and even compete among themselves to show their generosity on many religious occasions. In one respect, these celebrity monks are 'social channels', through which prospective donors uplift their social reputation by offering them expensive gifts, but the value of their 'symbolic capital' is also validated by trends and criteria set by lay donors to justify their patronage and religious investment.

Urban donors today generally offer cash in offering *dāna*, paying little heed to its subsequent religious implications on their monastic recipients. Monks and nuns, for their part in attending Buddhist functions, are given 'token fees', which is a kind of honorarium comprising banknotes in an envelope for conducting, for example, a funeral or a memorial service.[21] This kind of cash offerings was apparently uncommon before the 1980s in Myanmar, having been regarded as an unsuitable form of *dāna* that symbolically tainted the religious stature of monastic recipients. Transacting with money can also be a double-edged sword since there is always an implication of worldly pollution that one takes in by receiving and transacting with it.[22] Nonetheless, the notion of 'remuneration' recently proposed by Sihlé seems to have more relevance in contemporary societies where lay donors expect religious offerings to be quantifiable.[23] In Myanmar, there is a kind of going rate for the above-mentioned honoraria offered to monks or nuns, but the amount is not fixed and normally decided according to the donor's generosity.[24] In addition, the social standing of the lay donor, his/her financial resources and the recipient's 'symbolic capital' as defined by the degree of reverence the monastic can command may also determine the amount of offerings made. At Buddhist ceremonies, the honoraria envelopes, with the donor's names written on them, are placed on top of the usual pile of gift items, which is offered by donors to all participating monastics in the final section of the ritual.

As suggested already, social trends and commercial values have also come to affect the types of non-cash gifts offered to monks by urban donors especially in Yangon. These days, the monk's robes that are offered are made by expensive foreign labels, and luxury items such as iPads or expensive briefcases are offered if they are beneficiaries from monasteries of high repute. In the old days, wild honey harvested in remote forests was the most valued gift appreciated by elderly monks, but it has been superseded by expensive birds' nest essence with a medicinal quality, which is also sought after as a socially impressive and expensive consumer item. Adhering to traditional monastic practice, monks do not generally refuse any offerings from their lay donors. Unfortunately, the latter's recent tendency to offer rich foods, including expensive large prawns, Western-style fried chicken, high-calorie desserts and sports drinks, has had dire consequences for the health of monastic recipients. And many prominent monks now suffer from diabetes, high blood pressure and high cholesterol. This social phenomenon in Myanmar represents further evidence that the nature of religious offering is changing from a traditional religious transaction, with an emphasis on its meritorious outcome for the lay donor, to a more secular one whereby the offering becomes a means for donors to make a public statement of their rising social importance and economic power. In other words, Myanmar's contemporary urban milieu has propelled both parties away from social transactions focused on mutual care and support and towards a more calculating and competitive relationship, which is increasingly deprived of its moral and meritorious qualities with some dire consequences as discussed above.[25]

Giving in practice

This brings us back to the original questions of *why* Myanmar people 'give', and why they give at all? Is it out of kindness and compassion towards others, or ultimately to bring benefits to oneself? Within the self-focused intentions, is there a major distinction between the religious offering (making merit for a good rebirth) and social giving (enhancing one's public reputation)? And in an interdependent society, is giving a form of imposed favour or a kind of obligatory social tax, or is it a means of lubricating one's relationship with others – or both? Such questions are raised by the law of karma, which – while highlighting the importance of conducting wholesome deeds – does not really explain what is implied by 'merit'. It is obviously something good to be reaped, but its concept of 'meritorious return' only adds further uncertainty. As mentioned earlier, generosity is one of the most important socio-religious values for a Myanmar person; not only does it make one feel 'good' about being kind and giving, but it also impacts one's societal position and general reputation. In other words, 'generosity' has considerable symbolic value in Myanmar's Buddhist culture, and a person is respected simply for being generous and considerate, that is, parting with money easily, being hospitable and caring for others even in the absence of any expectation of reaping something in return.

In this respect, merit is not only relevant when thinking about the next rebirth, but it is also an important motive in a secular context for people to show their innate goodness, either through conducting altruistic services or by performing arduous tasks. I have already mentioned how eager Myanmar people are in offering help whenever occasion arises, amounting in many cases to competitive displays of generosity – almost as if they are on a constant lookout for opportunities to open their abundant stores of kindness. Having said that, the traditional way of merit-making – through offering *dāna* to the sangha – is still important in understanding the religious motives that underlie the generous giving in Myanmar society since offerings to the sangha continue to be a means by which Buddhists try to offset demerit and safeguard themselves against potential misfortune.[26]

Every now and then, Myanmar people prostrate themselves to the Triple Gem, in front of Buddha images and at pagodas where relics are known to be enshrined. They pay respect to Buddhist monks, to various Buddha-related images, to the Buddha's footprints and even to a Bodhi tree. People chant and count the Buddha's virtues in front of Buddha images at home and in temple *dhamma* halls, signifying how they pay respect to the merged entity of the Buddha as a teacher, his ritually consecrated body and relics, and his *dhamma* teaching. Remembering the Buddha and making an offering for him at the sites where his image is evoked are as meritorious for lay Buddhists as going on pilgrimage to India.[27] As expressions of their faith, Myanmar people put coins into donation boxes at sites that hold holy relics and in front of Buddha images when they pray in pagodas and temples. Each donation box is labelled with how the cash offerings will be used by the pagoda trustees: for example, for the 'lights' or candles, for tiles to repair the roof, to lay 'golden leaves' on the surface of stupas and so on. The reasons why people make offerings at religious sites may be similar to those when they offer *dāna* to the sangha, even though the former is made to virtual recipients: that is, in the hope of securing a good rebirth and achieving a sense of wellbeing. Therefore, *dāna* is commonly directed towards a symbolic entity, conceptualized as the Triple Gem or the Buddha, but at other times towards living people, both monks and nuns, who devote their lives to the dissemination of the Buddha *sāsana*.

Spiro, earlier on, listed the reasons for Myanmar people's veneration of monks and why they offered *dāna* to them.[28] First, every monk is held to possess special qualities of the mind and spirit, or *pārami*, a special kind of integrity, derived from the large amount of merit accumulated in his previous life. Second, a monk is respected for his moral discipline, as most men find a celibate lifestyle extremely difficult to follow, and for this reason they look up to a male person who can. And third, if a monk reveals such integrity and high spiritual qualities as listed in the first, this merits the donor's attention and continuous support. In other words, the moral character of the monastic recipient assures the lay donor that his/her offering is truly worthwhile. It should be noted that logically if a *dāna* offering was solely about the good intentions of the donor, it could be made to anyone in need, such as a beggar on the street. To this, however, many Myanmar Buddhists have replied that a person's status as a beggar is evidence of one's bad karma and consequent unworthiness for their offerings, and thus bringing no meritorious results. Spiro made the point that 'the merit deriving from *dāna* is proportional to *the spiritual quality of the recipient* rather than that of the donor'.[29] Hence, *dāna* has to be made only to the righteous beneficiaries endowed with *kutho kan*, which is 'good karma' that subsequently brings *akyò* (positive meritorious results) to the donor/giver. In contrast, the moral quality of a donor is not questioned when offering to the monastic community; he/she could be a criminal, even a violent one. And yet the donor can make merit as long as the person's intentions are 'wholesome' at the moment of offering. As Spiro put it, 'For the same amount of *dāna* the merit acquired by the crook is no less than that acquired by the saint'.[30] As such, the monastic recipient is never in a position to judge or refuse the offering, and will never pick and choose between donors according to their social or political reputation, provided only that they have approached the monastic with good intentions.

On the issue of merit acquisition, it was explained to me that there was a distinction between, on the one hand, 'how one feels' towards the recipient at the point of offering *dāna*, and, on the other, a premeditated notion of 'good intention', with the former being far more important for my informants. It meant that any doubt of the giver regarding the meritorious outcome of one's offering could offset its subsequent positive outcome. If the act of offering in question does not evoke a spontaneous sense of joy and fulfilment, it does not bring any meritorious return. For example, I witnessed some lay donors becoming visibly disappointed when a famous monk did not accept their food offerings, which he considered too rustic and 'not up to his taste'. They commented that it was not meritorious to offer him any longer if he was so selective as to what he ate. As one female informant told me, 'I would rather give to a nun whom I really respect than to any arrogant monk whom I don't think much of'. If the given donor truly believed in the meritorious outcome of her act in offering to a nun, despite the latter not being the socially preferred monastic recipient, the true reward was the donor's joyous state of mind. I will discuss this point about the 'appropriateness' of a monastic recipient more in detail in the next chapter.

Conversely, if one's generosity is misdirected, an act of donation could result in *akutho* or demerit. This also implies that an act of generosity requires tact and a good understanding of human psychology if it was to be truly effective. So the giver has to know what the recipient likes and/or needs, and understand the social and political dynamics in which the recipient is situated. The gift also has to be appropriate for the recipient so that it will not affect him/her negatively and cause an imbalance in the local social hierarchy.[31] In addition, if a person tries to bestow generosity on a reluctant recipient, but ends up angry when his/her *dāna cetana* (intention to offer) is rejected or not acknowledged properly by the recipient, such an angry state of mind is believed to also result in demerit. This calls to mind the powerful image of Myanmar monks during the Saffron Revolution, upturning their alms bowls and refusing to accept donations from the military and their families – a perfect example of the impact that a 'refusal of generosity' can have on the psyche of Buddhists. More specifically, when a prospective lay donor's offering is rejected and the person's urge to conduct a good deed cannot be realized – that is, when there is no one willing to accept their *dāna cetana* and nowhere for *cetana* to go – it causes great confusion, humiliation, anger and even panic because their hopes for a good rebirth have been dashed. The power of such a refusal is rooted in the general cultural-religious assumption that generosity and giving always have willing recipients, and that it is only through their 'receiving' that donors can reap their meritorious returns.

A typical Buddhist ritual

Almost every rite of passage and religious celebration in Myanmar is accompanied by commensality in the form of communal feasts called *ahlu*. The integration of religious offerings into communal feasts implies the significance of sharing a meritorious occasion and rejoicing in its outcome collectively. In a Durkheimian sense, an individual's good deed becomes celebrated by the whole community through commensality, which also reflects the country's tradition of hospitality. From a Buddhist viewpoint, the act of giving is regarded to make a person less ego-centred and allows him/her to regain an inner balance by ridding one's attachment to material things, but it also gives the person added value when it is witnessed and the meritorious occasion shared by the wider community.[32] The sponsorship of a monk's ordination known as *yahan-kan* or any ritual to support and nurture the sangha is regarded as highly meritorious, and the whole community comes together in support of such an occasion. Thus, the ideal of being a good Buddhist ultimately points to one's willingness to nurture and help disseminate the Buddha *sāsana* – nowadays seen as going into decline and eventually disappearing. In this respect, the outcome of social transactions cannot be measured simply in economic or in other practical terms; and conversely, religious donations cannot be separated from the realm of social reciprocity, due to the close interrelationship we observe between the religious and the secular.

A Buddhist ceremony or ritual, following the communal feast, is composed of two main parts. It starts by the recitation of *awkatha*, by the lay congregation, which we have already seen in an earlier section of this chapter. The principal monk sits on a raised golden pulpit, flanked by several monk assistants, facing the lay congregation. Buddhist nuns sit on the floor in the front, usually towards the left side of the room: senior nuns sit in front of the junior nuns who support them in their collective recitation. The main lay benefactor(s) occupies a central place in the front row facing the monks with other lay participants sitting at the back of the congregation. The officiating monk responds to the *awkatha* recitation of the laity and takes up his officiating role by confirming their adherence to the Triple Gem and soliciting the congregation to recite every line after him. Then, *Uposathasila* is the taking of the Five or Eight Precepts. By repeating the precepts recited by the principal monk, lay participants make a commitment to keep the vows publicly.[33] The second part is the sermon, in which the chief monk expounds various themes from the Buddha's teachings. The sermon can be short or long, and topics and style can also vary, but the most popular topic is often about the significance of *dāna*, comprising a meritorious deed. This is followed by a collective recitation of *paritta*. One or two of the eleven protection prayers called *payeik* or *paritta* in the Pali language are recited by a group of monks – and, increasingly, by nuns – believed to authenticate the ritual and bring special blessings on the congregation. Each *paritta* is believed to have a particular beneficial function, such as curing illnesses and injuries, even snake bites.[34] But more specifically, the recitation of any one of them at important life events is aimed at inviting good fortune. The two most commonly chanted *paritta* in Myanmar are *Mangala Sutta* (on Auspiciousness) and *Mettā Sutta* (on Loving Kindness), with the latter being particularly popular as a means of pacifying restless spirits, as well as soliciting protection from *devas* and deities to achieve a peaceful balance.

The most significant section of a Buddhist ritual comes at the end, when the principal monk announces the names of those who contributed to the ceremony, and while he recites a *gāthā* confirming the meritorious value of their act, the donors conduct *yezet-cha* (water libation ritual), pouring water slowly from a special pitcher onto a receiving plate on the floor. This is the moment when family members gather around to take photographs of the water pouring act to both witness and record the meritorious moment. The falling water, drop by drop in *yezet-cha*, is equated to the flowing blood, which points to the essence of life and its smooth continuation into the next. The water-pouring ritual originates in the mythological final battle between the Buddha, on the brink of attaining enlightenment, and his arch-rival Mara. As the *Suttanipata Sutta* recounts, Mara – resenting the Buddha's efforts to bring an end to suffering and bent on destroying him – attacks him with a retinue

Figure 1.2 *The ritual of* yezet-cha *(pouring water) points to the essence of life and its continuation into the next, confirming the meritorious deed done by the lay donors.*

of demons and unleashes the evil forces of anger, hatred, envy, hunger, lust, thirst, craving, sloth, torpor, fear, doubt and passion. As thunderstorms rage, the Buddha summons the help of the earth deity by pressing the four fingers of his right hand to the ground.[35] At the crucial moment, she rises and saves the Buddha by wringing her long thick hair, from which a copious quantity of water gushes out in evidence of his past meritorious deeds and that drowns Mara's entire demonic fleet.

This ritual sequence suggests a symbolic interface between Buddhism and nature-worship, and a connection between the donor's good deeds and the earth deity, customarily known in her role as the guiding moral force of nature. Thus, with water made to represent the current of *samsāra* into which a man is thrown, here is an agent that mediates the transferral of merit from the present to the future in a continuous flow.

When a Buddhist ceremony is about to conclude, all the participants join in the collective recitation of *ahmyá we*, the aim of which is to send out a wave of loving kindness to a range of spirits in the environment, soliciting them to share in the auspicious occasion and rejoice in the occasion. The calling out of *ahmyá* ('[to] all [of you]') in this recitation three times is followed by the congratulatory proclamation of *sadhu* ('well done'), also three times, to acknowledge the meritorious deed done by everyone in the congregation. The collective affirmation of the donor's good deed becomes truly efficacious for the participants when all rejoice in their mounting store of merit. The ritual is authenticated by a monk and witnessed by a symbolic earth deity, signifying the endorsement of the whole community of the meritorious deed.

Communal occasions for social giving

As discussed above, the generous disposition Myanmar people show towards one another is by no means confined to the monastic community. For example, free food is offered on one's birthday, or on any celebratory day in the Buddhist calendar, or whenever one feels the impulse to be generous to others. Prior to such a day, an announcement is made by the named benefactor and circulated in the locality that free food would be offered, ranging from soft drinks to snacks and to cooked meals. During the week-long holiday of Myanmar New Year in April and on the full moon days of October and November, lay Buddhists commonly practise *satuditha*, literally meaning 'four directions', inviting whoever passes by and offering free food, sometimes for several days in a row.[36] The traditional dishes offered on such an occasion are cooked rice and curry, *mohingar* (rice noodles in fish soup), *ohnaw khaswè* (noodles in coconut soup with chicken) or *shwe yin aye* (a sweet coconut drink made from agar jelly, tapioca and sago).[37] As well as marking the auspicious occasion, *satudhita* serves a practical function of helping those who cannot earn an income during the week-long holiday of *Thingyan*, when markets are closed and economic activity comes to a complete standstill. This custom of offering free food to everyone and anywhere represents further evidence that offerings in Myanmar need not have an overt religious component, but the value of generosity is fundamental to every public act and social occasion, providing the vital glue for one's interactions with others in an interdependent society. All these social occasions, nonetheless, are intertwined with religious meanings, and the sharing and a sense of goodwill produced by every such event subsequently result in cooperation and integration of people into wider networks, affirming a Durkheimian view of the occasion as having a socially cohesive function.

2

The laity

This chapter focuses on lay Buddhists' relationships with members of the monastic community, and especially on the social dimension of laypeople's merit-making activities. Many types of lay-monastic relationships underlie the numerous transactions that take place in Buddhist ceremonies and alms collection: some sporadic and temporary, and others regular, sometimes sustained over several generations. It also examines how religious offerings made during ceremonies can instigate a circular pattern of goodwill offerings – from lay donors to their monastic recipients, from senior members to junior members in the monastic hierarchy and, sometimes, back from monks to the laity – thus strengthening or confirming these groups' positions in relation to one another within the moral community.

In the Maussian transaction model, every giver requires a recipient-partner to whom a store of goodwill is released, and in return the giver is assured of his/her own innate goodness, perhaps similar to a sense of wellbeing reaped as a result. In practice, however, such an act of giving implies much more than a generic expectation of a meritorious return, since the notion of 'merit' is neither uniform nor static as has been generally assumed. My local informants described in great detail what merit actually meant, in terms of positive effects on their wealth, health, power, social status, attractiveness, popularity and so on. Some asserted that you get protection from misfortune and even accidents by making a lot of merit.[1] Yet, it is not exactly clear what 'merit' is and why the notion motivates Myanmar Buddhists to conduct good deeds. Rather, why does the act of offering *dāna* – conceived of as an aspect of doing one's moral duty – makes them so happy and feel good about themselves? It is reasonable to ask, then, what is the difference in moral and religious terms between feeding a monk and being hospitable to a guest, especially as generosity of any kind is almost always seen as a good deed and explained in the context of its meritorious outcomes. Indeed, Myanmar people assure one another that it is good to be generous by using the phrase *kutho ya-de*, 'you will gain merit'; but as pointed out earlier, *kutho* (merit) is an ambiguous term, rendering it difficult to explain what 'you' have actually received.[2]

The donor's state of mind at the point of making an offering has been mentioned in the previous chapter. Ingrid Jordt said, 'The goal of donation is to achieve *a state of mind* in which generosity emerges in the individual's intentions as unprompted volitional acts'.[3] To make the most of an offering, however, the recipient must be someone appropriate – normally, a legitimate member of the monastic community – and thus capable of justifying the donor's disposition for generosity. There already seems to be a consensus that 'the greater the holiness of the monk, the greater the merit of the benefactor',[4] but the criteria for the 'appropriateness' of a monastic recipient vary widely from donor to donor. Thus the decision to offer or not also depends on external factors and various personal attributes of the monastic recipient. Therefore, merit has to be treated as a fluid concept affected by social trends and the changing status of recipients; and thus, the people's frameworks for making decisions for donations are likewise ever-changing.

Becoming a lay donor

In Myanmar, there are social as well as religious implications for being called a *taga* (male donor) or a *tagamá* (female donor). The main donor to a monastery or a nunnery is called *kyaung taga* or *kyaung má*, and it is a great honour indeed to be referred to as such in religious events and on ceremonial occasions. This status also affiliates the person with other regular donors who support the same monastic institution and suggests that he/she is an important member of a particular donor group. Similarly, a donor who is the main sponsor of a male novice at his ordination is called *bazin taga* or *bazin tagamá*, who becomes known in association with this particular monk, and whose status can accrue more prestige if he eventually becomes an established monk scholar. Such terms of address, especially when the lay donor is associated with a particular monk, are much more than personal honorifics; they signify that the addressee has enhanced one's karmic positions, with a direct positive consequence to his/her social reputation and future rebirth. Of course, anyone can become a lay donor simply by offering *dāna* to the monastic community. However, those who commit themselves to care for and support a monastic beneficiary on a regular and long-term basis are the ones who accrue the most merit. And conversely, the most valued donor relationships from the viewpoint of a monastic recipient are those that involve continuous support and regular transactions.

U Nu, Myanmar's first democratically elected prime minister, boosted his political standing by making it known that he was a practising lay Buddhist, and his string of electoral victories in the 1950s was ascribed to his popularity as the *paya taga* (literally 'donor of the Buddha'). This position, however, curtailed his effort to extend freedom of worship to other religions, since the concessions he granted them in the early part of his premiership were criticized by the sangha as a violation of his role as the main patron of Buddhism. And yet, after making Buddhism Myanmar's state religion in 1961, U Nu came under mounting pressure from monks to give them special privileges; and the political upheaval that followed eventually led to his downfall in the following year.[5] Although arguably an extreme example, these events reflect the reality that, at any socio-political level, being well-known as a lay donor of the monastic community, that is, Buddhism, implies that one will meet the expectations of both sangha and society regarding one's religious and sometimes public role. In this respect, becoming a regular donor cannot be seen merely as a personal preference or a whim, since the act amounts to an announcement that one has joined the collective project for fostering the Buddha *sāsana*. At the same time, it connotes the assumption of certain duties, extending beyond the individualistic notion of meritorious return, as the donor is expected to conduct regular visits to his/her monastic recipients, and frequently transfer goods and funds to them often upon informal request. In practice, then, giving sporadic donations does not qualify one to be a *paya taga* or *tagamá* in the true sense of such a term. In other words, offering *dāna* is a matter not solely of acquiring religious merit, but of engaging in many kinds of transactions that connect a donor to a larger community of Buddhist faithful, bringing new social contacts and other beneficial opportunities in promoting oneself.[6]

Moreover, despite the act of offering *dāna* being – in theory – a person-to-person transaction between a lay donor and a monastic recipient, being a *taga* or *tagamá* usually implies a joint undertaking by a married couple or a *mithazu* (family unit), who reap the meritorious outcome collectively. As we will see in the last chapter, *dāna* is customarily made in the name of *mithazu kaung-mu* (good deeds done by the family unit) in the hope that the whole family will reap the meritorious outcome and be reunited in the next life.

Often, it is the senior female member of a family who acts as a sort of team leader in religious matters, and the details of religious donations are normally decided by her, with males acting in supporting roles. She takes the initiative in collecting funds, budgeting, contacting the monastery or the monastic recipients to whom the offering will be made, and organizing the details of when and how it will be made.[7] She is also responsible for the contents and quality of items offered to suit the particular needs of the monastic recipients. To make the giving more worthwhile, she even invests considerable time in researching the worthiness of individual monastic beneficiaries and/or their monasteries' moral standards before finalizing the total expenditure and other details, down to the level of what food will be served at the ceremonial feast.[8] As such, the onus for the success of an offering ceremony is on the woman in the household who makes the actual arrangements for it.

Pure intention and 'falling in love'

To describe their motive for giving, my informants have often referred to the notion of *cetanā*, a Pali word that literally means 'intention'; the term is also used to describe kindness or a generous disposition, especially when combined with the term *dāna*. Another term commonly used is *thada taya*, which means to have faith in the Triple Gem, but is also used in a phrase like *thada taya kaung-de*, implying that the person has a generous disposition and is always willing to offer *dāna*. Implicitly, the use of these words acknowledges the donor's inherent goodwill in meeting the needs of his/her monastic recipient,[9] who would otherwise have no other source of income.

However, when I sought to examine how intention and goodwill are generated in practice, I identified another factor that is not usually talked about, but which can motivate a layperson to act in a most generous manner: namely, a desire to offer *dāna* that arises in some strange and unpredictable way. It can be described like something 'out of the blue', an impulse arriving suddenly without any clear cause or reason (unless perhaps one blames one's karma). In such a situation, the lay donor may not know why he/she suddenly felt generous or compassionate towards a certain monastic recipient; sometimes, the donor's heart is simply touched by listening to an inspiring sermon or moved by a beautiful recitation in the temple. One donor told me that she was so inspired by the tranquil serenity of a particular nunnery that, overcome by a strong desire, she decided on the spur of the moment to donate her life's savings to support its resident nuns. Another said she became a regular donor to a particular nun after she was moved by her graceful demeanour and soft voice. Myanmar Buddhists take such an experience as a 'sign' and pay special attention to such momentary inspirations for kindness. Indeed, a special encounter between a layperson and a monastic recipient may be almost like 'falling in love', and an emotional attachment, albeit platonic, can also develop into a nurturing long-term relationship.

Here, it is worth remembering that the law of karma incorporates a notion of causality in which every deed has a corresponding effect, and every effect is caused by a corresponding deed. Following this logic, a 'sudden urge' or 'impulse' that results in a large offering could challenge the concept of karma, by appearing to deny that this deed has a cause, or to assert that 'something could happen' due to mere luck or chance. This point is perhaps especially pertinent in the case of offerings made to a Buddhist nun or a nunnery, as doing so is not regarded as a normative act, at least in comparison to offering to monks. Several informants told me that they did not understand why they felt the sudden urge to offer to a nun rather than to a monk. One male donor said no one in his family had ever donated to a nun, but he just felt the urge to offer a substantial sum to an elderly nun because he was deeply touched by her humility. He added that this event was totally unexpected even to himself, but since that first encounter he had become her regular donor, visiting the nunnery every month to offer her financial support.[10] When a spontaneous urge like this takes over, in other words, no one – even the family – seems to be capable of restraining him/her from offering (often large) sums of money to a monastic recipient – in this case a nun.

Such instances have sometimes led to mentions of the notion of *patanzet*, explained as a special pre-destined karmic affiliation. In this context, the surprise encounter that takes place between a monastic recipient and a lay donor is an evidence of one of the twenty-four interrelated links, described in the book of *Patthāna*, which reveals their shared journey in the cycle of spiritual striving. This concept is popular with devout Buddhists in Myanmar, who become visibly happy when describing such encounters as 'pre-conditioned'. That is, when they experience an inexplicable encounter, people prefer to explain it by reference to some past relationship between the same two people – possibly aeons ago – that predisposed them to meet again and again to jointly conduct meritorious deeds. In this way, the notion of a meeting by coincidence or luck is refuted, and a sense of order congruent with standard Buddhist cosmology is re-imposed. And yet, when such goodwill is generated by a seemingly chance occurrence, it opens the door to agency, implying that the individual decision made by the donor obliges him/her to take on a new kind of moral responsibility that was not preordained by past karma. Therefore, while karmic law is fundamentally deterministic, holding that every act and every decision is pre-conditioned and that every reality one encounters is the result of one's past actions, the notion of a 'chance occurrence' provides an outlet for randomness and a sense of free will. In this respect, the notion of 'chance' is also very appealing to people in Myanmar, who are famously attached to gambling and lotteries, perhaps for similar reasons. Tellingly, stories of 'winning' and 'losing' in both business and leisure contexts are staples of their daily conversation. It is almost as if people want to test their karma by placing a bet on their present life, hoping to somehow outmanoeuvre their bad karma in the bigger or smaller scheme of things. On the other hand, placing one's hopes in some highly unlikely occurrence can also pose a threat to one's general sense of security as dictated by the karmic law, which reinforces order as well as a sense of moral responsibility in a Buddhist society.

Terms and conditions of the relationship

As mentioned earlier, Myanmar's Buddhists strive to cultivate close associations with monastic recipients who are tangible means to enhance their social and religious standing. For this reason, prominent Buddhist monasteries in Mandalay and Yangon maintain waiting lists of prospective lay donors, each of whom hopes eventually to become the main patron of a bright young novice with strong academic and religious potential. These lists are not operated on a strict first-come, first-served basis; rather, the donor-matchmaking is left to the abbot or a senior monk teacher who decides, when the novice monk nears the ordination age of twenty, who his main donor will be.[11] The novice himself has little control over his future prospects and normally does not express any opinion of his in the donor-matching process, since it is considered the monastery's responsibility. If a novice is especially gifted academically, many prospective donors will jostle for the chance to claim this role, but it is customarily granted to an established donor who already has some other connection to the abbot or to the monastery in question. In one instance, a donor offered to fund an ordination for a novice he had known from childhood, but he was told by the monastery that there was no possibility of this happening since there were already a dozen donors hoping to do so. Even the novice's own family had no say in the matter, nor knew ahead of time who his prospective patron would be. The final decision was left to his monk preceptor. Once assigned to a novice monk, however, the main patron (and his/her family) would be expected not only to pay the costs of his ordination ceremony, and to offer donations to his host monastery, but also to provide for his daily necessities and any other expenses as required. Thus, the appointed donor carries a heavy long-term responsibility; indeed, becoming a monk's *bazin taga* or *bazin tagamá* is akin to being a surrogate parent for the duration of his monastic career. And unsurprisingly, such lay patrons always receive public acknowledgement in relation to their monastic beneficiaries.

Nonetheless, if one still wants to contribute to an already-ordained monk who has been matched with some other donor, he/she can resort to a custom called *theik-hka that* (a repeat ordination). In such cases, lay donors – sometimes including the monk's own family members – pay the expenses of ordaining him again after the first ordination and endeavour to make merit, which they could not have done earlier due to the matchmaking process described above. A 'repeat ordination' can happen more than once, or even many times in his monastic life, especially if a monk is popular; and it is evident from the existence of this practice that a monk is a valued medium through which his many followers aspire to make merit.

A popular monk normally has a circle of regular lay donors who are always at hand to meet his needs, and who compete among themselves to attract his direct attention. For instance, each supporter strives to respond the fastest if asked for help and maintains regular contact with the monastery to keep abreast of the monk's requirements. If a senior monk falls ill, each supporter hopes to be the first to arrive on the scene to take him to hospital and pay for his medical expenses. If the monk needs transport, several vehicles may be sent from his supporters arriving to gift him a lift. By means of these and other forms of tangible patronage, lay supporters associate themselves with the monk's good reputation, and this can be a major source of their social pride. Of course, not every monk is successful in his academic endeavours, and many drop out of monastic learning in the early part of their careers, or even decide to disrobe, to the dismay of their lay followers. Hence, a prospective donor always takes a risk when committing to a long-term investment in someone else's future and monastic career.

Circles of committed lay donors are especially likely to be found in the vicinity of prominent monastery schools and urban meditation centres. As Jordt explained of her research in the 1980s, 'Patron-client ties proliferated at the monk-donor nexus, resulting in networks that penetrated the state bureaucracy, the nationalized corporations, the universities, and the small businesses that operate in the formal and black markets'.[12] The formation of these donors' networks and active engagement with other donors often take place with those who frequent monasteries and take keen interest in religious affairs. Yet, the personal charisma that makes a lay donor influential in particular Buddhist circles is generated as a result of constant transactions with his/her monastic recipients and other lay donors both in formal ceremonies and in informal settings in the monastic community over a sustained period of time. As such, an influential patron is always aware of other donors' meritorious deeds in the Buddhist community and acknowledges one's own position in relational terms. At its best, this process spurs everyone within a circle of like-minded Buddhist faithful to offer more donations and do better in meritorious terms.

When a lay donor decides to support the monastery as a whole rather than a specific monk, his/her support is intended for all its resident monastics; and such a role demands a large and regular flow of cash for ceremonies, events and the many needs of the institution's senior monks. Some of these arrangements have persisted for several decades, sometimes even after the original donor and abbot who first formed the relationship, having both passed beyond living memory. Often, the relationships pass down in Buddhist families that have lived in the locality of the monastery. The names of prominent donors can be well known in provincial towns, and their past meritorious deeds are talked about as an integral aspect of local history.[13] In many ways, the generous deeds of these long-dead donors continue to have an impact on the reputations of their living descendants. As it can be imagined, it is increasingly difficult to take on such a heavy financial responsibility in Myanmar today, as inflation is rife, and yet the expectation that monastic beneficiaries will be fully provided for is even more pressing. I know of a female donor in a provincial town who struggles to live up to the reputation of her late father, who was a prominent patron of several important monasteries in the area. But because of crippling increases in the prices of food and building materials, it has become harder and harder to discharge the same duties for her. Indeed, the current economic climate means it is almost impossible for an average family to regularly support even one monk, making it difficult to sustain the reputations as generous donors that have been inherited from previous generations. The same female donor mentioned above told me that she spent almost half the income from her family business supporting her 'inherited' monasteries, but – despite it causing her tremendous stress – she was adamant that she wanted to continue the family tradition. As her case illustrates, Myanmar donors regard their supportive role with considerable pride, and defend it despite many difficulties, since their sense of worth as 'good Buddhists' and their families' reputations depend upon continuing to be known as generous donors in the locality.

Although the current state of Myanmar's economy has increased the financial burdens associated with lay donors' support of the monastic community, such relationships retain another beneficial dimension. That is, when monks or nuns are supported over a lengthy period, the monastic recipient and the lay donor come to know each other well, often developing a close bond akin to membership of the same family. When a major life crisis strikes – for example, bankruptcy, serious illness or divorce – it is common for lay donors to consult their monastic beneficiaries, and find solace in opening their hearts to those monks or nuns they feel closest to. And at the time of a patron's death, that person's family will almost certainly turn to the monastic beneficiary for moral support. I have encountered several cases of Buddhist nuns caring for their former donors who have encountered major misfortunes. In one, a former patroness had a stroke and became paralysed, upon which she was abandoned by her then husband. Since she did not have any children, her nun beneficiaries invited her to live with them at the nunnery and cared for her for several years until she passed away. I have also known a monk who took in a former patron who had lost everything through gambling, giving him a place to live and a role as caretaker in the monastery. It seems likely that many of the lay helpers we encounter in monasteries were offered similar kinds of practical help by their monastic beneficiaries in the wake of life crises. Although Myanmar's people tend to explain such situations by reference to karmic cause and effect, it seems natural enough that a relationship of mutual care would develop as a result of the long-term support given to a monastic beneficiary. And in such cases, in karmic terms, an unfortunate donor may simply be reaping the consequence of his/her meritorious actions in this life. In other words, these cases demonstrate that the relationship between lay donors and monastic beneficiaries entails much more than a normative material or monetary transaction.

Cases of mutual support also reveal how, as in any Buddhist culture, there is an acknowledgement of interdependence in every relationship, and people recognize the transitory nature of life, in which good or bad fortune may befall absolutely anyone. Therefore, offerings of material support to the monastic community by lay Buddhists are aimed not only at reaping meritorious benefits in the next life but also at least potentially about returns in this one as well. In other words, offering material support to and transacting with members of the monastic community on a regular basis can serve, albeit perhaps without the participants' conscious knowledge, as a form of life assurance or social security for many Myanmar Buddhists who have no other means of assurance.

The specifics of *dāna* offerings

In Myanmar, a Buddhist family will spend about a quarter of its income on *dāna* offerings; people save up for special religious occasions, and even those categorized as 'poor' will set aside a bagful of rice grain to support the monastic community. In fact, every Buddhist will try to provide *dāna*, either in cash or in foodstuff, but in practice, religious offerings can vary widely, being given in both cash and kind, and ranging from a daily practice of offering cooked rice to a large ceremonial feast at which hundreds of monks are fed.

It is commonly stated that the financial standing of a lay donor should not disadvantage one's moral position in terms of gaining a good rebirth. On this point, my informants emphasized that a regular alms-offering to monks was more meritorious than a sporadic show of lavish feasts, since it was not the public spectacle that was meritorious, but a sincere wish to support them. In other words, from rich to poor, all have an equal opportunity of achieving a desirable rebirth, rooted in the strength of their commitment to support the monastic community, and therefore status or wealth ideally becomes subordinated to the purity of intention. However, the social dynamics embedded in the country's donation culture imply that such an ideal is not always borne out in reality.

The items to be donated to the sangha are stipulated in the Buddhist scriptures, and thus theoretically limited to *parikiya shi-pa*, the Eight Requisites. These are a set of three robes, an alms bowl, a razor, a water strainer, a belt and a pair of slippers. Myanmar donors also offer low-value items for the monks' daily needs, and books and stationery for monastic students and teachers. In addition, since the majority of these donors still live in rural agricultural communities, it is also common for them – especially in the period following the harvest – to offer farm products to the monastic community. People donate blankets, mats, baskets, pots and handicrafts: collectively, a type of *dāna* invested with the donors' time and energy, which reaffirms their goodwill and the special bond between a donor and his/her monastic recipient. Those engaged in trade also offer whatever goods they have in surplus. For example, one woman was known as the monastery's egg donor, as she raised chickens and sold eggs in the market. Another donor who regularly offered *latpet* or 'pickled tea leaves' to local monks came from a family in the tea trade. There are also flower donors, fruits donors, petrol donors and so on. In short, laypeople offer the monastic community whatever items they can afford to give or have in surplus, whether purchased or otherwise.

There are many ways of contributing and supporting the monastic community, and *dāna* can also take the form of voluntary services offered to monasteries, such as repairing roofs and painting walls or even helping with the cooking when a large feast takes place. For instance, I met a group of an architect and engineers who offered their services at no charge to a monastery that was building a worship hall. On that project, carpenters, bricklayers and other manual labourers were paid their usual daily wages by another lay donor who wanted to earn merit by doing so; but people at all socio-economic levels try to make themselves useful on monastery premises in whatever capacity they can. I also came across an IT specialist from Mandalay who visited monasteries whenever he could to fix their computers for free. Thus, *dāna* does not always involve offerings of food or material gifts, but sometimes 'offering' consists of immaterial services that are welcomed by monastics who require them, as much as people would in the outside world. For this reason, merit-making needs to be understood not only as an act aimed at accumulating merit, but also as a kind of self-worth or value that accrues to a person as a result of making his or her skills useful to the monastic members in need of help.

In Myanmar's urban centres, where increasing numbers of people engage in waged work in factories and offices, *dāna* offered in cash rather than goods to monastic recipients has become more common. This trend towards cash offering seems to have accelerated in the mid-1980s, as a result of successive 'demonetizations' that took place then without advance warning by the Myanmar government, making banknotes invalid overnight.[14] The demonetizing measures were meant to impose control over black-marketeers and those in illegal trades, but as a result of them millions of people's savings were wiped out and had a huge unintended impact on ordinary people's attitude towards cash. One informant said, if money was just paper, after all, it was better to make the most of banknotes while they still had some value and make merit before they became worthless .... In the local usage, offering cash is referred to as *navakamma*, literally meaning 'new work' or 'new action'. The usage of this term reflects that, until recently in Myanmar, cash was not a commonly accepted form of *dāna*, except in the special circumstance of solicitations of support for major projects intended for the collective use of the community – for example, a pagoda or a worship hall in the village monastery – in which context the term *navakamma* was originally used. However, donors in Myanmar today use the same term when making cash donation to a monastic member, in the form of an envelope packed with new banknotes. In other words, the word itself seems to have survived an important cultural shift, away from offerings of cash to projects confirming one's communal affiliation and active support of the sangha, to a new style of such offerings reflecting practical convenience and individuality.

As discussed earlier, social ceremonies including *alhu* and *shinbyu* have become expensive affairs even for an urban middle-class family, and donations at such events are commonly made in cash for reasons of convenience, and perhaps due to the practice of announcing the amounts of donors' cash contributions at the ceremony. This might be what Spiro meant by the term 'quantified' resultant merit.[15] Nonetheless, as he rightly pointed out, 'The desired transformation in material and social status is achieved without any corresponding transformation in the self'.[16] Thus, cash donation has come to quantify one's meritorious deed: a modern-day criterion for assessing the meritorious outcome – up to a point – but without much spiritual uplift for the donors involved (unless one counts social reputation as a spiritual matter). Having said that, even in Yangon, offerings in kind or in the form of voluntary service are still preferred by committed practising Buddhists, reflecting money's connotation as worldly and 'hot', and offerings of it as deeply questionable, since it transfers worldly pollution – the very source of suffering – back to the monastic community.[17]

The specific content of an offering can also reveal the distance or closeness of the relationship between a lay benefactor and his or her monastic beneficiary. If a settled and regular relationship already exists between them, it is expected to be intimate and informal, insofar as the donor is aware of the actual needs of the monastic recipient and caters for them. In such a close relationship, in other words, offerings become more tailored to the recipients' preferences regarding size, colour and/or other specific features. As well as these matters of taste, regular donors also pay attention to the monastic's state of health, special dietary needs and so forth; and such attention to detail is also appreciated by the monastic recipient, cementing the relationship even further.

On the other end of the spectrum, people from non-Buddhist countries and others who are unfamiliar with Buddhist cultural practices may offer monastics items that are totally inappropriate, to the dismay of resident monks: for example, unwanted furniture, plates or cutlery.[18] I have seen foreign tourists in Myanmar offer monasteries soap they have picked up at hotels, plastic cutlery from airline flights and second-hand clothes to monasteries, probably on an assumption that such items could be of some use there. Receiving such items upsets monastic recipients in Myanmar who are not in the habit of receiving 'freebies' or anything second-hand, and, in fact, rather see themselves as doing a favour by accepting something from the laity in the first place. Such mishaps are usually caused by a fundamental lack of understanding and/or an absence of reverence towards Buddhist monastics, but also seem to reflect the givers' non-expectation of any meritorious return.

This may point to the fundamental difference between a monastic recipient and a beggar in a Buddhist society: lay Buddhists may give items of value to both, but to the former it is to make merit, and not to give away surplus coins or something they longer want. That is, the general consensus in a Buddhist culture is that the most *appropriate* items are to be offered and planted in the *punnakkhettamlokassa*, 'a field to plant the seeds of merit', so that those offerings are appreciated by the monastic recipients and every donor reaps the meritorious consequences. Hence, it is simply unthinkable to use the monasteries as a dumping ground for redundant furniture or vases that no one needs any longer.

Meanwhile, the issue of inappropriate donations highlights the vulnerable position of monastic recipients, insofar as they are not always fully in command of their vocational recipient role. In fact, they are ultimately at the mercy of capricious lay donors who can misuse their position or make the life of a recipient a misery, as will be discussed further in Chapter 4 in the case of Buddhist nuns.[19]

Meritorious occasions for offering *dāna*

There are many meritorious occasions for *dāna*, but Myanmar tradition holds that a *shinbyu* is one of the most meritorious deeds for a Buddhist family. Conducted when a boy reaches the age of seven or eight, and marking the end of childhood, he enters a monastery to observe and practise the vows of religious abstinence. A *shinbyu* is not only a rite of passage for a son, but is also regarded profoundly meritorious for the parents, whose symbolic role in nurturing the sangha is acknowledged by the whole community. The details of the ritual sequence are performed as if the parents were giving up their precious 'treasure' to the monastic community. Vessantra – the most selfless giver in the Jātaka story – is often invoked during the ceremony to highlight the generous disposition of a father who gives away his precious son. Such references to Vessantra's extreme generosity assure lay Buddhists of the value of their sacrifice in supporting the sangha and, interestingly, shift the focus away from the merit that might result from one's offering onto the value of selfless action.[20]

In practical terms, the parents' major concern about conducting a *shinbyu* is its high cost. Myanmar parents of average means will therefore save up for their son's *shinbyu* from the time of his birth, but still might go into debt to make the most of this auspicious occasion.[21] The ceremony involves various levels of offerings to the sangha, the host monastery and the community. The basic costs are spent on preparing monastic robes and the other requisites for a prospective novice; but customarily, new robes and daily necessities are also offered to all the resident monks and novices of the host monastery.[22] The communal feast conducted prior to the actual ceremony can go on for several days, attended sometimes by the whole village and relatives arriving from far. Despite its costs being borne in most cases entirely by the boys' parents and the procedure exceedingly costly, it is regarded as *mingala*, an auspicious duty for the parents and a way of reaping more merit. To minimize its heavy expenses, however, *shinbyu* is often conducted as collectively, with the young male offspring of a group of relatives and friends undergoing it jointly and sharing the temporary experience of living in a monastery. In rural villages, it is a traditional norm to have a *shinbyu* conducted by the whole community; and if some parents cannot afford to participate, it is common for relatives who do not have a son of their own to pay the relevant expenses as another way of making merit. For the majority of Myanmar Buddhists, the desire to conduct a *shinbyu* seems to stem from a strong sense of moral duty towards their Buddhist tradition, and people take great pride in seeing the young novices having their heads shaved and donning monastic robes.

The first part of a *shinbyu* is a lavish communal affair. A theatre troupe is normally invited to entertain the local people on the eve of the ritual, though the amount of money people spend on such appendages will vary based

Figure 2.1 Shinbyu *is an initiation ceremony for boys from Buddhist families in Myanmar. They are taken around in a procession before becoming temporary novices in the village monastery.*

on how much of a public spectacle the parents want to make. On the day, following the tradition of the Burmese royal court (despite its official abolition in 1885), each boy is dressed in long silk robes, crowned with the headgear of a nobleman and shielded by a white parasol. A public procession around the town takes place prior to the ceremony – with the boys seated on horses and sometimes on elephants, followed by a dozen beautifully decorated white bullock carts ridden by family and friends, and a retinue of dancers, musicians and a joker in tow. In large cities, such processions have become modernized, with many families hiring a row of Jeep guzzlers to show off the boys dressed in their full glory, which fulfils the same basic function of symbolic identification with worldly wealth before they go into a monastery to renounce it all. The dramatic transition from a noble prince with all material luxuries to a simple novice monk – governed by monastic discipline, fasting in the afternoon and celibacy – can be equated to initiation rituals that young males must undergo in various other cultures. After spending a week in the monastery, or as many days as they can bear, the novices leave quietly and without any pomp. Nonetheless, undergoing *shinbyu*, a boy becomes a potential monk who might eventually take up the responsibility of learning the *dhamma* and disseminating the Buddha *sāsana*.

It should be noted that Myanmar has no widely accepted ceremonial mode of initiating daughters as Buddhist nuns, and such occasions seem to generate little public celebration.[23] However, the social climate appears to be changing, amid the rising popularity of nun scholars, and the practice of temporary initiation for girls especially from urban areas has become more commonplace in recent decades.[24]

Among many meritorious occasions in transacting with the monastic community, some say that *kathina* – when robes are offered to the sangha as monks emerge from their long rains retreat – is the most important. The robe-offering ceremony is recorded in inscriptions as well as in old murals that date back to the twelfth century.[25] In Myanmar, *kathina* is conducted normally over a period of up to one month beginning at the full moon of October, but no specific date is designated for the actual robe-offering unlike in other Buddhist countries such as Cambodia, as noted by Holt.[26] Coinciding with the end of the rainy season, the offering season is highly anticipated, with many families saving up for months prior to the festive period.[27] This is not to suggest that lay donors are barred from offering robes to monks at any other time of the year; however, offering them during the *kathina* season is treated as a major communal event. It is customary for villagers, neighbourhood groups, trade or business guilds, council offices and schools to collect money from their members and affiliates for the purpose of making a joint offering to the sangha. It is also a time when people seek out monasteries that normally do not receive much support in remote corners of the country so that every monk receives a new robe and the donors' generous intentions are fairly and evenly distributed.

In rural villages in upper regions of the country, people traditionally grow and collect cotton balls, spin them in preparation for the loom and then weave the robes through the night; this weaving event is often the highlight of the robe-offering celebration. Even today, a robe-weaving competition called *matho thingan* is conducted on the eve of the full moon day at several prominent pagodas in November, most notably Shwedagon in Yangon. There, several groups of young maidens weave the *thingan* (monastic robes) all-night long, competing to finish the task before sunrise, and are watched by thousands of spectators and tourists, which adds a sense of climax to the celebration. The freshly woven robes, normally in a yellowish-brown colour, are then symbolically offered to the Buddha by being placed on his many images around the pagoda premises. By making these concerted efforts to support the weavers' task from its inception to its completion, the community reveals its enduring commitment to support the Triple Gem.

Offerings made during *kathina* celebrations are not limited to robes, however, and a variety of other items to be given to monks are put on display in public places before the ceremony. Inside community centres and town halls, it is common to see a *padeitha bin* or 'wish-fulfilling tree', which is a wooden triangular structure some five to six feet high, decorated with gifts and banknotes that hang from its branches for many days. In addition to the commonly stipulated Eight Requisites, these 'trees' hold sandals, umbrellas, incense and candles, soap, toothpaste, towels, hot water bottles, calendars, and even large items such as electric fans and rice cookers. Heavy-duty items that cannot be hung up – such as refrigerators or chairs – are displayed on the floor beside the tree. Holt describes this open display as an 'exhibition [that] serves as an inspiration for others to contribute as well, or as a barometer of the levels of charity achieved'.[28] Whether it inspires the spectators to offer or not, the term *padeitha* used to describe the 'tree' to be synonymous with 'abundance' and 'inexhaustible wealth'. The celebrated Myanmar writer Khin Myo Chit described the symbolic tree as being 'nurtured by people's acts of generosity'.[29] The ongoing popularity of such structures and their display may point to the strength of people's hopes that these trees would eventually bear abundant fruits they can all pluck. However, as the story narrated to the *kathina* congregation by the officiating monk points out, such a wish-fulfilling tree once existed at the beginning of the world, but it subsequently stopped bearing fruit, dried up and died, due to human greed and selfish hoarding. Hence, the *kathina* period is also a time when the laity are reminded of the moral story of *padeitha bin*: that they should not take more than they need at any one time and that people should take due care of the natural environment so that resources do not become depleted. Somewhat paradoxically, then, the ultimate aim of erecting these symbolic trees and decorating them with every item people can imagine the monks might need is to celebrate an ideal state of material abundance and total fulfilment, where there is no more greed or desire. At the same time, it also warns of excesses and the human propensity for greed that could eventually lead to suffering and the decline of Buddhism.

The meaning of meritorious giving

At any Buddhist ceremony, almost without exception, the officiating monk preaches on the theme of Buddhist morality, including the importance of *dāna*. He praises the donors for their good intention and reassures them of its meritorious outcome. In short, the main reason for Myanmar Buddhists to conduct *dāna* is because they want to secure a good rebirth, or even a better one than the present in their next life. Mogok Sayadaw U Vimala (1899–1962), who established the Mogok tradition of *vipassana* meditation, known for his sharp wit and inquisitive mind, frequently interrogated his donors about their ultimate – perhaps selfish – motives in offering him *dāna*. 'Is it because you want better rebirth or is it because you want *neikban*: *nibbana*? Why do you always want something? Why do you offer *dāna* if you want something in return?'[30]

As we have seen, being generous to one another is very much part of Myanmar's Buddhist culture, but the question of *why* people engage in so many acts of giving remains a complex one. In fact, religious offerings have wider implications beyond the lay donor's expectations of a good rebirth: for instance, enhancement of his/her social reputation, since a generous person is popular with a wide network of influential friends. It is also about how one is perceived as a good moral person in Myanmar society, and how a lay Buddhist tries to become publicly acknowledged as such. This may touch on the point raised by Venkatesan about morality and how religious ethics affect how people live and teach them how they 'ought to' engage with others in society.[31]

Yet, by the same token, to 'give well' requires cultural knowledge and tact, so that the giver must know what, when, and how to give, as well as to whom. If one's offering is not given properly and not appreciated by the recipient, it will not reap positive consequences. In other words, if generosity is misdirected to the extent that it fails to correspond with the recipient's wishes; and if imposed anyway, it can result in tension or even anger by the recipient. Thus, people in Myanmar are careful not to overstep the mark with their kindness in dealing with others, generally keeping it within their intimate social circles to avoid becoming overbearing to others, as reflected in their vernacular expression of *à-na-de*. On the other hand, monks and nuns receive whatever is offered to them, as doing so is an important part of their religious duty, but the details of transactions reveal the true nature of their relationship – as noted in my earlier discussion of how a lack of understanding can cause offence to monastic recipients. It is often stated that the 'pure intention' of the giver is what really matters, but 'merit-making' is a much more complex and a fluid practice than is generally stated.

Meanwhile, when our understanding of *dāna* becomes tightly focused on its meritorious outcomes, we come back to our initial questions of what 'meritorious' really means to Myanmar people and why offerings are directed predominantly at the Buddhist monastic community. Would it not be more meritorious to care for one's own infirm parents or support the disadvantaged in society? Spiro has already answered this question, stating that 'the merit deriving from *dāna* is proportional to *the spiritual quality of the recipient*'.[32] In the Anguttara Nikaya, the relative importance of the recipients is graded from the viewpoint of the 'merit worthiness', from an ordinary human being to the achievers of the rightful path to sainthood, culminating in the Buddhas.[33] Thus, from a Buddhist perspective, it makes sense to offer to the sangha rather than to a person in a state of beggary. In practice, this can be taken to extremes: among lay donors known to be generous patrons of monks and monasteries, there are also some who do not spend a penny to support their relatives. Such a case raises fundamental questions about the concept of 'merit' again: the innate intentions of lay donors and what they expect as the consequence of merit-making activities. Certainly, it could be argued that if one's kindness does not extend to those closest to oneself, like family members and friends when they are in need, then it seems no amount of generosity targeted exclusively to distant monks could uphold the original notions of what a good Buddhist should do or what a good deed should be.

The Buddhist scriptures list generosity as the starting point for any person in conducting a wholesome deed and stipulate that the act of *dāna* supports one onto the path to the final liberation. It is known that the practice of meditation or the self-discipline involved in observing the Buddhist precepts ranks much lower in the hierarchy of merit-making activities for Myanmar or Thai Buddhists.[34] Specifically, it is said that people observe the precepts not to acquire merit, but to avoid the 'demeritorious consequences'.[35] The net effect of all this seems to be that the sole criterion for the wholesomeness of their actions is their external engagement with the sangha and society, rather than with their own inner selves. This is what Spiro described as the distinction between Nibbanic Buddhism and Kammatic Buddhism.[36] As the emphasis shifts from becoming freed from *samsāra* to merit-making for a good future rebirth, the practice also shifts from inward to outward, from the practice of meditation to merit-making and from the transformation of the self to the improvement of one's social status.[37] Incidentally, one monk said to me that people in Myanmar spent too much time cooking and offering food to the monks, and too little effort is put into the practice of self-cultivation. As he put it, 'Offering is easy, but cultivating moral discipline is not'. Nonetheless, unlike the solitary practice of meditation, offering daily alms to monks and transacting with them in ceremonies appear to reassure many lay Buddhists that they are actually doing good deeds, sanctioned by the sangha and witnessed by their moral community. And conversely, meditation or an adherence to the Buddhist precepts is ultimately an inward practice that is self-centred and even seen as 'selfish' by some. As members of an interdependent society, Myanmar people seem to perceive and acknowledge their worth in the sharing experiences, in commensality and in reciprocal transactions with others, which ultimately generates a deep sense of wellbeing and a 'feel-good' factor for everyone. Therefore, 'giving is the means, par excellence',[38] and this is at the core of what the notion of 'merit' means to many Myanmar Buddhists.

Engaged Buddhism in practice

The culture of giving provides a fertile ground for people to help each other in a country whose emergency services and social welfare systems are still underdeveloped, and – particularly in Myanmar's provincial towns – many volunteer groups fill the void as we will see in Chapter 5. They spontaneously gather in times of crisis, providing aid to local families who cannot afford funeral costs or need transport for hospital visits, and sometimes even acting as undertakers themselves when other options are out of reach. Interestingly, many of these volunteers are middle-aged men who hang around idly in tea shops during the day or in beer gardens at night, but thanks to the ready availability of advanced telecommunications in recent years, they have been able to rapidly and flexibly fill these and other roles in the community. In the town of Sagaing, there are about a dozen loosely organized groups, comprising men usually from local families of merchants or shop owners, who are relatively free to offer their time and services spontaneously. Whenever they receive a phone call from a local family in need of help, members organize themselves into a group of five to eight and rush to offer whatever support they are required, as well as relaying news of births, deaths, fires and accidents, and collecting funds to pay the hospital or funeral bills for poor families. These volunteers also come together on auspicious occasions such as weddings, *shinbyu* or communal feasts when extra hands are needed to carry large pots and deliver drinks. It is customary for the host to thank the volunteers with ample alcohol and food, and for the members themselves; it seems yet another excuse to have a big party.

When I interviewed them about why they volunteer, and even pay for such an activity out of their own pockets, almost all of them replied, *ayan pyò-de*: that they were just 'happy' to help. Only two out of twenty-three informants mentioned 'merit' in their responses. Even when they were prompted to discuss the role of merit-making in their involvement, most said 'merit' did not even occur to them when they were summoned to help and insisted that karmic uplift for the next life did not enter into their decision to act. Many reiterated that they were just happy to be useful to others who were in dire circumstances. In this case, despite my usual scepticism about the underlying motives for people's conduct, these volunteers convinced me that even devout Myanmar Buddhists can simply revel in existential experiences that inspire simple joyous feelings and live in the moment. That is, every volunteering opportunity gave them a sense of purpose and fulfilment, reinforcing the connection to their own community. I came to realize that the deep sense of worth they gained from working with and for others in the community was the real 'meritorious outcome' for them.

3

Buddhist monks

Although Buddhist monks may appear to be the antithesis of politics due to their renunciant position, historically, they have played important roles in 'conflict resolution, promoting dialogue between warring groups and factions, and in the dialogical process for promoting peace'.[1] In fact, Myanmar monks have led a number of social movements in modern times and actively engaged with issues that concerned the 'common good'.[2] Moreover, during the country's five decades of isolation and military rule that began in the mid-1960s, the sangha was the only civil institution in the country that survived political oppression and intolerance; and monasteries served as gathering places where people exchanged information and discussed their daily problems. Since political reform started in Myanmar in 2012, monks have emerged as central actors in the rising phenomenon of Buddhist nationalism. Social tension mounted between Buddhist and Muslim communities during this period of major transition, accelerated by the widespread narrative of 'Buddha *sāsana* under threat'. Buddhist monks, asserting their role as moral authority especially during such times of uncertainty, also came out as vocal critiques of the country's rapid development and moral degeneration as a result. In this, some observers associated the sangha with the old order, blaming them for hindering the process of development promoted by multinational businesses and Myanmar's new government. The public behaviour of monk U Wirathu, who rose to notoriety as the face of 'Buddhist terror',[3] added another layer to the negative public perceptions of Buddhist monks as being anti-Muslim and inflammatory.[4] This also reflects a dramatic change in the media coverage of

Buddhist monks in Myanmar in recent years, who were once seen as heroic leaders of the non-violent Saffron Revolution and even nominated for the Nobel Peace Prize, but are now regularly criticized as chauvinistic, politically motivated and discriminatory. I will touch briefly on the case of Ma Ba Tha, the Association for the Protection of Race and Religion in the latter section of this chapter, but it is beyond the scope of this volume to provide exhaustive detail on Buddhist monks' political involvements. Rather, the aim here is to examine the fundamental workings of the sangha in transacting with society; and in this particular case, to understand the 'how' and 'why' they are popular with a wide socio-political influence, rather than the 'what', of Buddhist monks in Myanmar society.

There are more than half a million vocational monks registered with the Department of Religious Affairs in Myanmar today, most of whom come from rural agricultural communities where people have traditionally been loyal supporters of the monastic community. Most prominent monks in the modern history of the country – Ledi Sayadaw (1846–1923), Sunlun Sayadaw (1878–1952), Taungphila Sayadaw (1897–1986), Mahasi Sayadaw (1904–1982), Mingun Tipitaka Sayadaw (1911–1993) and so on – are also from these rural villages, where monastics have been held in deep reverence in a way that no politicians are. The vast monastic network, based on deep personal allegiances between teachers and students, and their lay supporters extend even to the borderlands of ethnic autonomous zones in the country. From the standpoint of Buddhist monks, however, maintaining a regular relationship with their lay congregations is essential not only for their day-to-day survival, but also to sustain the foundation of Buddhist faith by promoting moral duty and harmonious coexistence. For lay Buddhists, meanwhile, monks provide a focus for their daily worship, performing the role of a medium through which people 'plant' their good deed and are assured of its meritorious return. This relationship of interdependence is the religious ideal held to provide the moral foundation for a stable society.

It is usually assumed that the main tasks of Buddhist monks are learning the scriptures, meditating and disseminating the teachings of the Buddha. Yet, despite the Weberian perceptions of them as solitary recluses withdrawn from society, Myanmar monks perform a variety of roles for their lay supporters.[5]

For instance, they conduct funerals and officiate at memorials, give public sermons on morality, recite protective chants at housewarming events and offer blessings to those suffering from ill health. In the absence of adequate social welfare system or any infrastructure to support the population, monks fill the vacuum by providing various services: offering counselling, mediating in domestic disputes, taking in anti-social delinquents and offering shelter to the homeless. Furthermore, in the aftermath of natural disasters or at times of intra-communal tension, monasteries have offered a retreat for victims and even a shelter for political prisoners. As such, Myanmar monks occupy a pivotal position in society; they are looked up to as moral leaders and relied upon to guide the laity's social actions. Unavoidably, some monks end up being drawn by this closeness and/or by their own sense of moral duty into secular affairs beyond the bounds stipulated in the Vinaya, and thus often become embroiled in Myanmar's public controversies.

Daily transaction with monks

The people of Myanmar are willing, enthusiastic donors; and almost every Buddhist family engages in some type of alms transaction with the sangha, ranging from a daily offering of cooked rice to monks who come on their morning rounds, to communal feasts on the occasions of *alhu*. The majority population's urge to offer *dāna* seems to be rooted in a sense of moral obligation and a particular understanding of how a 'good Buddhist' ought to behave. Thus, engaging in a regular relationship through these offering transactions bonds lay supporters to their monastic recipients, affirming the former's sense of affiliation with the moral community and, thus, enhancing their Buddhist identity.

The commonest means of transactions with the sangha for a lay Buddhist is by engaging in the act of *sun-laung* (the offering of cooked rice). Almost every Buddhist celebration in Myanmar seems to start with *sun-laung*; visiting monasteries to offer *sun*, scoop by scoop to every monk waiting in a long queue or offering to those who visit the household every morning.

Within Buddhist families, one individual – usually a pious grandmother or an unmarried aunt – has traditionally taken up the role of looking after the monks who visit the household every morning to collect alms. This can be quite demanding, as the person in question has to get up early every morning to cook for the monks who begin arriving before sunrise, and they have not eaten since midday on the previous day. Piping hot rice is offered to them universally, while some households may offer additional food such as curry dishes in small containers, fried lentils, cakes and bananas, all of which are neatly placed in their alms bowls. Many novices are still children, and the alms bowls suspended from their lean shoulders sometimes appear bigger than their bald heads. As eager as they are to receive their first meal of the day, they leave as swiftly as they arrived, without uttering a single word or acknowledging the offerings in any way. A few elderly monks may arrive later, but most of the food offerings will be gone by around 7.00 am, to the satisfaction of the lay donor. Because this scene is repeated across Myanmar every day of the year, devout Buddhists are reluctant to go on holiday unless someone can be found to take over the daily chore of offering food to arriving monks. The situation can be likened to having a permanently dependent family member. Nonetheless, it is this level of commitment by lay Buddhists that not only sustains the monastic community, but also constitutes the foundation of their own Buddhist faith.

On their daily rounds, come rain or shine, monks follow the monastic norm of walking barefoot to their donors' residences. This can be strenuous and painful, and effectively limits their range to about a three-mile radius from the monastery. This relatively short distance both reflects and symbolizes the closeness of the relationship that exists between monasteries and their respective local communities. Many of the young boys in the neighbourhood must have had their first novice experiences in their local monasteries, learning how to read and recite Buddhist chants, and shown how to maintain discipline by the senior monks. The relationship between monasteries and their local communities is sustained over generations and the regularity of their daily transactions has provided a stable foundation for Myanmar society. Thus, it is noteworthy that lay Buddhists do not offer food to just any monk or novice who visits their household; an unfamiliar face is unlikely to receive any, even if he arrives in a monk's robe. In other words, alms transactions in Myanmar society are not casual ones, but are based on prearranged relationships in which both lay benefactors and monastic beneficiaries are known to each other, presupposing a regular and sustained relationship between the sangha and its lay supporters.

Monks as recipients

When people in Myanmar are asked why they respect the monks, they normally refer to the latter's self-control: in observing celibacy, not eating in the afternoons and giving up material comforts, as well as the degree of difficulty associated with these abstinence practices. Young monks in particular are admired for the fact that they can control their libidinous impulses and general material desires. Many people I talked to mentioned that they supported the monks because they practised detachment from worldly pleasures, which they themselves found difficult to do. One male informant commented that becoming a temporary monk was the most difficult experience he had ever undergone and said that anyone who can persevere as a vocational monk for life is worthy of any amount of *dāna*.

Nonetheless, as noted earlier, people are quite selective about their monastic beneficiaries and do not offer material support to just any monk.[6] In an earlier article, I described three types of monks to whom Myanmar people generally offer *dāna*,[7] listing their socio-religious attributes according to what is seen as their 'symbolic capital'. Classified as preachers, monk-scholars, or *arahant*s, each type transacts with lay followers in their distinctive ways, while laypeople, for their part, expect different spiritual returns from each of them. It should also be borne in mind that a monk's degree of closeness to his lay benefactor is determined to a certain extent by whether the donor is a member of his family, a close friend, a student or disciple, a regular donor, the main sponsor of his ordination (who might also be his regular donor), or a stranger whose identity is not known (i.e. an anonymous fan). Most lay supporters of preachers and *arahant*s fall into this final category of a constantly fluctuating 'fan base', which presents a contrast to lay supporters of monk-scholars, the majority of whom are known regular donors. In the case of these regular supporters, their donations and involvement with the monastic beneficiary tend to be constant and stable, and an established monk-scholar is normally supported by several groups of committed donors who attend to his every need.

In addition, a monk who displays exceptional self-discipline is highly respected, especially when the world around him is becoming more materialistic and filled with temptations; but gaps certainly exist between the idealized prototype of an aloof monastic and ordinary monks people transact with in their daily alms offering. Thus, the complaints we hear about the monks' displays of many kinds of worldly behaviour are likely to arise from a mismatch between social reality and the laity's unreasonably high expectations of what a monk should be, rather than from their behaviour itself being unreasonable. Another mismatch is highlighted when Western observers, who are brought up to verbally and frequently express their gratitude, complain that Asian Buddhist monks are unwelcoming or even rude as they do not show their appreciation when receiving alms.[8] Again, people have different

Figure 3.1 *Many of the committed lay donors are women, who take a keen interest in offering food to the monks.*

expectations of how Buddhist monks should behave and judge their outward conduct according to what they perceive as normative. Hence, the monks are sometimes criticized for adhering (too rigidly) to the monastic rules stipulated in the Vinaya, and at other times, criticized for becoming too worldly and departing from the ideal image of a detached renunciant. Myanmar monks I spoke to said that it was essential to show 'detachment' and follow the monastic rules when transacting with the laity.[9] However, they also told me that they were always grateful for the generosity shown by the laity despite not explicitly showing it. One said, 'my heart fills with *mettā* whenever I receive an offering from my donors', and added that he always sent out blessings under his breath in return for their kindness. After all, there is an understanding in a traditional Buddhist society that it is the monks' entitlement to receive *dāna* offerings and it is the lay donors who actually have to be grateful in having them as recipients.

During communal feasts of *ahlu*, monks invariably eat quietly with downcast eyes, and show no appreciation for the food being offered, or even any preference for one type of food over another. This seemingly disinterested behaviour is the result of a strict monastic training that obliges them to minimize the display of emotions in public, and which simultaneously serves to keep emotions in check. While the monks are being fed ceremonially, the donors huddle around and carefully focus their attention on the monks eating. Male members of the donor family mill around to top up their rice and soup bowls, making sure that the monks' every need is met. Women may keep a calculated distance but are just as keen as men to observe how the monks eat; and it is this act of observation itself – rather than, say, cooking – that becomes the focal point of their meritorious deed. As one female donor told me excitedly, 'imagine their stomachs filling up! It makes me so happy'. Another said that observing the monks eat made her feel *sei ayan kyantha-thi*: 'My heart becomes very rich'. Some described such feelings as *piti* (pure joy) and nothing was better than the feeling of their stomachs filling up! In short, watching the monks eat, albeit quietly and expressionlessly, seems to give Myanmar lay donors a profound sense of satisfaction, as a tangible evidence of their goodwill being 'ingested' and as a symbol of their roles as nurturers of the moral community.

Charismatic monks

In the modern history of Myanmar, there have been many saintly monks who attracted large followings due to their apparent moral purity and non-attachment to worldly power. Ferguson refers to Ashin Jāgara (1822–1894), later known as Shwegyin Sayadaw, the founder of Shwegyin sect in the mid-nineteenth century, as one of these special monks, renowned for his exemplary scholarship and moral discipline. It is said that King Mindon (1808–1878) of the Konbaung dynasty was so impressed by Shwegyin Sayadaw's saintly qualities that he granted him twelve monasteries.[10] Ferguson goes on to describe how the Sayadaw 'redistributed' the offerings he received to his many monk disciples, thus furthering the development of his new Buddhist sect. Another highly popular monk in more recent times was Thamanya Sayadaw U Vinaya (1910–2003), who was instrumental in transforming the uninhabited remote corner of Karen state into a 'civilized' place.[11] His holy presence in the 1990s attracted lay donors from all over the country, including politicians and army generals,[12] and a continuous flow of donations and transactions in goods and services resulted in the construction of a large self-sustaining community around him. While at the centre of this complex operation, Sayadaw ensured that Buddhist morality was practised, thus meat eating, alcohol and weapons were not allowed on the premises, and that donated goods were fairly redistributed and used for everyone in the community.[13] As time went on, Thamanya Sayadaw's followers multiplied, sharing his vision for the creation of a Buddhist utopia on earth: a place where all their material needs would be met and there would be no more suffering. Without having or welding any worldly power himself, in other words, the monk acted as a medium through which people sought to realize their dreams by offering their time, goods and services: a phenomenon Rozenberg described as a 'cumulative process of sanctification'.[14]

This type of centripetal position occupied by a charismatic monk can be likened to the eye of a storm – the calm centre of an ever-growing force created by people's devotion and desire for a betterment of their lives. As the 'storm' attracts evermore attention and donations from society, it gives rise to proliferating layers of transactional complexity, linking the monk's inner layers of close devotees and personal assistants to outer layers of frequent visitors and acquaintances, and beyond to a distant rim of anonymous well-wishers and first-time pilgrims. Each and every follower jockeys for position to get closer to the monk, making offerings and performing services in the hope of attracting his attention, even catching his direct gaze, which is interpreted as a sign of special blessing. As the term 'cumulative process' indicates, once a person is accepted into the inner circle of confidants, proximity to the monk gives him/her a certain level of influence in his moral community. And by becoming a communal gatekeeper who protects the monk's sanctity from the encroaching and ever-increasing crowd, one becomes part of the process of 'sanctification'. Incidentally, young children can approach a saintly monk with the utmost ease, perhaps due to their innocence and lack of concern for his 'powers'.[15]

Rozenberg described the extent of Thamanya Sayadaw's power and the respect he generated, especially among the ethnic Karens in the periphery, culminating in the construction of a large communal settlement near Hpa-an town in the Karen state.[16] In effect, this was the re-appropriation of an ideal monastery as a communal site, where people from all walks of life could come together and talk about their hopes and aspirations, and that would function (before the advent of the internet and social media) as a haven from their daily worries and political constraints. In this ideal schema, the moral purity of a saintly monk formed the focal point for the lay congregation, representing detachment, selflessness and non-reciprocity, which – ironically – would attract a large influx of people and resources to him. However, such saintly monks in Myanmar are becoming rarer by the day. The traditional habitat of such spiritual seekers, such as remote caves or the wilderness of the borderlands, is becoming cultivated; forests are being cut down, and secularism is taking hold in society. Moreover, as had happened with many of his forebears, the passing of the extraordinary Thamanya Sayadaw led his material legacy to sadly disintegrate almost as rapidly as it had emerged.[17]

Another charismatic monk worthy of mentioning in this context is Bodhi Ta-htaung Sayadaw U Narada (1931–2006), who resided on the rural outskirts of Monywa city, now the provincial capital of the Sagaing region. He was a renowned *weikza* or wizard (literally, someone with 'higher or esoteric knowledge'), known for his *samatha* concentration powers and special skills in *daloun* (alchemy). He attracted mostly rural devotees due to these unique skills, along with his unusual visions of the Buddha and his prophesies. As a result of his visionary dreams, many projects involving the installation of large Buddha images were initiated, and they eventually filled up every corner of his large monastery compound of fifteen acres. Sayadaw's first such project was launched in 1960 after he dreamed of planting a thousand bodhi trees in the arid wilderness of his native village outside Monywa. He later spoke of the special attraction to the bodhi tree that he had felt since young, as it was under such a tree that the Buddha was known to have attained enlightenment. Urged to plant bodhi trees by his dreams, Sayadaw spent many years doing so on his own, and then erected an image of the Buddha in a meditation posture under every tree. The story of a lone monk planting bodhi trees gradually spread by word of mouth throughout the region, and he came to be known as the 'abbot of one thousand bodhi trees'. Today, his

Figure 3.2 *The largest reclining Buddha in Myanmar in the outskirt of Monywa, which was constructed as a result of one monk's vision of the Buddha's spiritual power.*

monastery is best known as the home of Myanmar's longest reclining Buddha (101m in length), built in 1991, as well as for the country's tallest standing Buddha statue (129m in height), completed after his death in 2008.[18]

During the last decade of his life, Sayadaw's monastery premises continued to see random installations of many Buddhist statues and colourful artefacts, adding further to their general atmosphere of bizarre and eccentric creativity. His monastic education during his formative years having been cut short due to tuberculosis, Sayadaw was neither eloquent in speech nor sophisticated in behaviour, and thus never had much appeal to educated urban donors. Nonetheless, he managed to carve out a unique legacy of his own, supported by his creative imagination and aspiration to grandeur and spiritual heights, which resonated with many Buddhists in the rural agricultural communities.

In contrast to monks who operate in traditional religious landscapes of rural areas, Myanmar is home to an emergent class of so-called celebrity monks, whose sophisticated performances, linguistic skills and academic knowledge are attracting the attention of middle-class urban residents. Many are well-established preachers called *Dhammakatika*; and among them, the most famous monk is Sitagu Sayadaw U Nyanissara, who is known for both the power of his oratory and his political acumen.[19] His popularity stems in part from his knowledge of decorative homiletics in the Buddhist Myanmar tradition, incorporated expertly into his sermons, and this was the skill he learned from the famous monk-preacher of the last century Anisakhan Sayadaw U Pandita. The appeal of celebrity monks is enhanced by the select images they disseminate via social media, appealing to a new brand of trend-following young urban Buddhists. As such, monks in this category may display characteristics similar to popular rock singers or film stars, attracting material support from a wide spectrum of society. However, their lay followers, many of whom know these monks only by reputation or virtually (e.g. through images disseminated on the internet) are not necessarily devotees or Buddhist pious. In this respect, although their attraction may appear to be centripetal, the position of these monks may be vacuous, since there is no tangible or sustained spiritual relationship between them and their lay followers. Moreover, the criteria for supreme moral purity or detachment, the fundamental prerequisite for a monk to be considered extraordinary, do not have to be necessarily met by modern 'celebrity monks' or, indeed, relevant for those followers who are attracted to them in the first place.

Scholarly monks and popular preachers

On the main television channel in Myanmar, live sermons by prominent scholar-monks such as Bamaw Sayadaw (b.1930), the chairman of Ma Ha Na (the executive Sangha Maha Nayaka Committee appointed by the state),[20] are broadcast almost every day. Their sermons are also distributed on CDs and other tangible media, listened to by devout Buddhists at home and via their car stereos. Among these preachers, Dr Nandamala-bhivamsa (b.1940), commonly referred to as Pa-chok Sayadaw, the Rector of International Theravada Buddhist Missionary University,[21] is currently the most popular, being both a 'celebrity monk' and a well-established Buddhist scholar.[22] His *dhamma* talks are highly sought after due to his advanced scholarship, while those who enjoy his sermons commonly cite his extensive scriptural knowledge as the reason. Another such monk is the 'Oxford Sayadaw', Dr Khammai Dhammasami (b.1964), who is a rising star in *dhamma*-talk circles. A highly respected scholar fluent in several languages, trained in Sri Lanka and England, he holds a DPhil from the University of Oxford. His Shan ethnic background adds to his unique credentials, and he has recently established a Buddhist college in the Shan state to train monks and nuns from ethnic minority backgrounds. There is also Shwe Parami Sayadaw U Sandadhika (b.1967), an established scholar, a popular preacher and a writer. He rose to fame as a student when he came first in the whole country in the advanced level examination, but left the medical school option to become a Buddhist monk. He studied at Mahagandhayon Kyaung in Amarapura, a prominent monastery school, and became one of the most popular writers on Buddhism in Myanmar.[23] At the pinnacle of Buddhist scholarship, there are monks known as Tipitakadhara (Bearers of the Tipitaka), the prestigious title awarded by the Myanmar government for being the most erudite scholars of the Pali canon.[24] Currently, there are ten Tipitakadhara and, as evidence of their academic brilliance, they are the most respected and sought after monks in Myanmar. Unlike the traditional charismatic monks, who were often meditating monks rather than scholars, popular Buddhist monks in the contemporary scene are equipped with advanced knowledge of scriptures and high academic degrees, and they engage with the laity as *dhamma* teachers, as public speakers and writers who can disseminate Buddhism in a modern manner and even in several languages. Meanwhile, there are socially engaged monks such as Dhammaduta Sayadaw U Sekeinda (b.1958), who reaches out to the younger generation by his lively sermons based on moral tales from an early life of poverty, and his radio broadcasts aimed at children and uneducated masses are popular making the *dhamma* easy to comprehend. Perhaps he is the only Myanmar monk who openly claims that he can cook and sew, being the eldest child of ten siblings, which he credits his mother for training him in various domestic skills.

As far as the role of a typical scholar monk in Myanmar is concerned, he has an institutional role as abbot or principal of a monastery school called *sathin-daik*. These monasteries that function as Buddhist seminaries are dormitory schools privately run by monks for the training of monastic students. Senior monks who administer them are integrated into an extensive network of *dhamma* teachers and students whose relationships often overlap with those of preceptors (mentors) and preceptees in the monastic community. As a result of living together and due to the many years of tutelage and guidance, the relationship between a monk-teacher/preceptor and his students formed during the latter's formative years often develops into a close-knit unit akin to a pseudo-family. Spiro has suggested that monks are generally reluctant to establish interpersonal relationships for fear of developing 'emotional attachment',[25] but this is not the case in a monastery school milieu. Indeed, it is commonplace for student-monks to develop emotional attachments to their monk-teachers and treat them as if they were their own parents. As a rule, a student will never criticize his teacher and the teacher will always defend and act as the protector of his students. Occasionally, I have seen a monk-teacher reciprocating their loyalty with small amounts of cash called *moun-bou* (money for sweets), for example, when his students do well in exams or excel at some other

Figure 3.3 *Traditionally, Buddhists in Myanmar express their respect by taking off their sandals and prostrating themselves on the ground when welcoming a senior monk.*

task. If a student under tutelage is struggling financially, but academically promising, a monk-teacher may also ask his own donors to sponsor the student's education. Regular payments in such cases are similar to grants or scholarships as we know them, and thus different from *dāna* offerings; but it is still regarded as meritorious for a lay donor to be in a position to offer a student-monk this type of sponsorship.

As the above discussion implies, a scholar-monk normally has an intimate group of committed donors who have supported him from the early years of his monastic life. They look after him by sending him regular remittances, usually in the form of a monthly allowance transferred into his bank account, and calling on him frequently to check that his every material need is met. The support of these donors can also extend to his monastic students; and depending on the level of the teacher's popularity and influence, wealthy donors may even take on the role of benefactors to his whole monastery school. Not coincidentally, a prominent monk-teacher will generally be known as Sayadaw 'of such-and-such monastery', reflecting the interweaving of the institution's good reputation and his own. In addition to those from his own group of regular donors, a monk-teacher receives a continuous flow of *dāna* offerings from those who donate primarily to his students and other junior monks in the monastic hierarchy, despite his lack of personal relationships with most of them. This serves as an expression of gratitude felt towards the monk-teacher by his students' families and donors, and supporters of his monastery more generally. Consequently, a prominent monk-scholar often finds himself in a position of extensive influence over his students and their respective sets of lay supporters even down the monastic hierarchy, and such extensive support base forms the crux of his powerful position in many monastery schools.

In the high echelons of Myanmar's sangha, all senior monks nominated and appointed to the executive sangha committees, even at its regional and township levels, are in the category of *pariyatti* monks, which forms an exclusive group of *dhamma* teachers and scholars who make important decisions regarding monastic affairs and oversee the general conduct of monastic members including nuns. They also form horizontal relationships of friendship and collaboration with fellow monks and nuns in the lineage of their respective scholarly affiliations. Important news and information are passed down in these monastic alumni groups and shared within the network of *dhamma* fellows, who can be relied upon to support each other in times of major crisis. Their internal circles and monastic networks can be regarded as an autonomous sphere of influence that cannot be penetrated by any outside source of power such as local secular authorities or the military. As will be discussed in Chapter 5, personal contacts in the monastic network can be particularly beneficial during major disruptions caused by natural disasters or political upheavals, facilitating the distribution of food and passing on vital information quickly and securely when other means of communication fail.

Monks as benefactors

Tambiah once argued, 'Monks are always receivers and laypeople always givers'.[26] However, as noted earlier, Myanmar monks are not always on the receiving side in social transactions. On the contrary, they are active givers who redistribute whatever they have received to other monastics; and on certain occasions, for instance, on their birthdays, they reciprocate the favours they have received from their lay supporters. Because the worth of a monk is ultimately determined by his compassion and goodwill, it is also seen as important that he tactfully redistributes the offerings he has received in order to maximize their utility to the moral community. If an offering is given in the form of food or other consumables, the redistribution process can be straightforward, as the monk consumes only what he needs and gives away any food surplus. If a monk receives a material item he does not need, he could offer it to another monastic who might find a better use for it. However, large items such as cars or fridges normally become the common property of the monastery. The original monk recipient might also give away an item to a different lay donor other than the one who gave it to him in the first place if he regards it as too lavish or otherwise inappropriate for a monk to have. As well as being seen to generate meritorious returns for monastic givers, these redistributive practices within the monastic community result in the monk recipients/givers widening their general influence. Nonetheless, the manner in which one 'gives away' – that is, so that it does not offend the original giver and/or revert to him/her – and the occasions on which it is done are as important as the offering itself, since mistakes in this area could have far-reaching negative results.

Thus, nothing is wasted in monasteries; any leftover foodstuffs are given to the needy of the neighbourhood, and dogs and cats living on and around the monastery premises are also fed. As such, all monasteries operate a social welfare system for their local populations, and a number of people survive on its daily handouts in return for providing menial services.[27] Holt also stated from his recent observations that in Myanmar, 'the monastery is often a redistribution point for wealth and excess'.[28] At best, such transactions may result in a cycle of reciprocity that can sustain people inside as well as outside the monastic community. Hence, the material surplus from the original *dāna* offered to monks is filtered back to the local community, and the practice of reciprocity mediated by monastic members results in broader sequences of giving and receiving in communal life. For example, if a male former donor becomes unemployed or homeless, an abbot may express his gratitude by allowing him to stay at his monastery or by paying him to do some chores around the premises. As such, over the long term, a monastic beneficiary will at times become the monastic benefactor to his former lay donor, returning the various types of favours and offerings accumulated over the years.

Some Buddhist monks also give out symbolic tokens of their special spiritual powers: for instance, the forest monks in Thailand make amulets and give them out to lay devotees who come to seek their protective powers.[29] Devotees also believe in the emanating power from the monks' special chants and accept the recitation of sacred words in the ancient formula as a protective gift from the monks to them.[30] Sometimes a short protective formula or *yantras* is granted in its material form to a lay devotee, also described by Justin McDaniel when he was given a *takrut* (a kind of amulet with rolled inscriptions placed inside a sealed tube) by his abbot with an abbreviated inscription of *Ratana Sutta*.[31] Amulets are not as popular as sacred commodities in Myanmar as in Thailand, but many Buddhists go on pilgrimage to worship relics and visit charismatic monks to receive their blessing. Often it is granted in the form of chants or an item that has direct association with the monk, for example, a piece of robe so that his magical powers are transferred to protect the recipient from unseen danger.

On my several visits to the monastery of Bodhi Ta-htaung in Monywa in the late 1980s and 1990s, I met the Sayadaw rumoured to be a *weikza*. Unusually, for a saintly monk, he offered every visitor a 'gift', sometimes a small rosary or a miniature black or green Buddha statue, or at other times a *daloun*: a small black metal ball produced by his alchemy. A gaunt figure who rarely spoke and appeared almost indifferent to the stream of people coming to meet him, he occasionally smiled, and even invited visitors to have a meal if their visit coincided with the lunchtime at his monastery. Other known *arahant* such as the late Taungphila Sayadaw in Sagaing gave out a spoonful of dry ash to all visitors, who would queue up to gratefully receive it in the mouth, as if it were some kind of spiritual medicine. Konlon Sayadaw, another charismatic monk in the Shan state, was widely rumoured to be an *arahant* and possess *dagò*, a kind of spiritual power beyond the influence of any secular powers.³² I have written elsewhere about how the monk would give out small pieces of his old robe to visitors, who believed in his protective power.³³ Many miracle stories surrounding his life generated an almost inexplicable fervour, and many Myanmar people felt compelled to visit and meet him in person. Faced with this influx of curious and admiring crowds, it was almost as if the monk *had* to distribute token gifts to dissipate the weight of adoration directed towards him rather than conferring on them his authoritative power.

When a symbolic item of this sort is given by a monk to a lay person, the recipient would generally describe the act as *ketin-thi*, implying that the monk granted him/her some part of his protective spiritual powers. The transmission of such powers is also held to occur by way of physical touch or the consumption of his leftover food. My informants told me that such a gift had the effect of *andare-kin thi* (protection from danger). The 'dangers' from which they needed protection might be worldly ones such as car accidents, contagious diseases, or thefts, or the negative influence of spirits or curses sent by jealous rivals. Because of the association with such a special monk, the granted object – albeit worthless in itself – becomes mysteriously imbued with his magical potency. When anything as powerful is given, it is customary for the recipient to first lift it above his/her forehead to show gratitude to the monk, and then to carefully wrap it in a tissue or put it in a separate container to take home. Once there, the powerful item will be kept on the Buddhist altar with other religious paraphernalia as a reminder of the special transaction with the saintly monk and worshipped as his physical remnant. Lay followers seem to believe that by being close to the material source of *dat* (spiritual power), they have received some of it, and that the monk in question would offer them ongoing protection deriving from his deep *mettā*.

Birthday celebrations of monks

Birthdays are important social occasions in Myanmar society laden with symbolic meanings. It is generally an occasion for making merit, patching up past fallings-out and giving everyone a chance to start afresh in enhancing their karmic state. This may sound odd to those accustomed to receiving celebratory cards and presents on their birthdays in the West; but in Myanmar, it is the birthday person who customarily treats his/her friends and family to a meal, releases animals back into the wild, and offers donations to mark the auspicious day. Myanmar monks and nuns also use their birthday celebrations to express their gratitude for the support given to them during the year, and in recent years the birthdays of prominent monks have become widely celebrated events. They typically throw a large feast and distribute presents to their lay supporters, especially when reaching the age of sixty, with the seventy-fifth birthday referred to as the diamond anniversary, eightieth as the ruby jubilee and any age over that as an additional bonus. These events have become even more grand and lavish as monastic students and lay followers gather to celebrate a monk's lifetime achievements. The birthday celebration allows a monastic to reverse the normative flow of gift offerings and become the principal benefactor, using the opportunity to bestow gratitude on those who have provided him/her support. The following quote from Rozenberg gives us a description of the July 2000 celebration of the eighty-ninth birthday of Thamanya Sayadaw, then at the height of his popularity:

> Though it is common in Burma to celebrate the birthday of highly venerated living monks, no birthday ceremony, no matter how famous and venerated the monk, has ever reached [… such] scale and complexity of that of Thammanya Hsayadaw.[34] In the early 1990s, at most one hundred invited monks congregated to take part in what was a local celebration. Since then, in accordance with the ever-growing fame of the great monk, the birthday has developed into a national and even international event, involving tens of thousands of religious and lay participants.

He described how people showed excessive devotion to the monk, resulting in a continuous flow of affection and generosity, but their devotion was also reciprocated by the monk on a large scale on his birthday.[35] Rozenberg, however, noted the danger in which the saintly monk's great wealth, accumulated almost entirely through the receipt of offerings, could eventually threaten the public perception of his 'saintliness'.[36] Besides a monk like Thamanya Sayadaw did not need any more merit as he was just biding his time for the past karma to work itself out. Thus, a reasonable interpretation of what occurred may be that this popular monk gave out token gifts on such an occasion to express his gratitude as well as offload the heavy weight of devotion directed at him. But ironically, such a reverse gift granted from a saintly monk appears to become an ultimate 'pure gift', which cannot be reciprocated by any lay person.

As the above discussion implies, the birthday of a prominent monk can be a grand show of his influence in the Buddhist community, as his current and former students, friends, monastic colleagues and lay donors all come together to celebrate the special occasion. When the seventy-fifth birthday of Insein Ywama Sayadaw was celebrated at his monastery in Yangon in March 2014, essays emphasizing his high academic and religious achievements written by his students were printed as booklets and distributed several months prior to the event. During the three consecutive days of celebrations, hundreds of vehicles were hired to transport elderly guests and prominent senior monks who came to give celebratory talks. On the first day, 400 monks arrived from all over Myanmar, many of whom were Sayadaw's former students, and were given local banknotes equivalent to about $50 USD each, along with a high-quality suitcase and books. On the second day, the 600 monks and novices resident at his own monastery were given $10 USD each and the same presents. On the third day, 100 senior monks and Sayadaw's former students residing in Yangon arrived and were each offered $150 USD, along with a set of robes and a high-quality briefcase. Last, on the same day, 120 nuns were also invited and given briefcases as well as $50 USD. On all three days, well-wishers and guests were offered lunch at the monastery and everyone was given small commemorative gifts inscribed with the Sayadaw's name and words. The total sum he spent on flowers, decoration, lighting, sound effects, transport and food consumed by more than 3,000 guests for three consecutive days must have come up to around $30,000 USD. Of course, his regular donors also contributed towards the sum; some as *sùn taga* (donor of the celebratory lunch) and others specifically to pay for transport costs and so on; but in accordance with the long-standing custom in Myanmar, it was the birthday monk himself who paid the bulk of the expenses, not merely to celebrate the occasion but also to accumulate merit.[37]

The case of Ma Ba Tha

We have seen that the relationship between a monk and his lay donors is the product of continuous transactions between sangha and laity, and it often develops into a close bond that forms the crux of his wide support base in Myanmar society. As we have seen, laypeople's support of the monastic community is remembered even after considerable lapses of time, and donors honour the meritorious deeds of their family members by offering continued support to the monks and monasteries once patronized by past members of their family. Thus, an act of generosity by a lay donor generates a certain momentum, showing that the relationship of interdependence between the monastic community and its supporters generates, spreads, and multiplies the generosity over time, with transactions flowing in both directions. In this respect, the social and political influence that Buddhist monks exert in present-day Myanmar cannot be understood solely by reference to their political actions or rousing rhetoric in the social media. Rather, to be effective and authoritative as a public religious figure, a monk must have a solid support base in society, which cannot be sustained by media attention or other forms of virtual popularity alone.[38] Therefore, the rise and fall of many political monks in recent years should be seen in the context of rapid transition and structural change the country is undergoing, and specifically the introduction of social media and the lifting of censorship in 2013. Myanmar's people, having struggled for decades in an isolated society where freedom of speech was curtailed, and fear and suspicion reigned, suddenly encountered an open and free environment marked by advanced communication technology and an influx of global information. Dramatic secularizing effects were felt immediately.

Bénédicte Brac de la Perrière claims that a new generation of political monks emerged after the democratic reforms that started around a decade ago, and more specifically in the aftermath of Cyclone Nargis in 2008, which acted as a catalyst for Buddhist monks to become a new collective force.[39] Sangha dynamics also seem to be changing accordingly, since younger monks today access information directly via the internet and can make their own judgements about events of public importance without deferring to the traditional sangha authorities.[40] Thus, the post-2012 Myanmar has been marked by a widening gap in how public issues are dealt with between, on the one hand, this new media-savvy generation of younger monks and, on the other, an elderly and inward-looking high-monastic echelon. Notably, the gulfs between rich and poor, between urban and rural citizens, and between those who have access to outside information and those who do not have also widened; and it is perhaps inevitable that differing views, regional disputes and generational clashes are coming out of the sangha.[41]

Against this backdrop, the activities of Ma Ba Tha (a privately run national association of Buddhist monks) and Ma Ha Na (the executive committee of state-appointed monks) must be understood if one is to achieve a rounded view of the recent political engagement of Buddhist monks in Myanmar. Ma Ba Tha, an acronym for Amyotha-batha Thathana Saungshauk-yei Apwe (Association for the Protection of Race and Religion), was founded by monks in June 2013, with the mission of defending Theravada Buddhism in Myanmar from various external threats.[42] Although the monastic backgrounds of many of its senior members are similar to those of state-nominated Ma Ha Na, many observers were surprised by the speed and force with which it emerged as a national Buddhist movement. Media reports categorized monks affiliated with Ma Ba Tha as 'nationalist', and civil society groups were quick to label them as 'anti-Muslim' or 'anti-women'.[43] However, these reports tended not to take notice of the multiplicity of voices emerging from the Buddhist community.[44] Incidentally, a research conducted by McKay and Khin Chit Win found that a large number of laywomen and Buddhist nuns from across the country supported Ma Ba Tha as it advocated the protection of women's rights, while providing legal aid and pastoral care to women, and carrying on the type of work the monastic community has always done.[45] Hence, contrary to general media report,[46] Ma Ba Tha monks were seen to be a custodian of women's rights who banned polygamy and protected Buddhist women especially in interreligious marriages. The movement also had a large following among Buddhist nuns as many of them had studied directly under the monk-scholars who were figureheads of the widespread Buddhist movement.

Looking closely, Ma Ba Tha's formation does not seem to be the result of any concerted political agenda on the part of monks, but it started following the increased intra-communal tension after 2012, along with a view shared by monks and laity – and to some extent, justified – that Buddhist morality in Myanmar was in rapid decline. As violence and intra-communal tension escalated in many parts of the country, many monks took up a public stance of both self-defence and aggression in their role as custodians of the Buddha *sāsana*. A strong frustration with the inability of state-appointed monks and their failure to control the extremist sermons of militant monks such a U Wirathu led to Ma Ba Tha members calling for the reform of the executive committee of Ma Ha Na. They wanted a change in the sangha's relationship with the government. The influential monk Sitagu Sayadaw suggested at the 2014 conference that Myanmar ought to follow the path of Thailand, Cambodia or Laos: countries that did not have a Ministry for Religious Affairs, and where monks were overseen by a national sangha council independent of any state control.[47] Sayadaw stated the need for Myanmar sangha to be independent from any form of political intervention so that monks could contribute to a moral society founded on Buddhism, which was broadly the wishes of Buddhist monastic community.[48]

However, this should not be taken as a suggestion that the leaders of Ma Ba Tha were fringe figures within the sangha whose actions were motivated by their lack of influence. The majority of its monk members were known *dhamma* teachers or scholars affiliated with prestigious monasteries, representing the height of Buddhist scholarship in Myanmar today.[49] It can be said that Ma Ba Tha's open, democratic internal discussions also broke with the traditional protocol of the sangha hierarchy, whereby the decisions of senior members and teachers were not necessarily followed. On the other hand, the openness of these discussions allowed a variety of viewpoints – including anti-Muslim sentiments – to seep out into the media, despite members of the executive committee genuinely adhering to non-violence and impartiality. Ma Ba Tha made an important mark in Myanmar's recent history, shedding light on various political and moral issues faced by a society in major transition. However, it did not succeed in becoming a sustained national movement and, as quickly as it emerged, it quietly fizzled out, ordered to disband by Ma Ha Na in 2017, and the use of its name was banned by the high court in the following year. Nonetheless, the nationalist sentiments have not abated in the face of international criticism, and the patriotism incited by the movement has led to formation of many small groups of monks and lay supporters, continuing their work to disseminate Buddhist values and morality, and preserve the Buddha *sāsana*.

Epilogue

Just as it is impossible for Buddhist monks in Myanmar to remain fully detached from the *dāna* offerings they receive on a daily basis, it is also very difficult indeed for them to stay aloof from the social and political realities that surround them. The interests of monks, especially those who are scholars operating in extensive networks of teachers and students, are intricately bound up with those of their intimate lay donors and the numerous other supporters who form their wider support base. This phenomenon is exemplified by the venerable Insein Ywama Sayadaw, chairman of Ma Ba Tha, renowned for his knowledge of the Vinaya. He developed an effective method to study the Abhidhamma and produced two Tipitakadhara monks under his tutelage. Incidentally, he was an active member of Ma Ha Na until he resigned from the position before the NLD (National League for Democracy) re-registered in 2011 as a political party to contend elections.[50] He was also one of the monk-teachers arrested in the aftermath of the 1988–1989 uprising due to his wide-ranging influence over his loyal monastic students, and the threat he therefore posed to the military government of the time. Monk-teachers with his level of popularity have a centripetal power to attract any number of monks and lay participants to his sermons, and subsequently summon their material support through an extensive network of monastic students and colleagues, regular donors, and general well-wishers around the country.

It should also be borne in mind that, on the final day of Sayadaw's birthday celebrations, Daw Aung San Suu Kyi, the leader of the NLD and state councillor, who had endured a tense relationship with the monk in recent years, arrived to offer him birthday wishes and sought his blessings in return. It was a poignant moment: a celebrated politician and a respected monk coming together and acknowledging both their differences and their complementary roles in building a new society. It showed how Buddhism and politics in Myanmar shared a 'moral field' in which both could come together to remedy past conflicts and lubricate their social and political relations.[51] As we have seen, in this typical use of monks' birthdays, a widely popular monk can utilize such an occasion to consolidate his power base, by instigating a reverse flow of generous offerings, and confer his authoritative power associated with the reverse gifts on the receiver, which is probably not a comfortable position to accept for a temporal political leader.

4

Buddhist nuns

This chapter examines the socio-religious transactions of Buddhist nuns in Myanmar society and highlights their crucial position as a bridge between the monks and laity. Importantly, though these nuns are unquestionably monastics and initiated into their monastic communities, many still view them as 'not fully ordained', and the public in this matter follow the official viewpoint of the country's sangha. In practice, Buddhist nuns are the most active *dāna* contributors to the sangha, which reveals the layers of complexity in their role as monastic women, including a certain discomfort they express with the *dāna* offerings they themselves receive as mendicants. Nevertheless, it remains unclear whether their desire to reciprocate the donations they have received from the laity arises because they are insecure in their religious position, or because women are more receptive to such cultural norms of social reciprocity.[1] In other words, a woman from Myanmar, whether lay or monastic, is likely to have been socialized into the mindset of being a 'nurturer', and thus a Buddhist nun might find it easier to act as a 'giver' than be a full-time 'receiver'.

The interactions Buddhist nuns have with their lay donors, however, vary considerably, as their relationships are affected by many factors including the nuns' social and religious credentials. Some nuns are less economically secure than others, depending on sporadic donations from pilgrims and visitors, while others may have a steady income from committed donors who support them on a regular basis. The recipient nun's academic qualifications, the reputation of the nunnery she is affiliated with, her charisma or lack of it, the kinship distance from her lay donor, and so on, all have direct effects on the nun–donor relationship. Besides, every monastic member has distinctive qualities that may appeal differently to potential donors, and nuns in particular experience a wide range of treatment by the Buddhist laity and not merely due to the lack of consensus about their religious position. And while many nuns – especially those without ranks – struggle to make ends meet, there are also prominent nun-teachers who are highly respected and given much more support than ordinary monks.

Offering *dāna* to Buddhist nuns

The majority of Buddhist nuns in Myanmar are Eight Precepts observers, who are celibate and fast in the afternoons, but there are some who observe Ten Precepts and do not engage in any secular transactions. Few as they may be, the latter group are respected for their moral purity, which derives from the fact that they decline to handle money, in contrast to their Eight Precept counterparts, who regularly engage in cash transactions. As we have already seen, Myanmar people are notably generous towards the sangha, but taking on a monastic beneficiary, in practice, implies a long-term commitment. Moreover, socio-cultural norms oblige the Buddhist population to support the monks, but not necessarily nuns, so being a regular donor to a Buddhist nun implies a serious and special undertaking.

As discussed in an earlier chapter, those who decide to donate to nuns have been inspired by a special experience or some other personal reason that transcends normative practice in a Buddhist society. Feelings of empathy towards the disadvantaged and the urge to help those who are desperately in need can be strong motives for offering support to others in general. Yet the reasons that motivate those donors who support the nuns can be difficult to explain or at times even mysterious. I have seen Myanmar people decide on the spur of the moment to offer *dāna* to a specific nun, often without being able to explain why. As one of my informants put it, 'Why would anyone want to make offerings to these poor women? But I suddenly felt the urge to offer them'. One nun-teacher remarked innocently that it was indeed *thuzein-thi* (strange or awe-inspiring) that a one-time visitor would suddenly decide to offer her *dāna*. She said she had never solicited donations or asked for support, but sometimes people just became suffused with generosity after listening to her talk and offer her donations. She suspected that people generally did not expect a Buddhist nun to speak so well and that when they found that she could move them, they therefore felt obliged to offer her *dāna*. Others explained that offerings of *dāna* to a nun were probably associated with feelings of surprise, humility or inspiration brought on unexpectedly. There are, however, exceptional lay donors, such as the family of U Aung Than Sein in Yangon, who donates exclusively to nuns, and he has been doing so continuously for the last thirty years. What is remarkable about this donor family is the strength of commitment made by the head of household to regularly donate to 3,000 nuns twice every month, who line up on both sides of his street to receive local banknotes equivalent to about $2 to $5 USD each (depending on seniority). When asked why he made such a commitment to support so many nuns, he said he could not remember how it started but was certain about how he felt; he wanted to help them as the nuns' life was far more difficult than that of the monks and said that it was his responsibility to offer them material support.[2]

During my first fieldwork as a Buddhist nun in the mid-1980s, Myanmar was still cut off from the outside world and in the final stage of the decline of U Ne Win's government. As the country was then one of the world's poorest, as measured by United Nations GNP statistics, I was taken aback by the large amounts of offerings and cash I received from local donors who were often surprised to encounter a foreigner living in a humble hut. When queried about why they offered me donations, my informants would reply that they thought I was making a great sacrifice by living as a Buddhist nun in the countryside, enduring a life of deprivation and hardship. The notion of 'sacrifice' they often referred to involved not only the standard practices of abstinences, but also a monastic life of apparent inconvenience and lack of material comforts. There was no air conditioner, no fridge, nor indeed any modern appliances to support comfortable living in the nunnery then, and there was no hot water or a separate bathroom to wash in. The nearest public toilet was five minutes' walk away, and it took me another half an hour to reach the post office to make a domestic phone call. Such inconvenience, from the standpoint of local Myanmar people, appeared as a great penance – and especially so, for someone from a 'developed' country. In other words, it was the fact that I was so deprived of material comfort that made me, as a 'foreign nun', a worthy object of their *dāna* offering.

Spiro mentioned the great respect Myanmar people showed towards celibate monks, and the amount of emphasis they placed 'almost exclusively on the sacrificial character of their lives'.[3] He was referring especially to the attention and empathy directed at male monastics (and not females), whose main source of suffering was seen to be sexual deprivation, more than any other abstinence practices. Comparatively speaking, people do not view the practice of celibacy by women as a deprivation; at least as far as the Buddhist nuns are concerned, and feel sorry about the other kinds of deprivation they endure, such as having to endure bald-headedness. They also often mention the great sacrifices that nuns make by giving up the many symbols of femininity such as their long hair as well as their fertility by never becoming a mother or a wife, but the focus of such talk was rarely about the practice of celibacy per se.

I randomly selected a dozen informants who were regular donors to Buddhist nuns and asked them why they offered *dāna* to a nun rather than to a monk. Their replies were often based on reasons that were quite personal to each one of them.[4] One female informant said, *thana lò*: 'because I feel pity' that they have endured such a hard life, while others mentioned, *kyinyo lò*: 'because I admire and respect her'. Women, in particular, were sometimes overcome by a strong urge to help and support the nuns but at other times offered donations because they felt guilty about enjoying a comfortable life themselves. In some ways, then, making offerings to nuns and donating to the victims of natural disasters may be associated with similar sets of emotions such as pity and sadness. In another respect, these emotional responses reveal the conflicting nature of people's perceptions of Buddhist nuns: as objects of both pity and respect, looked down upon as well as looked up to and admired for the sacrifices they were making, and yet abhorred for the level of deprivation they were seen to be experiencing. Unsurprisingly, the responses of lay Buddhists in Myanmar today can likewise be varied and contradictory, since there are usually no clear criteria to inform their decisions about whether to support the nuns or not.

Transactions with regular donors

Buddhist nuns are mendicants and sustain themselves by a weekly round of alms collecting, during which they receive rice grains and cash. In return, they chant blessings in unison, the most common of which is *jamabazei janthabazei, sutaung pyet bazei* – meaning 'may you be happy, may you be healthy, may all your wishes come true', and so on. Similar phrases are recited on every occasion of their transactions with the laity, as rewards for offering *dāna* and acknowledgement for any good acts performed towards them. In comparison to monks, who receive offerings in silence, with downcast eyes, and without any show of emotion, the nuns' vocal and vibrant expressions of gratitude seem to solicit more generosity from the Buddhist public. Whenever nuns transact with their lay donors, they acknowledge people's kindness by infusing them with *mettā*, and many standardized chants or *gāthā* (verses) are recited to bless and honour the donors.[5] In their daily lives, every meal starts with a special chant that sends out loving kindness to those who have offered them food, acknowledging their good deeds and extolling the virtues of the Triple Gem. Thus, their every transaction with society focuses on conferring loving kindness on those who have made offerings to the monastic community. In normative transactions, such recitations are performed according to short standardized formulae, but on special religious ceremonies, they are specially composed, and elaborate displays of full recitation are made, sometimes by professional ceremonial reciters. The contents of the recitation acknowledge the generosity of donors and send out a message of gratitude and loving kindness aimed at filling the lay congregation with a general sense of wellbeing.

In addition to large quantities of uncooked rice they regularly receive, nuns are given various food items such as dried fish, fish paste or eggs, brought by lay donors to their nunneries. At harvest time, nuns are also invited to local villages, where they receive agricultural products such as onions and garlic, groundnuts, lentils and oil. Fresh vegetables and meat are purchased with donated cash, while other necessities such as books, stationery and robes are usually donated on a number of religious occasions.[6] The collective ceremonial feeding of resident nuns at a particular nunnery also takes place as a typical form of *dāna*. As a common practice, donation items are offered individually to each monastic, and when cash offerings take place, nuns form a queue and receive an envelope with banknotes from the donors one by one. In small nunneries, donation income in the first instance is used to pay for household expenses, since nuns are not exempt from paying electricity or water bills, and various forms of taxes collected by the local authorities.[7] In a large nunnery school, where a group of regular donors helps with paying utility bills and other major expenditure, nuns may keep the individual cash offerings they receive for personal uses.[8] Nevertheless, being members of the Buddhist monastic community, nuns also have to factor in various expenses for communal events and social affairs: for example, for making offerings to monks especially during the robe-offering season. Therefore, most sustain their religious lives by living as thriftily as possible and saving up their donation income to operate in the community as full vocational members.

To be fully active, however, it is essential that a nun secure a number of regular donors so that she can devote herself to matters of religious significance. However, it is difficult for an ordinary nun to find a virtuous donor who would commit him/herself to supporting her on a regular basis, and those with little education or without any rank struggle to make ends meet. As a result, young nuns and students end up depending on their immediate families and wider kin networks (despite theoretically having renounced them) until they become established as *dhamma* teachers and/or acquire non-family-member donors.

The reciprocal relationship between rural agricultural communities and the monastic community has always provided the foundation for Myanmar Buddhism, and if they are from rural villages, as the majority of Myanmar's nuns are, they tend to depend on their wide network of family and relatives for staple rice and for other agricultural products customarily offered them during the harvest time. Also, in villages in upper regions of the country, people commonly used to ask a Buddhist nun to symbolically adopt a sickly child – male or female – so that he/she would be given special protection by her, including in the material sense of acting as the child's guardian. In such cases, though they may now be rarer, the child retains a close relationship with the guardian nun throughout one's childhood and, once an adult, expresses his/her gratitude by looking after her in old age. In this respect, nuns can have a close male benefactor as a result of such a relationship, and there have always been male donors in villages who acted as important benefactors for the Buddhist nuns.

Meanwhile, relationships of mutual support can be essential for a laywoman, especially when she encounters family problems or other vicissitudes of life, and in such times of crisis, a woman commonly turns to a nun acquaintance for moral support and advice (since there are no other social services to support them in most cases). In fact, many of the long-term donors to nuns are laywomen, some being unmarried who dedicate themselves to supporting monastic women. Commonly called *apyogyi* or 'big virgins', these unmarried women are often breadwinners in society, administering relatives' businesses or running their own, and usually take up the role of deciding donation expenses as well. A very high percentage of schoolteachers, college lecturers and nurses are unmarried in Myanmar, and many regular donors to nuns are these single professional women, who may feel more affinity towards the nuns than their married counterparts. Sometimes, the beneficiary/benefactor relationship develops into a close friendship, similar to a bond with a biological family member. In such cases, the female donor may speak of the relationship with her nun beneficiary as 'pre-determined' and justify their closeness in karmic terms, that is, that they were meant to come together and support each other in this world.

As the relationship develops, female donors in particular tailor their gifts more carefully to suit their monastic recipients. For example, for an old nun, a warm overcoat or blanket; for a young student, a good pair of glasses. In recent years, students have also been offered iPads or Kindles, and teachers given smartphones. Being monastics, nuns are not normally in a position to state or otherwise exhibit any personal preferences, but they may reveal their true likes and needs to their close donors. The degree of attentiveness and care Myanmar donors show towards their monastic recipients, or even to a foreign guest, can be overwhelming. In this context, it is understandable that monks do not express their likes or show any sign of gratitude towards their lay benefactors; otherwise, they would run the risk of being swamped by gifts from enthusiastic donors, who seem only happy to fulfil their every wish. Having said that, the relationship between a regular donor and his/her monastic beneficiary seems to thrive when the two parties know each other well and share intimate information: the nun revealing what she really likes and wants, and the lay donor fulfilling her actual needs, rather than just offering standard donation items. Nevertheless, it can take many years for a relationship to achieve such a level of trust and dependency.

Being a full-time 'dependent'

A precept Buddhist nun in Myanmar is a mendicant, who survives on receiving alms; yet her incomplete religious status makes it difficult for her to enjoy this position of full-time recipient. Moreover, although there is no obligation for a nun to reciprocate the *dāna* offered, the failure to do so seems to strangely erode her confidence as a religious person. In contrast to the feeling of wellbeing generated by the act of giving, receiving seems to arouse a sense of indebtedness, and thus discomfort, among many people. This phenomenon is even more daunting for the nuns, whose monastic status as constant recipients evokes the more disquieting sense of dependency. According to my nun informants, the feeling that they should reciprocate lingers on, and, being enmeshed in a culture of excessive giving, they also want to repay the kindness of their lay donors in one form or another. In this respect, *dāna* offered to a nun does not seem to bring about the kind of liberation it might for a monk. On the contrary, it creates an emotional burden or even a sense of guilt on her part.[9] Therefore, it is important to look beyond the standard notions of gift offering and explore more deeply the cultural and psychological aspects of religious transactions if we are to understand how both parties are affected by the consequence of their giving and receiving.

As we have seen, regular donations offered to a Buddhist nun often end up confining her in a kind of gift-debt relationship with her regular donors to whom she is unrelated by blood. One could state that in theory the nun-recipient has no obligation to reciprocate, but in practice, she becomes caught up in the social morals of reciprocity. Once established, a regular relationship between a nun beneficiary and a non-relative benefactor can be morally taxing, and in many cases, the nun is locked into semi-exclusive relationships of 'reciprocal dependence' with few donors whom she feels morally obligated to care for or otherwise 'serve'. Far from having figured among her early goals when choosing a monastic life, such relationships seem to simply accrue from the social and moral implications of every unreciprocated gift and eventually overwhelm other aspects of her religious existence.

The difficulties of becoming a *dependent* of this type can be hard to imagine for those who have been socialized into becoming independent in their adult life. In other words, if one fundamentally believes that independence is a superior state to dependence, it is impossible to appreciate the deep implications of interdependence in a Buddhist culture: an ideal that could never be achieved if everyone were independent and did not appreciate the need to work with others towards (or as) a higher religious goal. That is, in the tradition of Theravada Buddhism, monks and nuns are vocational recipients whose religious life centres on receiving the generosity of lay benefactors, whose acts of offering, in turn, are the main expression of what a good Buddhist considers one's duty.

My own monastic experience has given me considerable insight into the difficulty of nuns' actual lives. The most difficult aspect of being a monastic was finding myself in the role of a full-time receiver: accepting whatever was offered and then waiting patiently until the donors would offer me what I really needed. The deeply unsettling feeling that one's whole existence depended on the goodwill and charity of others was shared by many of my nun informants. Specifically, they mentioned how hard it was not knowing when the next offering of food would come, as they could not dictate the generosity of their lay donors, yet had to depend on it totally, however infrequent or inadequate it was. In other words, becoming a vocational monastic implied a profound loss of control and spontaneity, or even autonomy; whereas for the laity, every opportunity for making merit remained open. Nevertheless, the nuns generally exhibited exceptional humility in accepting their dependent state and subjected themselves to other people's whims in their monastic life.

The types of transactions that a Buddhist nun engages in with her lay supporters, meanwhile, are determined by the respect she can command from society. That is, a nun can in some cases rise above the whims of her lay donors and reverse the power relationship if she has established herself sufficiently in the monastic community. Educated nuns are also confident and authoritative in their actual dealings with their lay donors, which seem to positively affect the relationship to their favour. In addition, if she is a Ten Precepts observer, a nun can retain her sense of autonomy as a monastic who engages in neither cash transactions nor social reciprocity. In this way, a Ten Precepts nun can overcome the ambiguous position of being a precept nun and stand on par with monks, as far as her moral position is concerned.[10]

Symbolic capital

Prospective lay donors are constantly on the lookout for worthy monastics endowed with special spiritual qualities and who thus deserve their attention, care and material support. As we have already seen, male members of the sangha are the normative recipient for lay donors' generosity, but a Buddhist nun can also attract their attention, especially if she is endowed with academic and religious credentials. In fact, gender is not a final determinant of lay donors' decisions in Myanmar about which monastic to offer *dāna* to. It is also relevant to discuss the concept of merit in greater depth here. That is, 'merit' is believed to accrue to the donor as the result of making an offering to a worthy monastic; however, it is not a static concept as some scholars have assumed it to be.[11] The question of who is a meritorious recipient and who is not can also be highly subjective, as well as varying along with the nature of one's own relationship with the monastic beneficiary. That is, people's decisions regarding *dāna* are influenced by traditional norms and trends in society, and monks are therefore still likely to be regarded as its most legitimate recipients. But, as noted in Chapter 3, the lay Buddhists of Myanmar do not simply make offerings to every monk they come across in the street. Among the various types of Buddhist nuns in Myanmar, those affiliated with respected nunnery schools and/or who have passed the state *Pathamapyan* are considered the most worthy recipients. As noted earlier, educational degrees and similar external credentials can allow them to overcome the disadvantages they encounter as ordinary precept nuns. Incidentally, having a *Dhammacariya* title – that is, a Buddhist degree that allows one to teach the *dhamma* granted by the state – is almost a prerequisite for monastic members, whether male or female, to attract the support of society. Individual skills such as an attractive chanting voice or a kind and pleasing personality can, however, also spur prospective donors to commit themselves to a specific monastic beneficiary. Thus, 'symbolic capital' – defined as 'resources available to a social actor on the basis of prestige or recognition, which function as an authoritative embodiment of cultural value'.[12] – can play a major role in justifying people's religious investment and in sustaining their long-term relationships with their monastic beneficiaries, by assuring lay donors that their association with a well-qualified monastic will be socially uplifting.

The success of a nunnery as a monastic institution, meanwhile, is often measured by quantifiable elements such as the number of large buildings on the premises, the number of resident students and good regular donors, and the general grandeur of the place as reflected in its facilities and infrastructure. The rapid development of a monastery managed by a prominent monk is expected by society, but when a Buddhist nun is able to build a successful nunnery, it is often seen as an anomaly, and despite the unfairness of this public perception, it can serve to attract the laity's attention. Meanwhile, a nunnery's success can also lead to suspicion being directed towards its abbess. For instance, when a new nunnery school in Sagaing started producing successful students in the *Pathamapyan*, many passing with distinction, it caused a stir. But rather than remarking on the quality of its nun-teachers or their methods of effective teaching, many observers voiced suspicions that the nun-students were cheating or receiving special favours from monk examiners due to their connection with an eminent monk scholar. This kind of negative perception is one of many examples of nuns' struggle to enhance their socio-religious position in addition to the common barriers thrown up by their social milieu. In fact, the nunnery's rapid success was built on its modern management style, strict discipline, and sheer hard work by all its nun-teachers and students. And yet people continued to ask them probing questions about whether they engaged in astrology or had 'won the lottery' to acquire the funds they had and if their nun-teachers were related to General Than Shwe, the then chairman of the military government. Such questions imply the general discriminatory attitude laypeople tend to express towards women whenever they show high competence that exceeds normative expectations, revealing a deep-seated prejudice that too often leads Buddhist nuns and other women to accept their own subordinate position in society.

Relationship with monks

Buddhist nuns are not only 'other-worldly' mendicants, but also pious followers of the sangha, who provide material support to and uphold the authority of monks. That is, nuns stand on the threshold between the two opposing, yet complementary worlds: *lokiya* (this-worldly) and *lokuttara* (the other-worldly), sometimes serving to keep them apart, but more often as a bridge between them. The nuns offer *dāna* to monks on every religious occasion available, and whenever they themselves are offered expensive items or have any surplus funds left, they save them to be re-offered as *dāna* to the sangha. The nuns also look after the general welfare of the monastic family, caring for young male novices as their honorary mothers and for old, infirm monks as their symbolic sisters. They seem to thrive when performing these close, nurturing roles and providing various other altruistic services whenever the need arises. Serving the sangha in this way, however, does not seem to undermine them or render them subservient as far as the nuns are concerned; on the contrary, it appears to give them a deeper meaning to the time they invest in the sangha's general welfare.[13] *Weiyawesah* (devotional services) for the sangha are regarded as bringing meritorious returns to the person offering them and especially so in the case of menial work.[14] Meanwhile, it is normally the nuns with no rank who actively seek out such servile roles, and the amount of time and effort they expend in these activities reveals how much their religious identity rests on achieving close affinity with the monks.[15] The presence of nuns conducting many different and often menial chores also seems indispensable in fostering communal cohesion; and by merging their interests with those of the sangha, nuns have carved out a position of informal authority within the monastic community.

It has to be remembered that the Buddhist nuns in Myanmar are celibate and few have had the experience of becoming a biological mother, but in spite

Figure 4.1 *Buddhist nuns offering* dāna *to a monk. They are enthusiastic supporters of the sangha, providing material support to and upholding the authority of monks.*

of or perhaps because of this, many aspire to perform a maternal role in relation to the monks. If a nun establishes herself as *bazin medaw* (honorary mother) to a specific monk, she receives special treatment as his 'nurturer': for example, being seated in the front row during ceremonies in acknowledgement of her close association with him. In parallel to the pride lay donors take in being called *bazin taga* or *tagamá*, discussed in Chapter 2, nuns aspire to become *bazin ama* (honorary sister) or *bazin medaw* of a monk. This kind of close association with a monk is generally established via a senior nun taking a special interest in a male novice in the early part of his career, often as a result of a chance encounter. It should also be noted that such a special relationship between a monk and a nun can only happen if there is *yeikzet* (predestined relationship) between them, which cannot be easily sought or formed.

In practical terms, being referred to as *bazin medaw* to a monk means that a nun has paid for his ordination ceremony and supported him throughout his monastic life by providing him with whatever necessities required. At times, the relationship of a monk 'son' to his symbolic 'mother' seems even closer than the one he enjoys with his biological mother, and it is also common for a monk to conduct a public funeral for his *bazin medaw*, but rare for him to do so for his biological mother. Elsewhere, I have written about the celebrated scholar nun Daw Dhammasari and her special relationship with U Vicittasara-bhivamsa, the Mingun Tipitaka Sayadaw, who was one of Myanmar's most respected and erudite monk scholars of the twentieth century.[16] Daw Dhammasari was more than thirty years older than the monk, but having known him since he was a young novice, she acted as his maternal confidante. She was referred to as the Tipitaka Medaw, since the accomplishments of the 'son' in such situations generally accrue to the 'mother', and in this case, he was granted the country's first *Tipitakadhara* title for his detailed knowledge of the Pali canon. It is recorded that when she died in 1971, Mingun Sayadaw was the chief officiator in the ritual at her funeral, paid for all the expenses, and conducted it in a grand manner to publicly celebrate her life as a Buddhist nun.[17]

Buddhist nuns perform a variety of other voluntary roles for the sangha, one of which can be likened to that of 'vigilantes', patrolling not the city streets but the other-worldly threshold, to protect the monks from corrupting influences of the secular world. For example, it is nuns, not the monks, who tell monastery visitors how to prostrate themselves and instruct them how to use honorifics and speak to monks properly whenever transacting with them. I have also seen nuns reprimanding female devotees for stepping on the shadows of monks, acting too informal with them, wearing flimsy and skin-hugging clothes when visiting monasteries, and not showing enough respect to the sangha. As such, Buddhist nuns not only bridge the two worlds, but act as an essential buffer between the sanctity of the monks and external presences that may unwittingly threaten it – especially, though not exclusively, laywomen. Monks, in contrast, are generally more relaxed and casual in their dealing with lay visitors, and my observations suggest that the presence of laywomen does not seem threaten, annoy or worry them as much as it does the nuns. Nonetheless, in ceremonial situations, monks and nuns work together as a complementary team, with the monk – representing the sangha's authority – literally talking down to the congregation from a high platform, while the nuns ensure from the floor that no one threatens his exalted position, physically or otherwise. This is a clear reflection of the monastic community's hierarchical structure, which defines where each member stands in relation to the others. Yet there are many other factors that define individual monastics' actual relationships, which are not as cut and dried as might be generally assumed.[18] For example, contrary to stereotypes, not all nuns spend their time cooking for the monks and serving them, and scholarly nuns in particular spend less time conducting menial tasks, due to the relatively high proportion of their time that is devoted to studying and teaching. Senior nuns may offer certain services on special occasions or when they are summoned by their monk-teacher or some other specific abbot they are obligated to but do not regularly engage in any menial chores for the sangha.

In the case of a nun-student and a monk-teacher, however, the former sometimes acts almost as his symbolic daughter and may be addressed as *thami* (daughter) by the monk in informal settings. And in a monk-teacher's old age, a former nun-student may look after him – though never addressing him as *apei* (father). Such close relationships may be looked upon with suspicion, but nuns in Myanmar who are precept observers – and thus not confined to strict Vinaya rules – are relatively free to decide how to follow their monastic conventions. They are also summoned to deal with domestic situations that involve monetary transactions on behalf of monks who do not handle cash and even sometimes work as bookkeepers in large monasteries. During the relief operations in the wake of the 2008 Cyclone Nargis, Buddhist nuns supported the monks in logging relief goods, keeping financial records and organizing aid operations. However, the nuns who did so were generally not publicly visible, and their contribution was thus underappreciated relative to that of the monks. This lack of visibility is an issue that Buddhist nuns are likely to want addressed, especially as it also impinges on their relatively low levels of material support from society.[19]

The nuns' involvement in cash transactions is, in part, merely an extension of a wider social practice in countries in mainland Southeast Asia: that is, women's performance of important roles in the domestic economy.[20] It is well known that women in the region have always engaged in trade and market transactions and enjoyed active roles in running family businesses and small holdings, and thus their ability to receive and handle money and look after monastery accounts is congruent with their general social profile. The situation in Myanmar seems similar to that in Thailand, where *mae chee* (nuns who observe the Eight Precepts) are involved in the monastic economy, with some even receiving alms on behalf of the monks.[21] In monasteries in urban centres and other Buddhist countries in Southeast Asia such as Cambodia or Vietnam, male novices and lay helpers may fill such roles and work as accountants or administrators, especially in prominent institutions or meditation centres. Nonetheless, in Sagaing Hill, in Myanmar – where hundreds of monasteries and nunneries have coexisted side by side for centuries – monastics have worked out practical arrangements whereby nuns perform certain types of work that complements and supports that of monks.[22] In practice, the main issue with this seems to revolve around who can be trusted with monastery finances, rather than who mediates between sangha and laity, and Buddhist nuns are generally seen as the most trustworthy caretakers of the monastic community. Hence, the practice of nuns looking after monastery finances seems to be a natural outcome of their close relationship with monks and their disinterested position vis-à-vis the community's money. Nonetheless, Buddhist nuns themselves do not perceive their influential role in monastery finances as an indication of their religious worth; indeed, they tend to downplay it, since the (negative) image that arises from their involvement in cash transactions associates them further with the secular realm, from which – as we have seen – they are constantly striving to distance themselves.[23]

Relationships with other nuns

In addition to their multitude of transactions with the monks and the laity, nuns unsurprisingly engage in an intricate web of give and take within their monastic network of nun colleagues, friends and allies. Seniority, that is, the length of her service as an initiated member of the monastic community, is the most general expression of a nun's monastic position. When introducing herself, she is normally asked, *Bene wa ya-tha le?* 'How many *wa* (Buddhist Lent) have you spent [as a nun]?' This question gauges the level of her commitment to the monastic vocation, with very high numbers being taken as evidence of her single-minded dedication. She is also embedded in a monastic hierarchy of teachers and students, preceptors and preceptees, and head nunneries and

Figure 4.2 *Nun-students pay ritual obeisance to their teacher. A close relationship with their teacher is what sustains the students throughout their monastic life.*

branch nunneries, and in the context of these vertical as well as horizontal relationships, loyalty and devotion are highly valued. Other factors that add to the standing of a nun and her position or influence in the hierarchy are the level of her education and the scholarly lineage of her affiliation. Having been initiated by a respected nun preceptor or having been trained by one or more prominent *dhamma* teachers adds to her religious reputation, and it is common practice for a monastic student to maintain an attitude of deference towards those senior monastic members, regardless of whether they are monks or nuns.

Nun-students pay ritual obeisance to their teachers, abbesses and senior members of the community, prostrating themselves to the floor and offering token gifts at regular times during the year: at the Myanmar New Year in mid-April, and before and after Buddhist Lent in July and October. On these and other occasions, junior members seek for forgiveness for whatever unwholesome deeds they have committed during the year, and senior members reciprocate by offering blessings and *ovada* (moral instructions). Abbesses and teachers also publicly acknowledge the heavy responsibility of guiding the younger generations of nuns. Although formalized to a certain degree, the high frequency with which such ritual transactions occur between senior and junior members confirms their respective positions in the community and helps them strengthen communal cohesion and stability.

Meanwhile, each nunnery operates almost like an autonomous sociopolitical unit separated from the outside world, and the daily conduct of all the nuns affiliated with the same nunnery is regulated by its particular communal rules, customs and norms.[24] The frequent and informal interactions of resident nuns establish intimate relationships of mutual support, providing them with a safety net in times of tension and difficulty. Just like laypeople living in the outside world, nun neighbours living on the same nunnery premises exchange pleasantries and surplus food, and borrow and return mundane items such as sugar, utensils, candles, books and, sometimes, even cash. To an arguably greater degree than in secular communities, however, every borrowed item is remembered, even over long periods, and if a nun forgets a favour she has been granted, she is reminded of her 'debt'. If the nun persists in failing to honour the fact that she has become 'indebted', she might be reported to the abbess, and the issue adjudicated by senior nuns. Problems and squabbles within the nunnery are not customarily discussed with anyone from outside it, since nuns are careful not to damage their public reputation lest that negatively impact their donation income. However, serious problems between nuns, which normally involve land or property disputes, may be taken to the Township Council of Nuns or resolved by an influential Sayadaw in the community.[25] Most nunneries operate a system of surveillance aimed at minimizing the external damage caused by internal disputes, but keeping all the relevant situations under wraps is becoming increasingly difficult, especially with the development of social media and the rapid proliferation of smartphones in the last decade.

Just as every nunnery operates as an autonomous unit, every lineage also works as a closed hierarchical grouping that protects its members from outside threats and other forms of interference. A scholarly lineage is comprised of a monk or nun-teacher and his or her students, maintained by a strict code of loyalty to the teacher who may also be their preceptor or mentor or both. Hence, it is almost unheard of for a Myanmar student to openly criticize his or her teacher or even rebuke the relationship. Sometimes, a monk-teacher may officially accept a nun-student into his scholarly lineage, and in such a case, she is equally qualified to become part of his close circle of monastic disciples.[26] In nunneries, too, even those that do not operate lineages formally, there are always several groupings led by nun-teachers that can grow into exclusive factions. That is, a nun-teacher can decide which students to exclude from or include in her study group, and by imposing her own criteria and standards, she can increase her influence in the monastic institution. It is a common complaint in nunnery schools that teachers accept only the brightest and most obedient students, to the detriment of others, and yet, this selectivity in the recruitment of potential students can be a valuable investment in one's own future position in the monastic community. From the nun-students' standpoint, meanwhile, having a prominent teacher who also supports them as mentor and guide assures their long-term success and helps secure the support of lay donors through their teacher's network of contacts. By the same token, nun-students who fail to gain acceptance into the inner circle of disciples of such an influential teacher struggle generally and have to find monastic allies (often blood relatives) or other non-standard means of support if they are to make headway in their monastic career.

As these examples imply, senior nuns and teachers have wide discretion as to how to confer their generosity on junior members who are disadvantaged or have no regular support. Within the so-called inner circles, a nun-teacher commonly redistributes or shares the surplus of donated items originally offered to her with her students and disciples, who in turn pass down anything they do not need to others, such as the nunnery's lay helpers, as part of a top-down system of monastic redistribution in which nothing goes to waste. The more senior and prominent a nun is, the more she is expected to instigate such a reverse flow of goods, and her reputation may rise according to the level of compassion she confers towards others who are ranked lower in the community. Arguably, therefore, an important criterion of effective and popular leadership in the monastic community is knowing how to accept the right amount of goods and judge what and how much to pass on to those who are more in need and possibly also under her influence. However, the wise sharing of resources expected of a nun-leader is not always possible in practice, due to the fundamental insecurity of nuns' socio-economic position in Myanmar, and there are also some who become excessively possessive of material items they have received, probably as a kind of compensation for their economic insecurity.[27]

Nuns' relationships with their families

Every Buddhist nun is a renunciant, who in theory has renounced her secular persona and severed all familial ties when she joined the monastic community. Nevertheless, if she finds little support from society, a student or a junior nun simply cannot afford to break with her family and relatives, and will continue to seek their material support. Moreover, in a traditional culture like Myanmar's, where unmarried daughters commonly care for their parents in old age, a daughter-nun is still seen as a potential carer and may be summoned back home to look after her infirm parents if no one else in the family is available to take up that role. However, by the time this occurs, some nuns may be well enough established to ensure that parents (especially mothers) are cared for in their own nunnery.[28] Parents also tend to be reluctant to let go of their daughters completely, even after their initiations, and – if they can afford to do so – continue to offer material support as a means of preserving the emotional bond.

When a nunnery is founded, it is in most cases the nuns' relatives who collect the necessary funds for building the accommodation and expenses for other facilities on the premises. Sometimes, parents donate their life's savings so that their daughter can purchase a plot of land to start a nunnery. And although such transactions are originally made in the form of *dāna* offered to a nun recipient (i.e. the daughter), family members often perceive the resulting nunneries as their private holdings and continue to claim control over them. This issue does not usually arise if the original nun-daughter remains in charge of the nunnery; however, when such a nun dies and her non-relation nun disciple, for example, takes up residence, her surviving family members are likely to complain that a nun who is not part of their kin group is living in the building they had originally built for them. In some cases, nuns' family members reaching old age move into the nunnery buildings as if these were their private residences. Such situations cause terrible problems for resident nuns who are not related to these lay donors, since the former can neither claim ownership of the buildings they live in nor assert control over the communal assets.[29] Elsewhere, I have written about how severe such problems can become when the succession to the position of abbess is involved, since it is common for her family members to try to assert control over the whole nunnery institution via a new nun-relative candidate, to the detriment of the deceased abbess's close non-relation disciples.[30] One could easily argue that once anything, whether a small item or a plot of land, is offered to the monastic community, its ownership should be transferred either to the sangha as *sanghika* (sangha property) or more generally to the *sāsana* as *sāsanika* (*sāsana* property) and used by every monastic resident in community. This would imply that the original lay donor could no longer claim or assert any control once his/her property was given away. Nevertheless, disputes over such property that has already been donated remain commonplace, as the properties and assets of nuns are still regarded as 'private holdings', not as 'communal' as in the case of monasteries.

This brings us to another vexed area: what constitutes a 'field of merit'? As we have seen, the Buddhist monk is regarded as an ideal monastic recipient, who provides lay donors with an open 'field of merit'.[31] But what about the Buddhist nuns? The main donor to a monastery or a nunnery is referred to by the prestigious title of *kyaung taga* or *kyaung-má*; 'male or female donor of the monastery'. However, such a position ensuing from a large religious investment comes with a heavy responsibility, including a strong expectation of his/her ongoing financial support for the same institution. In addition, such support might consist of the main patron being frequently consulted by resident nuns on matters of importance regarding the nunnery's management and involvement in the general welfare of monastic residents. And much like a parent looking after the children, he/she is expected to participate in every ritual and commemoration ceremony that concerns the whole institution. In this respect, an expectation naturally arises that the main donor will retain some level of influence and control over the running of the monastic institution – especially in the case of nunneries, which, unlike monasteries, do not have lay trustees.

In the Buddhist nunneries where I conducted research over a decade in the Sagaing Hill, I observed that it was commonplace for resident nuns to suffer as the result of the sense of entitlement asserted by the original patron's immediate family or even the descendants. Many resident nuns find themselves in a situation akin to that of a tenant who has no say or rights over the property in which they live. This is because immediate family members and other relatives of the original donor who paid for and donated a building to a nun or nunnery continue to assert their ownership of it even after the demise of the original nun recipient and/or the original lay donor. Currently, resident nuns may therefore feel obliged to seek permission from the deceased donor's family members if they want to continue living in it. This can subsequently become a major issue if the nuns' building needs maintenance or renovation, and if the donor's family – despite not having the funds to repair it themselves – refuses to allow lay donors from outside their kin base to do so.[32] In such scenarios, despite the buildings having been built specifically as *dāna* offerings and given away to the nuns initially, they continue to be regarded as private 'merit fields' for the original donors' family, who tries to protect them at any cost. Logically, this implies that a traditional nunnery is not an open 'field of merit' where everyone can come and plant the seeds of their goodwill, and as such, this helps to explain why a Buddhist nunnery in Myanmar does not normally grow into a large institution.

Any solutions?

Buddhist monks in Myanmar are members of the sangha, and there is a clear consensus on where they stand in relation to society as well as how they ought to behave in their relations with others both within and outside the monastic community. The Vinaya provides the legal framework for monks' behaviour in transacting with their lay donors, which both guarantees their religious status and protects the collective interests of the sangha. Buddhist nuns, in contrast, have long endured an ambiguous position that is both 'other-worldly' as far as their monastic affiliation and religious identity are concerned, and 'this-worldly' in terms of their legal and civil status. This implies that the relationships nuns have with society and their own families are fundamentally different from those of the monks, who can publicly claim their other-worldly status by their ordination and official affiliation with the sangha. Having said that, every nun I spoke to saw herself to be a full monastic, who had renounced the world, and identified herself with the other-worldly domain. And yet the tension remains and that seems to feed into their self-perception and innate insecurity. In addition, the economic lives of Myanmar nuns are not as secure or comfortable as those of monks generally, and thus, they are more susceptible to negative financial implications of being mendicants whose status is not officially endorsed. Elsewhere, I have articulated the nuns' relationships with society in terms of the 'social distance' they maintain with their lay donors.[33] The upshot of this is that, the further a nun moves away from the comfortable relations she once enjoyed with her family and wider kinship network, the heavier the moral pressure becomes to reciprocate the *dāna* offered to her. As a result of such moral burden, she can become confined to a kind of servile relationship in relation to few regular donors who are not related to her. However, the nun's own family members can also create a parallel set of problems by not letting her go entirely and expecting her to look after infirm parents even though she has earlier relinquished family ties.

So many nunneries remain under the influence of original lay donors or their descendants. If the 'merit field' of a nunnery is closed, its donation income will obviously be limited, and it is the resident nuns who – lacking any power to rectify the situation – suffer the consequences. This is one of the many reasons why Buddhist nunneries in Myanmar, unlike monasteries there, have not developed into large institutions supported by large numbers of unrelated donors who plant their good deeds in open 'merit fields'. Again, the situation highlights the limitations of Myanmar's nuns' religious standing, which is not regulated or protected by the Vinaya.

By looking at their transactions with society, it becomes clear that the nuns' key problem is rooted in their ambiguous religious position: that it is difficult for nuns, unlike monks, to achieve full renunciation in the absence of legal protections for their other-worldly position. Due to the expectations of their immediate families and other relatives, and social practices that bind women to social reciprocity, Buddhist nuns in Myanmar are constantly being pulled back to this-worldly places where they have originally departed from. And the question remains as to why it is always women who have to carry the heavy burdens of family ties and perform caring roles, even after renouncing them.

5
Donor groups and social outreach

Traditionally, various types of lay Buddhist groups were active in towns and villages in Myanmar, supporting specific religious causes during communal festivities, and many continue to be the core of social activities. This chapter examines the various modes of offerings made by lay Buddhists today along with many religious activities of donor groups that extend into the secular area of social giving. The difference between Buddhist donor groups on the one hand, and charities and INGOs (International Non-governmental Organizations) on the other hand that have multiplied in Myanmar in the past decade is that members of the former are lay Buddhist enthusiasts who contribute to giving from their own pockets with the goal of making merit. Some of these groups gather on an ad hoc basis, and others meet regularly to work on their respective socio-religious projects. They also encourage one another to conduct good deeds and rejoice together on religious occasions when they share merit, which adds to their collective sense of purpose and feelings of belonging to the moral community.

Wealthy lay Buddhists may donate frequently to the monastic community and meet regularly at ceremonies and other functions at Buddhist monasteries or nunneries. At times, they compete against each other to offer large sums of money to prominent monastery schools and famous meditation centres. Nonetheless, donor groups today are observably diversifying and members are no longer restricted to traditional family/kin or neighbourhood structures, which include work and project-related groups. This phenomenon has been accelerated further by the rapid expansion of communications technology in recent years, which has reduced the price for connecting with one another and expanded Myanmar people's social networks and helped to link groups of strangers who share common goals or religious beliefs.

Traditionally, offering *dāna* to the monastic community was always regarded as a primary duty of lay Buddhists and social giving was ranked much lower among their priorities. However, after foreign aid was seen to pour into the country especially following the devastation caused by Cyclone Nargis in 2008, public opinion began to shift, with many people in Myanmar – including celebrities – showing considerably more interest in giving to the victims of natural disasters. Thus, the transition from religious offering to social giving or charity is another theme that this chapter will explore. The majority of Myanmar's Buddhist population has always regarded their monks and nuns as more trustworthy than either politicians or 'strangers', including foreign aid organizations. In this new climate, senior monks and abbots have played an essential role, by linking international aid organizations, through their extensive monastic networks with local monasteries in the Delta region, sheltering families in need and supporting domestic operations that were delivering aid supplies. Hence, despite demands placed on monks to accept a new mode of transactions, such as a corporate accountability model of filling reports and accounts when receiving, they are becoming important moral partners to secular agents often from the international community. Moreover, being socially credited 'intermediaries' for humanitarian causes, monastic members are also making it more acceptable for lay Buddhists in Myanmar to donate to secular causes of charity and social giving.

Merit-making as a collective act

As discussed in an earlier chapter, mutual support among family members, relatives and close friends are the norm in Myanmar's society, and people are always helped and supported within close circles of those regarded as *mithazu* (family members).[1] A donor group based on kinship, however, can be extended to neighbours and friends, invited by the core person to make merit alongside her family members. In contrast to the informality and affinity they express towards members of these family units, people are generally cautious about engaging in reciprocal relationships with those outside them, on the grounds that even seemingly minor favours could give rise to patron-client or dominant-subordinate relationships. Thus, Myanmar's Buddhists do not normally conduct merit-making activities with those outside their kin-based groups, and offerings are generally made by families or by groups of close friends.

In many monasteries in Myanmar, every section of a wall, or perhaps some entire building, is inscribed with lay donors' names. In these inscriptions, it is customary to see the names of married couples or larger family units, but rather uncommon to see those of individual donors. The most common practice is to place the two names of a donor couple: the husband and wife forming the core unit, on the top line – as U (Mr) X plus Daw (Mrs) Y – with those of other family members of their donor group below; and the vernacular term to describe their collective giving is *mithathu kaung-mu*. Since the family structure of Myanmar is not patrilineal like in China or India, there are traditionally no family names that are dominant and the full names of both the husband and wife are listed jointly. This is associated with the belief that any close relationship formed in the present life is the consequence of religious offerings made conjointly in the past, so couples customarily make *dāna* together so that they will be reborn together again. This custom also points to the official union of two families coming together to conduct good deeds and the resultant merit that accrues to both of them. In some cases, siblings make religious offerings together, especially when they are unmarried, and this too is considered *mithathu kaung-mu* accruing merit to the family as a unit.

Dāna offerings are most commonly made on the birthdays of family members, or on days especially relevant to a deceased member of the joint family. At times, offerings are also made to speed the recovery of a family member who is ill. Incidentally, it is usually the mother or grandmother who is tasked with remembering all the birthdays of her children or grandchildren, in addition to the birthdays of parents, siblings and in-laws; and it is the matriarch who summons all the family members to partake in making merit on such days. As families in Myanmar tend to be large, these occasions may occur up to several times in a month, at a substantial aggregate cost. In most cases, the expenses are paid for by senior members of the family, but in the spirit of filial piety, junior ones also pay for their elderly parents to make merit and celebrate their birthdays in old age. I have observed siblings handing banknotes to their elderly mother so that she could at least conduct the act of offering to monks in person, and thus make merit of her own accord (despite the money not actually being hers). In other words, though offering *dāna* is fundamentally a religious occasion dedicated to the acquisition of merit, it involves the coming together of whole families, sometimes across several generations, to confirm their close bond in the present as well as in the next life.

The sending out of *metta* at the end of every Buddhist ceremony, however, raises the question of whether merit can accrue collectively to all participants rather than to a specific individual donor. When asked this question, my informants assured me not only that it was possible, but also that the power of group recitation of loving kindness made it even more efficacious in earning merit for each member, and even for spirits in the environment. Donald Swearer, in his study of the consecration ritual of Buddha image in northern Thailand, introduced the 'grand merit-making celebration', in which the collective recitation of a particular text was also an opportunity for all participants to make merit.[2] Myanmar Buddhists generally seem to believe that merit can be made together, even over the generations, and the meritorious act in itself links these individuals together. However, this may fly in the face of Myint Win Maung's dictum that it is contradictory for people to recite *ahmyà* ('to all') and send out loving kindness to everyone and every spirit, and yet still try to take credit and accrue merit as an individual.[3] Likewise, it could readily be argued that – rather than writing down one's name on every item donated to the monastery, from the smallest cup to every envelope containing a cash honorarium – Myanmar donors should just write the phrase *ahmyà kaung-mu* (offering from everyone and to all), without revealing the identities of individual donors. Indeed, using this phrase of *ahmyà kaung-mu* would enable everyone present to accrue merit without any one of them monopolising the associated merit or honour. Lay Buddhists in

Myanmar customarily offer *dāna* to the monastic community as an indicator of their faith, but the question remains as to whether such merit can accrue to a group rather than to an individual: that is, whether one's karmic state can be improved by doing a good deed as part of a group. As we have seen, Buddhist offerings are usually collective acts conducted by family and friends, work colleagues, or even the whole village as part of annual community events. It is worth wondering whether, as Myanmar people gather in religious ceremonies both to participate in and to witness the good deeds being enacted, the context of reaffirming and rejoicing in the relationships they have with one another may be more relevant to them as a community than the strictly religious interpretation that focuses on the individual.

It is commonly believed that merit could be transferred to others, especially to loved ones like family and friends, and even to those who are already deceased long time ago. My own observations also confirmed that people in Myanmar were joyous when sharing with others in the performance of good deeds, and that few if any claimed the resultant merit as his or her own. Holt numbered *anumodana*, the giving of thanks while sharing in the joy of offering *dāna*, among one of the key concepts at work in the ritual process.[4] He noted, 'What it reflects is a conscious recognition of why an action is karmicly fortuitous'.[5] Therefore, although the concept of karmic law applies fundamentally to individuals who are expected to take moral responsibility for their past and present actions, the day-to-day practices of people in Myanmar suggest that they are more eager to spread merit collectively rather than assigning it to a single individual.

Traditional donor groups in community

Although collective offering made by families is the most common form of merit-making in Myanmar, local traders and neighbourhood associations in provincial towns are also active in organizing *dāna*, especially during the annual robe-offering period of *kathina*. In rural agricultural communities, too, committees of village elders facilitate community-wide planning of offerings to the village monastery as well as communal feasts, as distinct from the daily offerings of alms by every household. The recess periods especially after the harvest are reserved for many ceremonial events, including villagers going on pilgrimages together. Similarly, in many towns, administrative wards called *yaquet* organize their own offerings of monks' robes to local monasteries followed by large communal feasts. This offering period coincides with the cool and dry season of the year (November to January), when ceremonial feasts become frequent, weddings are conducted, and sons become noviciated. Long processions are often seen in many provincial towns carrying boys dressed as princes on horses and bullock carts, followed by traditionally dressed young women and men carrying flowers and offerings. Before *dāna* items are donated to monasteries, they are hung on the 'wish-fulfilling trees' and displayed in the public hall of each ward, whose residents competitively display their offerings as quantifiable evidence of their collective generosity. For a few nights before these goods are donated to monasteries, the occasion is celebrated with stage shows, singing competitions and comedy theatres known as *anyein*. Vendors gather in the evenings to sell noodles, barbecue and other local food and, in some cases, there are funfair rides, shooting galleries and funhouses for the children. In many small towns, these Buddhist celebrations provide the community with an important occasion for social mingling, and some households prepare and offer free drinks and food to everyone who come in the spirit of collective generosity.

The town of Sagaing, about half an hour's drive from Mandalay, currently has a population of about 78,000.[6] On its outskirts, a few miles east from the town, there is a large Buddhist monastic community that flourished under the patronage of Buddhist kings and queens during the last Konbaung dynasty (1752–1885). The monastic community of Sagaing Hill currently has a population of about 12,000 Buddhist monks and nuns, with many prominent monastery schools in operation. The town, which has thrived in part due to its connection to this monastic community, retains many of its cultural and religious traditions, and local donor groups continue to organize traditional forms of communal celebration at seasonal junctures. Local elders told me that it was common for residents to congregate at a *zayat* (public hall used for socio-religious purposes) located in every neighbourhood to listen to monks' sermons on the evening of every full-moon day. After Burma, as it was then called, came under the military rule of General Ne Win in the mid-1960s, its socialist policies discouraged both communal gatherings and religious celebrations. As these occasions for entertainment and celebration came under increasing surveillance, communal events in towns became fewer; and with many young people moving to large cities or going to work on foreign ships, residential donor groups disappeared one by one.

Today, however, at least three such groups are still active, and come together during the *kathina* period in some areas of Sagaing town, in Moezar, Poedan and Kwat Thit wards. Residents of the Moezar *yaquet*, located next to the central market, are renowned for throwing a large *dāna* display accompanied by a communal party, normally in December, a month after the end of the *kathina* season. The Moezar group is made up of market traders and brokers, and residents living around the market area, who form an ad hoc committee of trustees and oversee the preparation for the event. Committee members solicit donations from the local population to purchase robes and other items to be offered to monks, which are duly hung on their 'wish-fulfilling trees' as described in Chapter 2. Large markets in Mandalay, such as Zeijyo – a hundred times bigger than that in Sagaing – are well known for their elaborate displays of *kathina* offerings. Each donor group is composed of market vendors in a particular trade, such as gold, silver, fruits or 'pickled tea', who compete against the other trades to present the best display of offerings to be donated to the sangha. Although the majority of market vendors in Zeijyo are women, *dāna* groups there have traditionally been led by men, and influential traders see such leadership positions in religious events as reflecting their reputation as successful businessmen who are also generous givers with an abundant store of merit.

There are also voluntary groups at important Buddhist sites known as *weiyawesah athin* (association offering menial services) that engage in cleaning the premises and offering various miscellaneous services to the religious sites. They are composed of pious locals who gather either on an ad hoc basis or regularly (e.g., on any particular day of the week) to offer menial services to pagodas and monasteries. At important pagodas such as the Shwedagon Pagoda in Yangon or at the Maha Myamuni Pagoda in Mandalay, there are numerous lay associations and volunteer groups that look after and maintain these sites and premises. Some groups cook for and offer alms food to the monks who reside there, and others provide general security, overseeing events on every *ubòk-nei* (special abstinence days governed by the lunar calendar), when such places become crowded with worshippers and visitors. A lay association at the Maha Myamuni Pagoda is well known for its ceremonious washing of the face of the main Buddha image conducted every morning, using specially scented water and done only by male members. Whoever leads them, these groups are supported by regular members who sign up to participate in their weekly or monthly activities and contribute to the maintenance and management of important pagodas and other Buddhist sites. The area around Sagaing town has the second largest number of pagodas in Myanmar, some of which dating back to the fifteenth century. Especially the twelve pagodas in the area are regular places of worship, each being assigned a specific month of the year whose full-moon day is dedicated to honouring it as the pagoda of the month.[7] On such days, hundreds of visitors come to worship on the premises, and local donor groups meet a few days before to decide on their respective roles and responsibilities. These include cleaning and preparing the premises, purchasing religious amenities such as flowers, candles and incense, decorating the central worship hall where the ceremony takes place, printing the programmes, and informing the locality, as well as cooking food for the more than 5,000 monks who will arrive on the day. Families in the locality have contributed their services to these religious sites for several generations, and the current 'regulars' clearly intend to pass their roles on to their own children to maintain the tradition.

Sometimes, local donor groups are summoned by monasteries in the area: for example, when there is a large religious function such as a public sermon by a prominent monk preacher, and if the host institution does not have enough human resources or funds to accommodate large numbers of visitors. The core members of any such group tend to be made up of middle-aged men and retirees in town, though some contain a large proportion of college and high school students who offer their services during school holidays. Although these activities are religiously motivated, the participants seem to gain much contentment from taking part, perhaps because these also serve as occasions to get together with like-minded members of similar age group and from the same community. Such groups' social functions are perhaps especially important to younger Buddhists, being much like secular youth groups, that is, respecting seniority within the group and learning the moral ethos of the community.[8]

While many groups focus on reaping the meritorious outcomes of performing menial chores and services, there are also Buddhist study groups whose aim is to learn important chants as a means for the *thathana-pyu* (dissemination of Buddhism). These so-called recitation groups are normally led by former monks or sometimes by local *pyinnya-shin* (persons learned in the Buddhist scriptures), and their lay members learn the liturgies and practise to recite them correctly. As a prerequisite for this, they must observe the Eight Precepts and practise morality, and then learn the eleven *paritta* one by one. In addition to these chants, they may learn other important verses recited in Buddhist rituals, such as *Dhammasetkya* or even the difficult passages from *Patthāna*, the seventh and final book of the Abhidhamma. These groups not only earn merit by reciting these powerful words, but also act as a bridge between the monastic community and its lay congregations by passing on the recitation methods and disseminating the Buddha's teachings. Although composed of majority laypeople, they are often invited to Buddhist ceremonies or functions, where they lead the congregation in recitation and add their vocal support to the officiating monks.

In addition to *dhamma* learning groups, there are pilgrimage groups that congregate at certain times of the year to visit important pagodas or historic Buddhist sites together. Some of the wealthy donors of these pilgrimage groups invite monks and nuns so that they can also visit important Buddhist sites abroad such as Bodhgaya in India or Kandy in Sri Lanka, and they pay for their travel expenses as a way of making merit. Other group types include meditation-retreat groups, whose members stay in meditation centres together for a week or more, and support one another in persisting with the practice during its designated duration. This, too, is seen as a good opportunity to share in meritorious deeds. Thus, donor groups function in an array of different ways: from learning Buddhist chants and practising meditation, and to providing menial services to the local Buddhist community. Through collective participation and submerging their egos in religious services, and by offering their time and service in many other ways, lay Buddhists come to realize the significance and value of being interdependent in society.

Established lay associations in modern Myanmar

Turner described how hundreds of Buddhist lay associations sprang up across Burma at around the turn of the twentieth century, which she described as the driving force behind Buddhist modernism and innovation.[9] However, few have survived the test of time and are active today, and Malun Sanhlu Athin (Malun Rice-offering Association) is perhaps the oldest rice-offering group that is still in operation. This association was established in 1896 by a wealthy trader U Kyauk Kyair together with other devout elders who lived in the Malun quarter in Mandalay. They started the association to provide rice in support of the monastic community that fell on hard times due to the loss of royal patrons after the fall of the last Buddhist kingdom in Mandalay. The initial members of Malun Sanhlu Athin were rice traders who went around nearby

Figure 5.1 *Twice a year, boats of the Malun Rice-offering Association arrive from Mandalay to offer rice bags to thousands of monks and nuns in Mingun, Minwun and Sagaing.*

agricultural villages to collect surplus rice grains from rice mills and farmers. But the association now collects rice from all over the country and distributes at regular intervals thousands of rice bags to vocational monks and nuns residing in Mingun, Minwun and the monastic community of Sagaing Hill. Twice a year, boats piled with sacks of rice grains arrive from Mandalay across the Ayeyarwady River to the northeastern pier in Sagaing, and monastic residents await them eagerly in bullock carts and trucks nowadays.[10] Abbots and abbesses and those with special Buddhist titles are given extra bags; but for many ordinary monks and nuns, these rice distributions represent essential provision of staple food that sustains them for the whole year.

Lay Buddhists have also been enthusiastic supporters of Buddhist monastic education and there are many lay associations in the country that continue to support monastics' scriptural learning. These groups conduct private scriptural exams several times per year to complement the state *Pathamapyan* administered by the Department of Religious Affairs of the Religious Ministry, which is held only once annually, in March. The private scriptural exams are supported by the sangha, and senior monks help with setting the exam questions and marking them. Funded by private donations from well-wishers, the associations that offer these scriptural exams seem to have a bottomless well of support from the wider Buddhist community, with some donors offering specific awards and prizes in the form of *dāna* to monastic students who pass with distinction. Many of the lay supporters in question appear to see themselves as *sāsana taga*: that is, taking on the responsibility of supporting and disseminating the Buddha *sāsana* by enhancing the academic standards of monks and nuns. In fact, the key members of these groups tend to be *pongyi lutwet* (former monks who have disrobed), who have elected to continue their former responsibility for supporting monastic education, despite having become laymen.

Historically speaking, the popular drive to support and maintain high standards of monastic education began after the fall of the country's Buddhist kingdom in 1885. When the last Buddhist king, Thibaw (1859–1916), was sent into exile, and the country became part of British Indian Empire, many monks who had lost their royal patrons disrobed, and Buddhism went into decline. The British authorities who had suspended all Buddhist examinations earlier allowed the revival of *Pathamapyan* in 1895, as a way to encourage the monasteries to teach secular education.[11] Promoting Buddhist scholarship was nothing new, as Turner stated, in preserving the *sāsana*;[12] however, it was around this time that lay Buddhists, some of them wealthy traders in Mandalay and Yangon, rose to the challenge of supporting the monastic education. Community leaders also played a central role in administering private exams for monastic students and raising the standard of Buddhist scholarship.[13] Among these groups supporting Buddhist scholarship, perhaps the most enduring are: Cetiyangana Pariyatti Dhamma Nuggaha Athin, established in 1894 in Yangon; and Pariyatti Thathanahita Athin in 1898 in Mandalay, founded by a group of traders led by U Tun.[14] Despite being administered by lay enthusiasts, these two associations are said to have changed the way Buddhist scriptures were taught, as their examinations determined which texts would be assigned by teachers and, thus, they came to hold institutional power over large monasteries.[15] Both associations started to offer private exams for monks from 1902 onwards, but their scriptural exams were said to be notoriously difficult. Especially the Sakyasiha exam convened by the Mandalay Association was known as the 'monk-killer'.[16] With only a handful of bright monks able to pass it each year, special prestige and titles were granted to those who could meet its high standards of scriptural knowledge. Even today, to have the honorary title of *a-bhivamsa* (higher lineage) attached as a suffix to his Buddhist title as a result of passing the Sakyasiha is regarded as one of highest academic achievements for a scholarly monk in Myanmar.[17] Many more lay associations came to support Buddhist education around this time, such as the Buddhabatha Thathana-pyu Athin (Society for Promoting the Sāsana) in 1900,[18] but most are no longer in operation today.

After Burma's independence in 1946, more lay associations came into existence founded by wealthy and educated laymen, who wanted to promote Buddha *sāsana*, especially in the country's nation-building process to promote confidence and solidarity. Perhaps the most noteworthy is the Buddha Sasana Nuggaha Association (BTNA), founded in 1947 by Sir U Thwin, which led to the opening of Mahasi Thathana Yeitha two years later under the guidance of monk-scholar Mahasi Sayadaw U Sobhana. The centre, run by subscriptions from members and donations from the general public, became famous due to its association with prominent politicians such as U Nu, the first prime minister of Burma. He saw the benefits of Buddhism to provide an ethical foundation to the country's majority population and incorporated practice-oriented Buddhism into the social and economic projects of his government, highlighting self-discipline and hard work to achieve economic prosperity. BTNA was crucial in promoting *vipassana* meditation; and Mahasi meditation centre, through its institutional link with state departments, enabled the government to draw on the popularity of its meditation. It also developed into one of the most influential meditation centres in the country and its network expanded nationally and even to other countries.[19]

'*Dāna* cliques'

Jordt likened the lay-donor groupings to 'business cliques' as they conducted collective merit-making activities around the above-mentioned Mahasi mediation centre in Yangon. Their lay members formed commercial networks and created group endowments, pooling their fixed monthly donations and other types of income so that they could conduct religious activities together.[20] These cliques seemed to act as a kind of insurance fund for each other and their lay members trusted each other even to the extent of asking for a loan. They were mostly businesswomen or retirees who planned to spend the rest of their lives living on religious premises, including especially at the Mahasi meditation centre. However, it would be hazardous to generalize the activities of *dāna* cliques (or indeed their status as cliques) from this lone example, given the profound differences between monasteries or nunneries, where laypeople normally do not reside, and meditation centres, where some do. Nonetheless, the mutual trust noticeable within members of such groupings and the strong internal networks they forge through common religious practices and Buddhist worship are worthy of further consideration.

As we have seen in previous chapters, prominent lay donors are regular attendees at Buddhist functions and ceremonial feasts, and are well known for their close associations with monasteries, and individual monks and nuns they worship in their communities. Many such donors, but especially female ones, lead influential donor groups that focus their offerings on feeding the monks at large monastery schools. One group of this type, called Visakha, currently comprises about thirty regular members, led by a woman who was formerly a member of the above-mentioned 'clique' at Mahasi meditation centre. Each member of Visakha has to pay an annual fee an equivalent to about of $120 USD, with quarterly instalments allowed, to sustain its regular religious activities. These funds are pooled and managed by the key organizer mentioned above, whom the members must trust fully and follow as well.

Some lay Buddhist groups meet regularly wearing colour-coordinated uniforms, while others meet only on an ad hoc basis for offering *dāna* on a specific occasion. In the more permanently constituted groups, the members collectively decide on the frequency of their *dāna* offerings, with some groups offering once every three months, and others only once a year, such as during the *kathina* period. There are also donor groups formed by several wealthy families from a small town who visit monasteries and make offerings to them in the name of the whole town. Other groups have a uniformly wealthy middle- and upper-class membership; the Leijunthu group, for example, charges prospective members a fee of $10,000 USD when joining the group. It makes elaborate offerings at prominent monasteries at certain times of the year, and its prestige has made it very attractive to status-conscious businesspeople in Yangon. As such, Leijunthu seems to fit Jordt's description of a *dāna* clique akin to a business clique. Members of this and other groups with a similar level of prestige may already perform the role as *kyaung taga* of such-and-such monastery, or a *bazin medaw* of such-and-such monk, whose high reputation rests in part on their close association with their prestigious monastic beneficiaries. As Jordt noted, 'renowned donors are persons of influence, and their status is closely linked to that of the monks', with the pairing supporting the status of both lay benefactor and monastic beneficiary.[21] Nevertheless, members of these famed and prestigious *dāna* groups are not always serious meditators or keen students of Buddhism. Having similar interests and rarefied high social backgrounds, these donors exchange pleasantries and gossip, openly talk about the amount of money they have recently spent on *dāna*, talk about celebrity monks, and even arrange marriages for their daughters and sons. They also see it as important to control whom they mingle with during ceremonial offerings, and many arrive wearing formal silk clothes and expensive jewellery.

As briefly noted above, prominent lay donors within the same clique also compete head-to-head with regards to the amount and frequency of their offerings. Sometimes, rivalries between lay donors 'over who will count among the closest supporters or even as the chief donor' can turn bitter.[22] However, when it comes to supporting an influential monk (or occasionally, a nun), these donors come together more, due to the centripetal power of the monastic recipient concerned. For instance, if an abbot under their patronage falls ill, all members of a donor group will likely offer to pay his hospital bills, or at least discuss a way of distributing the costs among themselves. A member of such a group will also tend to regard its other members as trustworthy, usually because they were introduced to one another by the monk, who would otherwise lose face if they fell out. Thus, members also compete to demonstrate their trustworthiness as well as their generosity and kindness, since these fundamental moral values, and the associated self-perception of being a good Buddhist, are essential in keeping them together as a moral group.

Today, thanks to recent improvements in communications in Myanmar, including cheap smart phones and SIM cards and the proliferation of social media, lay Buddhists from all walks of life are joining various types of existing donor groups and forming new ones as well. Especially during important religious celebrations, volunteers and other lay enthusiasts become active in collecting funds and even contribute large sums from their own pockets. For example, Thirithuka Wutshwe Athin is a lay association that congregates monthly at the Shwedagon Pagoda in Yangon and its members are mostly young volunteers, both men and women, who stay the night to cook a meal for more than a hundred resident monks on the pagoda premises. This group exemplifies a new phenomenon in Myanmar society, as its members, previously unknown to one another, were brought together via social media due to their shared desire to make merit in this way. Importantly, many of these new groups convene temporarily for the sole purpose of offering *dāna* and dissolve after they have done so. In this respect, they are different from traditional donor groups, which also function as a support network in times of hardship, and members remain in contact even when they are not conducting *dāna* activities. And yet, the features we observe in digitized communication and virtual relationships in the world of social media today can facilitate these donor groups to expand their activities beyond the traditional confines and create more imaginative types of donor communities.

State involvement

During successive military governments, generals and politicians tried to enhance their moral reputation by paying homage to influential abbots and monasteries, presenting themselves as official supporters of the Buddha *sāsana* due to their positions of unelected power. Every Buddhist occasion involving generals' transactions with senior monks was photographed and disseminated in the media, in elaborate propagandistic displays of the former's generosity. When the sacred tooth relic was brought from Beijing, China, in 1994, SLORC (State Law and Order Restoration Council) perceiving itself in the lineage of past Buddhist kings created a huge merit field for the nation, granting large donors with certificates of honour, in its pursuit to appear as a legitimate political ruler. It was also at a time 'when constitutional authority of the modern nation-state [was] debated and in a socio-cultural milieu where power [was] often seen as vested in charismatic individuals rather than in political processes or civil contracts'.[23] Carbine confirmed that this phenomenon reflected an attempt by the state to 'promote political legitimacy and national integration vis a vis the *Sasana*'.[24] As such, the generals' every transaction with the monastic community revealed how the traditional Buddhist cosmology, imbued with symbolic meanings, continued to affect Myanmar's political culture for both religious and political reasons.

Under military rule in the 1980s and 1990s, many lay donors who supported Myanmar's monastic community were involved in black-market activities. They included timber and tobacco brokers, gold and gem merchants, some seen as connected with foreign commercial interests, and others with insurgent groups. The military regimes therefore focused considerable effort on hampering the influence of independent entrepreneurs and traders in order to capture the wealth and other resources of business communities that operated outside the state control. One mechanism for this used by the SLORC in the late 1990s was to pressurize businesspeople to make large donations to state projects such as those for building schools, repairing roads and painting the exteriors of major buildings. Donors who contributed were rewarded with access to building materials at concessionary rates, along with many other social and economic privileges.[25] But the attempt by the military government to impose control on wealthy donors' groups to re-direct their resources and goodwill towards the state, and draw them away from the Buddhist monastic community, was not especially effective, largely because the donors concerned felt that these public works led by the state were insufficiently meritorious.

While lay donors in the private sector continued to support the monastic community, in part as an expression of their frustration with and resentment of Myanmar's military rulers, soldiers and other public-sector workers were paid wages barely high enough to cover their expenses to support their families. As such, it was difficult for government employees to become active members of lay donors' groups, irrespective of how devout they were. The monastic community itself did not discriminate against any particular types of workers or traders, but monks – having no political agenda of their own – naturally were influenced by the political viewpoints of their main benefactors; and the majority of their lay donors were anti-government. In return for their material support, senior monks helped their regular donors by allowing them into the extensive monastic networks, through which information was shared and personal contacts were made. From the viewpoint of lay donors, reciprocal relationships with monastic beneficiaries, based on trust and piety, were much more beneficial to their business interests than the occasional conferral of privileges by the state.[26] Nonetheless, joining a *dāna* group simply out of political ambition or to serve one's own business interests would likely have been futile, since most or all of its other members would have genuinely upheld the religious authority of the monks, relating to one another through the lens of their Buddhist faith and genuine support for the sangha.

Under successive military regimes, whenever a new military officer was appointed to an administrative position in a town or a district office, he would go customarily – accompanied by his wife – to pay his respects to influential abbots in the area and make a token *dāna* offering to each one of them. Such donation activities were in effect a formality to publicly announce his arrival in the area, as opposed to genuine expressions of Buddhist piety. Although this is not to suggest that piety was always entirely lacking, it would have been obvious to any Myanmar bystander that a one-off formal offering of a few sacks of rice grains and a pair of monastic robes could not be compared to the continuous and, in the aggregate, high-level support offered by genuinely devout supporters. Senior monks, too, were generally critical of political power being displayed in this way. One prominent Sayadaw remarked to me that it was a nuisance to have anyone from the military government visit him, since a whole procession led by police officers and a retinue of officers' and soldiers' cars blocked the road to the monastery, sometimes for many hours and even the whole day, making it difficult for his donors to make their regular visits. It was obvious from this that the monk valued his ordinary, and yet committed lay donors much more than any army general coming for an official visit – a mere performance rather than anything heart-felt, and a way of appropriating Buddhism to maintain state power and the semblance of legitimacy. However, it is worth mentioning that after NLD won the national elections and became the majority party in 2015, democratic reforms started in earnest, and the protocol of military officers paying official visits to senior abbots in their area of control has also ceased. Ironically, the surveillance as well as patronage of the military government had sustained a semblance of relationship between state and sangha, in which army generals (who were also government Ministers) and senior monks engaged in frequent reciprocal transactions. In the new democratic era, however, the distance between both parties seems to have widened and a balanced relationship lost, in that the sangha, regarding it no longer has the support of the state, has started to assume socio-political roles in protecting its moral community as we have seen in Chapter 4.

There were times when the Buddhist monks refused to accept the gifts from the army and politicians, which was possible then since both parties had a common stake in the Buddhist merit-making scheme. The most recent instance of this occurred during the Saffron Revolution in 2007, when monks refused to accept any alms food from soldiers or from family members of the country's military rulers. This was in response to the harsh crackdown on the monks demonstrating against the hike in fuel and food prices that brought much hardship to people's lives. Upturning one's alms bowl as an act of protest, known in Pali as *pattam nikkujjana kamma*, implies a major moral rebuke to lay Buddhists.[27] The monks refused to be co-opted into what Schober described as the 'economy of merit', and thereby made a powerful statement to excommunicate the military and their families 'from the Buddhist field of merit'.[28] That is, if no monastic recipient would receive their goodwill in the form of an alms offering, then those people will not be able to improve their karmic standing or accumulate merit for future rebirths. Jordt reported that when monks on their morning rounds bypassed the homes of military officers, it had a ripple effect, as 'the wives of key military personnel refused to cook for their husbands' – illustrating the profound consequences of the act of refusal, not only for society at large, but also for individual households.[29] Such was the power of its moral message that many monks who protested in this way were arrested for showing their defiance to the military regime. Although non-reciprocity of this kind tends to be used only as a last resort, this incident demonstrated that interdependence between the religious and secular populations was still seen as essential to sustaining the Buddhist faith that both shared.

Socially engaged groups in Myanmar today

Recent rapid socio-economic transition, coupled with improvements in Myanmar's transport and telecommunications infrastructure, has enabled local donor groups to extend their activities far beyond the traditional confines of villages or hamlets. Residents of rural communities have always anticipated receiving mutual help and cooperated beyond the boundaries of the village with people forever visiting each other to collect funds and attending celebrations in other villages. However, what is different today is people of multiple villages cooperate for social projects that are not confined to merit-making activities, such as repairing the monastery roof or constructing a pagoda. The activities and communal projects of recent years have been marked by wide-scale cooperation: for example, multiple villages raising funds to purchase an ambulance for their area.[30] Thus, while religious transactions with the Buddhist monastic community continue to form the crux of communal activities, Myanmar's people are expanding their social engagement beyond its traditionally religious foci.

A range of social welfare projects conceived and funded by lay enthusiasts and local well-wishers, which can be referred to collectively as 'community-based' projects, are aimed at supporting a particular local community, for example, by establishing a free school or building a medical clinic in a remote village. Importantly, most such groups differ from traditional donor groups, insofar as their primary aim is not about religious merit-making, but social development and enhancement of the residents' quality of life. Many are funded locally, and their projects are relatively small in scale. And although many are initiated by lay Buddhists to start with, some end up being delegated to a local monk who can ensure a continuous flow of donations, mobilize volunteers in time of need and assure that their operations are conducted fairly.

In addition, a trend for social giving has emerged among Myanmar's urban middle classes over the past decade. As part of this, the country's film stars and other celebrities have become more visible in offering donations to the poor and disadvantaged, and some of them have set up their own charity organizations to support them. U Thukha (1938–2005), a writer, award-winning film director and devout Buddhist, was one of the pioneers in this area, founding the Free Funeral Service Society (FFSS) in 2001.[31] After his death, the FFSS was taken over by his protégé Kyaw Thu, star of more than 200 films in the 1980s and 1990s, who has since devoted his time and resources to offering free funeral services to people in need from all ethnic and religious backgrounds.[32] This work, however, included a battle against general prejudice in society. U Kyaw Thu said that negative feelings about those involved with funerals were so strong in the beginning that some township authorities would not allow FFSS hearses to drive through their neighbourhoods, and many actresses refused to appear with him on the screen as they believed his funerary work would bring them bad luck to their film careers. Nevertheless, younger celebrities have established charitable organizations more recently, with actor Ye Deik launching one in 2011 to support children made homeless by natural disasters, and his colleague Pyay Ti Oo raising funds through private events to offer scholarships to medical students from disadvantaged backgrounds.[33]

Even when aided by celebrity status and leveraging it to attract attention and collect donations from fans not only throughout the country, but also in the Myanmar Diaspora, social welfare groups run by laypeople have proved far more difficult to sustain than traditional Buddhist *dāna* groups supporting religious causes. This problem for the former appears to be inherent in the secular and large-scale nature of their activities, which go against the grain of the Myanmar tradition whereby charity outside the family circle – where if occurred at all – was mediated by monks or nuns, who stood in a pivotal position in society and were thus able to link different groups of people without coming under the influence of any one of them.

The popular monk U Dhammapiya responded to the funerary needs of residents of Sagaing after encountering many stories of poor families not being able to pay the expenses when he was invited to officiate at funerals. In 2010, further inspired by his involvement in relief activities following the Cyclone Nargis, he purchased two vehicles using funds from his close donors, and formed a welfare organization called Thukhakari, headquartered at his Oak Gyaung monastery.[34] A few years later, he established a medical clinic there that offers free treatment three times a week, supported by medical doctors, nurses and other staff working on a small honorarium. Thukhakari has had a less difficult journey than it might have done, due to the precedent set by the Byamaso Social Welfare Association, founded in Mandalay half a century ago, when public attitudes towards social welfare projects were far less sympathetic than they are now.

Importantly, whenever a social welfare association funded by private donors becomes influential in any area, it tends to come under heavy scrutiny from local authorities that see its popularity as a threat to their political base. Byamaso, for example, encountered an aggressive takeover attempt from the local office of the Ministry of Health,[35] and FFSS met with governmental harassment, and was ordered to choose between relocating to an area away from the town centre or the organization closing altogether. The military government also targeted 'civil society' following the anti-government demonstrations in 2007, and Kyaw Thu was arrested for giving his support to protesting monks (though the inter-faith nature of FFSS may have added another layer to official suspicion of him). These events should be seen in the context of the country's five decades of isolation. That is, despite the political reform efforts of the last few years, Myanmar's democratic foundations remain weak, and its civil society and the 'third sector' underdeveloped. To this day, social welfare organizations funded by lay individuals are classified as *pokgalika* (private groups), and regardless of whether they have any political intentions or not, these organizations are seen as a threat by the authorities whenever they grow beyond a certain level of membership, influence or social profile. In short, among the many obstacles to social engagement and charity work in Myanmar, arguably one of the greatest is that when a group comes to be seen as too influential in civil society, it is immediately re-cast as a potential threat to the political status quo.[36]

Interacting with international aid organizations

Cyclone Nargis struck Myanmar in May 2008, directly affecting almost 2.5 million people. This led to an influx of humanitarian aid and donations from the international community, as part of the largest relief effort the country had ever known. The disaster also sharply increased people's interest in and favourable feelings about social giving. Humanitarian aid from overseas, which had been long restricted in Myanmar, started to arrive anyway.[37] Some of it was in the form of cash offered to senior monks who had good connections with local authorities and monasteries in the affected regions. Despite the severe repression Myanmar's monks faced following the large-scale anti-government uprising of the previous year, many supported aid operations due to the absence of domestic NGOs then, and they involved themselves directly in the distribution of food and supplies to remote villages. In this, monks relied on their extensive monastic networks, both of monastic teachers and students, and of main monasteries and their branches. However, the sudden and large influx of cash from foreign charities and other secular organizations also caused confusion initially, as well as a gradual change in the attitudes of monastic recipients as they became exposed to a new transactional mode that required transparency and a Western corporate model of accountability. To comply with its requirements, some had to adopt practices such as 'the systematic use of vouchers, an accounting system, or templates that were provided' by their international donors, and even had to issue financial reports to them.[38] Nonetheless, transparency could never have been fully assured, since monasteries and religious organizations did not pay tax to Myanmar's government, or even register their activities with the local authorities in the manner that secular organizations did. Besides, monastics in Myanmar were already seen to be accountable, since their high moral credentials were a key plank of their religious identity. Meanwhile, the arrival of INGOs and donations from foreign well-wishers meant that the domestic Buddhist community came under new kinds of pressures in transacting with the outside world, with even local donors having to abide by internationally mandated procedures that more closely resembled corporate transactions than traditional religious offerings.

The involvement of foreign aid and other international organizations in the aftermath of the cyclone also led to a broad critique of Myanmar's government, which was already being widely criticized for its human rights record, with local officials being chastised for their lack of experience and inefficiency. The Myanmar government, for its part, suspected those foreign entities and their ethical, humanitarian stances to be mere façades, hiding dangerous political and religious agendas; and that, despite their emphasis on transparency, these organizations wasted large sums on overheads, or even misappropriated them.[39] As Bornstein has noted, 'Social welfare, in general, is highly political and morally laden political territory'.[40] Hence, the relations between international organizations and those in power in Myanmar were marked by mutual suspicion and frustration from the start.[41] Stepping into this vacuum of trust in the crucial early stages of the relief effort, Buddhist monks played a major role in delivering food and other necessities to people in the affected areas, with rural monasteries becoming temporary shelters and venues for organizing the large-scale distribution of food and supplies.[42] It was only then that the non-victim general public and INGO employees came to recognize the efficiency of their monastic networks and the critical role monastic members could perform as relief work intermediaries.

During the aid operation in 2008, prominent monks served as conduits for large amounts of donated cash. Sitagu Sayadaw, for example, liaised with regional monk representatives and monasteries who took responsibility for transporting and distributing aid supplies directly to families in their congregations in the flooded regions. In the eight months of his involvement, it is estimated that Sitagu handled more than $5 million USD, and that his relief operations delivered goods to 'over 1,500 villages and 2,264 monasteries, including [...] over 2,000 tons of rice, and many other goods and equipment'.[43] These supplies were not exclusively imported by formally constituted aid organizations; but many came from local donors in the country, or from the Myanmar Diaspora. Myanmar donors in particular expressed that offering to a prominent monk such as Sitagu Sayadaw enhanced the value of their donations, even though he was, in effect, acting only as a delivery medium. In the aftermath of the disaster, Sitagu monastery is also said to have collaborated with other faith-based groups in renovating schools and religious buildings, including hundred temples, sixty-four pagodas and sixteen churches.[44] As this example suggests, monastics in Myanmar were seen as – and indeed, largely acted as – responsible recipients and reliable conduits of goodwill donations to those suffering in the most dire circumstances.

On the other hand, despite foreign donors' optimistic sense that they were making a difference by helping a worthy cause, they were giving to total strangers in a country about which most of them knew very little. In this transaction, the 'giving' aspect took clear precedence over the nature or specific identities of the recipients in Myanmar. Most international donors probably had no knowledge of the general socio-cultural contexts in which local people lived, let alone of the layers of volunteers and monastic intermediaries who worked tirelessly to help the victims without any support from the government. In any case, after their initial involvement, most Buddhist monks handed over relief duties to professional aid organizations and local authorities, and they went back to their congregational work officiating Buddhist ceremonies and teaching the scriptures.

As we have seen, it has been traditionally assumed that Buddhist monks and nuns receive alms and *dāna* offerings, and monks in particular act as the 'field of merit' for the lay donors. However, Jaquet and Walton highlighted how this conception was affected by the inclusion of the monastic community within the broader realm of civil society.[45] For it is precisely by being 'detached' and 'other-worldly' that monastic members have been able to perform essential roles in so many areas of Myanmar's public life, receiving people's goodwill and relaying it farther afield. Besides, in a strictly religious sense, laypeople's generous intent would not produce any meritorious results in the absence of these recipients. During the relief operations, it was widely observed that monks who accepted donations on behalf of the families of victims distributed them fairly and selflessly. As well as being trained in disciplined conduct, monastics are also equipped with various kinds of socio-cultural skills, providing education in rural areas, and acting as moral and spiritual guides for the Buddhist majority. As a matter of fact, since the Cyclone Nargis, offering for social causes and offering *dāna* for religious ones have begun to converge conceptually, and are increasingly seen as equally meritorious by lay donors in the country. One can even state that Myanmar's monastics are performing a wide range of 'welfare' roles that are not sufficiently provided for by the state authorities. Hence, they are active in areas of healthcare, poverty alleviation and Buddhist moral education, as well as disseminating news of such activities through social media. One apparent advantage of this is that if social work is administered by Buddhist monks and nuns, the secular authorities normally do not interfere with it. Still, the monastic involvement in society remains a sensitive and contentious issue. Jaquet and Walton mention, 'Navigating a societal context in which norms for religious donations and social work as well as monastic involvement in "secular" development issues are in flux'.[46] Nonetheless, the current situation amounts to a mere competition to provide essential services between the secular and the religious spheres – a competition that cannot ultimately be healthy or productive for the further development of civil society in Myanmar.

Towards a society of interdependence

In hindsight, the title of this book should have been *The Culture of Receiving*, as this would have drawn attention to the disproportionate importance of the receiver as against the giver in Myanmar's Buddhist culture. In any case, I hope this book has shown how that culture expresses generosity in a wide range of material and immaterial ways, and highlighted how frequently giving, as one of the prime duties of practising Buddhists, occurs – both inside and outside of religious contexts. Nevertheless, although giving in various forms is often discussed in the scholarly literature, receiving is rarely talked about, arguably due to a widespread preconception that the receiving state indicates dependence, and thus subordination. In other words, receiving seems to carry a negative connotation, amounting to a stereotype of an always-already imbalanced relation between the benefactor and the beneficiary: for example, in the context of international aid, when the flow of goods or cash is from a developed country to a less developed one, or in charity of a more immediate kind, when they flow from the relatively privileged to the underprivileged. In this book, in contrast, I have tried to understand the 'dependence' of monastic members not in this stereotypical context, but as an important aspect of 'interdependence': a system in which giving only becomes meaningful when the giver has a willing recipient.

In practice, as we have seen, interdependence is not an easy ideal to achieve, and a relationship of mutual dependence does not work if people consider independence to be a more natural or otherwise preferable position. That is, the more emphasis we place on independence and equality, the fiercer competition in society is likely to be, and the greater the unhappiness that will arise from the idea and/or material fact of inequality. Buddhism, however, teaches that *dukkha* (suffering) is inevitable in life, as everything is in a state of flux and time waits for no man. There is a universal notion of equality in the Buddhist teachings, rooted in the inevitability of illness, the ageing process and death. But more importantly, it is *only* on the level of this existential reality that equality is understood. Meanwhile, the law of karma (if you believe in it) disposes everyone to differences in potential, as well as to a sense of moral responsibility. Everyone is born with a different store of karma as the result of their past deeds, so the present life situation inevitably presents distinct challenges and struggles for each person. And if one accepts the logic of this 'karmic difference', the notions of mutual dependence and reciprocity take on a new meaning.

A dictionary definition of interdependence says 'the condition of a group of people or things that all depend on each other'.[1] The interdependence I refer to here, however, is not about co-dependency but about depending on others for a sense of worth or relinquishing self-responsibility. The term may be best understood as a form of symbiosis we observe in biosphere or in the ecosystem, rather than in international relations or in global economics where interdependence is sustained by the calculating interests of respective participants. The Buddhist tradition includes a highly developed current of thought rooted on the principle of cause and effect, and described in the core teaching of the twelve links of *Paticca-samuppada* (Pali term for 'interdependent co-arising' or 'dependent origination'). This holds that: "Everything is interconnected. Everything affects everything else. Everything that is, is because other things are. What is happening now is part of what happened before and is part of what will happen next".[2]

For Thich Nhat Hanh, this was the realization of 'interbeing'; and for the Dalai Lama, it became the notion of 'universal responsibility'.[3] 'Interconnectedness' is a particularly critical concept in Mahayana Buddhist teachings on *sunyata* (emptiness), which is explained as the experience of non-duality. That is, nothing has its own tangible and inherent self-nature, and everything depends on something else for its current existence. Although most people may not experience such non-duality in their everyday life, the concept may be understood through reflection on interrelatedness in the natural environment, or on events in the global economy or international politics. Buddhism teaches us that a harmonious society cannot be achieved by a dichotomous positioning of 'us' and 'them' or by othering the other, since after all, everything in our worldly existence affects everything else.

Although this book is about a majority Buddhist country where people are known for their generosity, I have sought the essence of an interdependent society by closely examining the position of 'dependence', chiefly through the transactional relationships that take place between the Buddhist monastic community and its lay supporters. However, as the foregoing discussion implies, it can be quite difficult to appreciate the role of monastic recipients or others who are dependent if one is socialized into thinking that independence is better than the alternative. A person who harbours strong negative feelings about becoming dependent in sickness or in old age, for example, is unlikely ever to truly appreciate the meaning of interdependence in society. But, as we have seen, people in Myanmar still find meaning in mutual help rather than in self-contained reliance and are more eager to protect their collective interests than to assert their individual rights. In many ways, Myanmar's society emphasizes the collective over the individual; and even where it does not, individual interests are often realized through pursuit of the common good.

Many of the accounts in this book have focused on Buddhist monks and nuns whose primary duty is to receive from their lay donors: the givers. Monks, especially, provide a 'field of merit' in which people 'plant' their goodwill and 'reap' the merit that grows from it. Nevertheless, the givers require their recipient counterparts to generate positive value. As such, monastic recipients make up an important segment of society – both locally and nationally – that not only initiates generosity but also facilitates the laypeople's communication and transactions with one another. As a result, they are indispensable socially and economically as well is in purely religious terms. Sometimes a monk acts as a medium through which people realize their utopian dreams and, at other times, as a necessary intermediary in the transformation of social giving into merit. In other words, the monastic community acts both as a generator of merit and as a medium through which the notion of generosity is accommodated and processed. By performing their roles as full-time recipients of people's goodwill, Buddhist monastics in Myanmar initiate the turning of society's vital wheel of interdependence. Nor are they inevitably on the receiving side in such transactions; they are also active givers who redistribute whatever they have received and, on certain occasions, reciprocate the favours they have received from their lay supporters. Monasteries also function as social welfare organizations for nearby populations, with many laypeople surviving on their daily handouts and providing menial services in return. At their very best, such transactions result in a cycle of interdependent reciprocity that can sustain people both inside and outside the monastic community.

Glossary

Myanmar/Burmese words (B), Pali words (P), Sanskrit words (S) and Thai words (Thai)

a-bhivamsa suffix that means 'higher lineage'
à-na-de an expression to imply; I feel bad or I do not want to become obliged
abbhānumodanā (P) calling *sadhu* and rejoicing in the good deeds done by others
ahlu religious offering
ahmyà we recitation to send out loving kindness
ahmyà kaung-mu offerings for all
akyò good meritorious consequence
alagà waste, meaningless
ameimya nei mother's day
andare-kin thi to be given protection from danger
anyein comedy theatre
apasahyana (P) upholding a respectful attitude towards authoritative figures in the Buddhist tradition
apaciti (P) showing reverence
apei father
apyogyì 'big virgin', old unmarried woman
arahant fully enlightened Buddhist saint who has extinguished all desires
asariya puzaw pwe ceremony to pay respect to former teachers
athin association, society
awkatha (P: *okāsa*) devotional chant recited at Buddhist ritual in Myanmar
baka kyaung monastery schools run by monks for social welfare purposes
bazin ama symbolic sister to a monk
bazin medaw honorary mother to a monk
bazin taga/bazin tagamá male/female sponsor of a monk's ordination
bhāvanā (P) mental cultivation
cetanā (P) intention, generous disposition
chai-de to like
chit lò because of love
dagò special spiritual power
daloun metal ball produced by alchemy
dāna (P) Buddhist offering, donation, generosity
dat spiritual power, electricity
dhamma desanā (P) preaching and disseminating the *dhamma*
dhamma savana (P) listening to *dhamma* sermons
Dhammacariya official degree that accredits a person to teach the *dhamma*
Dhammakahtika Buddhist preacher, teacher of morality
ditthuju kamma (P) having faith and believing in the powers of the Triple Gem
ede guest
gāthā (P) verses
kadaw paying obeisance
kasii-ne thi to be mean, stingy
kat-thi the act of symbolically offering food to monks
kathein (P: *kathina*) annual robe-offering ceremony or the offering period

ketin-thi to be granted protective powers
kutho/akutho merit/demerit
kutho kan good karma
kutho kaung-mu meritorious deed
kyantha-thi to be rich
kyaung taga/kyaung má male donor/female donor of a monastic institution
kyinyo lò because of respect and admiration
latpet pickled tea leaves
lokiya (P) this worldly
lokuttara (P) the other-worldly
mae chee (Thai) precepts observing nuns in Thailand
matho thingan robe-weaving competition during the kathina season
mettā (P) loving kindness
mettā bhāvanā method of contemplation focusing on loving kindness
mettā kammaṭṭhāna method of contemplation on death and rotting corpse
mingala (P) auspicious occasion or auspicious duty
mithathu family, family members
mithathu kaung-mu good deed done by the family as a unit
mohingar rice noodles in fish soup
myiena-nge-thi to be 'small in the face', unpopular
navakamma 'new work' or 'new action', generally refers to cash donation
neikban (P: *nibbana*) nirvana, enlightenment
noh-set te protocol of greeting and paying each other recognition
ohnaw khaswe noodles in coconut soup with chicken
ovada moral instructions given by a monk or by someone senior
padeitha bin (P: *padetha*) wish-fulfilling tree
parahita social welfare, charity
parikiya shi-pa Eight Requisites for monks

pārami (P) Ten Perfections leading to enlightenment, special integrity
pariyatti (P) doctrinal study of Buddhism
patan-zet pre-destined encounter in the twenty-four links described in *Patthāna*
Pathamapyan Buddhist scriptural exams conducted by the Myanmar government
patipatti practice of meditation
pattam nikkujjana kamma (P) protest act by monks upturning their alms bowls
pattānumōdanā (P) transference of merit
pattidanā (P) sending out loving kindness to spirits and other sentient beings
paya taga donor of a pagoda, patron of Buddhism
payeik (P: *paritta*) Eleven protective chants
piti joy
pokgalika (P: *puggalika*) private holding, private group
pongyi kyaung monastery
pongyi lutwet a monk who has disrobed
ponnya kariya withu se-ba (P: *dasa puñña-kiriya vatthu*) Ten Ways to acquire merit
puññā (P) merit
pyinnya-shin learned folks
pyò-de to feel happy
sadhu (P) well-done
samatha (P) method of meditation, one-pointed concentration
sanghika sangha property
sāsanika *sāsana* property
sathin-daik monastery or nunnery that functions as a Buddhist seminary
satuditha literally 'Four Directions', offering of free food
saya kadaw pwe traditional ritual of paying of respect to teachers
sayadaw abbot, monk

sei kyantha-thi to be happy in the heart
shinbyu noviciation ceremony for a boy to become a Buddhist novice
shwe yin aye sweet coconut drink with agar jelly, tapioca and sago
sīla (P) morality, observing the Buddhist precepts
sun cooked rice (offered to monks)
sun-kywei religious feasts when monastic members are ceremoniously fed
sun laung offering of cooked rice to monks
sun taga donor of celebratory rice offering
taga/tagamá (P: *dāyikā/dāyaka*) male donor/female donor
tamin cooked rice, foods in general
thabaw kaung de lu generous person
thada tayà having faith in the teachings of the Buddha
thadingyut light festival in October
thami daughter
thana lò out of feeling pity
thathana (P: *sāsana*) the teachings of the Buddha, Buddhism
thathana lokngan supportive work to disseminate the *sāsana*
thathana-pyu dissemination of Buddhism
thathana taga donor or supporter of the *sāsana*
theik-hka htat repeat ordination
thingan monastic robes
thingyan Myanmar New Year and water festival
thuzein-thi strange, 'awe inspiring'
takrut (Thai) amulet with rolled inscriptions placed inside a sealed tube
ubok-nei (P: *uposatha divasa*) abstinence days assigned by the lunar calendar
ucha to clasp one's hands together in show of respect
Vinaya monastic rules and regulations, 227 rules for Theravada monks
vipassana (P) insight meditation for 'clear seeing'
wa period of rain retreat, Buddhist Lent
wadwin three months of rains retreat
weiyawesah (P: *veyyāvacca*) offering service to the community
weikza (P: *vijja*) literally 'higher or esoteric knowledge', wizard
yahan ordained monk
yahan-kan ordination ceremony for a monk
yantra (S) mystical diagram, from the Tantric traditions of India and Tibet
yaquet residential ward, basic administrative unit for town residents
yeikzet pre-destined relationship
yezet-cha water libation ritual
zayat public hall used for socio-religious events

Notes

Introduction

1 In Japan, social occasions for gift-giving take place twice a year: *ochugen* in the summer, two weeks before *obon* when ancestors are honoured, and *oseibo* in the winter, normally at the end of the year.

2 *The Gift* was first published in French as 'Essai sur le don. Forme et raison de l'échange dans les sociétés archaiques' in *L'Année Sociologique* in 1925.

3 Some of these criticisms were led by Alain Testart, 'Uncertainties of the "Obligation to Reciprocate": A Critique of Mauss', in *Marcel Mauss: A Centenary Tribute*, ed. Wendy James and N. J. Allen (New York: Berghahn Books, 1998), 97–110; and James Laidlaw, 'A Free Gift Makes No Friends', *Journal of the Royal Anthropological Institute* 6, no. 4 (2000): 617–34. For a more recent work that critically engages with Mauss, see *The Gift and Its Paradoxes: Beyond Mauss* (Farnham: Ashgate, 2014) by Olli Pyyhtinen. Against these criticisms, Graeber describes how we have all become indebted to each other by exchanging gifts. David Graeber, *The Debt: The First 5000 Years* (New York: Melville House, 2011).

4 Michael Carrithers, 'The Domestication of the Sangha', *Man, N. S.* 19 (1984): 322.

5 Michael Ames, 'Magical-Animism and Buddhism: A Structural Analysis of the Sinhalese Religious System', *Journal of Asian Studies* 23 (1964): 21–52.

6 Jonathan Parry, 'The Gift, the Indian Gift and the "Indian Gift"', *Man, N. S.* 21, no. 3 (1986): 462.

7 Ibid., 468.

8 Maria Heim, *Theories of the Gift in South Asia: Hindu, Buddhist, and Jain Reflections on Dāna* (New York: Routledge, 2004), 34; Reiko Ohnuma, 'Gift', in *Critical Terms for the Study of Buddhism*, ed. Donald S. Lopez (Chicago: University of Chicago Press, 2005), 107.

9 Joanna Cook, 'Alms, Money and Reciprocity: Buddhist Nuns as Mediators of Generalised Exchange in Thailand', *Anthropology in Action* 15, no. 3 (2008): 14. She said, 'The practice of alms donation de-emphasises the personal relationship and creates a new reality wherein they may face each other as if they were strangers not caught in relationships characterized by reciprocity'.

10 Ian Strenski, 'On Generalized Exchange and the Domestication of the Sangha'. *Man, N. S.* 18, no. 3 (1983): 472.

11 Maurice Godelier, *The Enigma of the Gift* (Chicago: University of Chicago Press, 1999).

12 Alain Testart, 'What Is a Gift?' *Hau: Journal of Ethnographic Theory* 3, no. 1 (2013): 249.

13 Ibid., 250.

14 Ibid.

15 Nicolas Sihlé, 'Towards a Comparative Anthropology of the Buddhist Gift (and Other Transfers)', *Religion Compass* 9, no. 11 (2015): 369.

16 Richard Gombrich, '"Merit Transference" in Sinhalese Buddhism: A Case Study of the Interaction between Doctrine and Behavior', *History of Religions* 11 (1971): 203–19.

17 Sihlé, 'Towards a Comparative Anthropology of the Buddhist Gift (and Other Transfers)', 367.

18 Ibid., 353; 362.

19 Ibid.

20 Ibid.

21 Parry, 'The Gift, the Indian Gift and the "Indian Gift"', 455. Also see James Laidlaw, who showed concern about the definition of 'pure gift', as he thought it was not clearly defined.

22 Gloria Goodwin Raheja, *The Poison in the Gift: Ritual, Prestation, and the Dominant Caste in a North Indian Village* (Chicago: University of Chicago Press, 1988), 32.

23 Ibid., 188.

24 Ibid., 188; 189.

25 Heim, *Theories of the Gift in South Asia*, 61.

26 Raheja, *The Poison in the Gift,* 32.

27 Parry, 'The Gift, the Indian Gift and the "Indian Gift"'; Ohnuma, 'Gift'; Heim, *Theories of the Gift in South Asia*.

28 Cook, 'Alms, Money and Reciprocity', 12.

29 I refer to Trautmann in my 2013 book, as he describes *dāna* to be the opposite to my view and states that it is a 'soteriology, not a sociology'. Thomas Trautmann, *Dravidian Kinship* (Cambridge: Cambridge University Press, 1981), 279.

30 Juliane Schober, *Modern Buddhist Conjunctures in Myanmar: Cultural Narratives, Colonial Legacies, and Civil Society* (Honolulu: University of Hawaii Press, 2011), 123.

31 *The Path of Purity: Visuddhimagga*, trans. Pe Maung Tin (London: Pali Text Society, 1975), 252. It is stipulated that the sangha is 'worthy of offerings, of oblations, of gifts, and worthy of reverential salutation'. Obviously, not all monks are as 'well practised, upright, righteous, and law-abiding', to be worthy recipients.

32 Stanley Tambiah, *Buddhism and Spirit Cults in Northeast Thailand* (Cambridge: Cambridge University Press, 1970), 68.

33 Sihlé, 'Towards a Comparative Anthropology of the Buddhist Gift (and Other Transfers)', 361.

34 Hiroko Kawanami, *Renunciation and Empowerment of Buddhist Nuns in Myanmar-Burma: Building a Community of Female Faithful* (Leiden: Brill, 2013), 136.

35 Ibid., 133.

36 John Davis, *Exchange* (Buckingham: Open University Press, 1992), 23. He state that *kula* comes into this middle category.

37 Kawanami, *Renunciation and Empowerment of Buddhist Nuns in Myanmar-Burma*, 133.

38 Peter Jackson, *Buddhism, Legitimation and Conflict: The Political Functions of Urban Thai Buddhism* (Singapore: Institute of Southeast Asian Studies, 1989).

39 Ann Blackburn, *Locations of Buddhism: Colonialism and Modernity in Sri Lanka* (Chicago: University of Chicago Press, 2010).

40 Ingrit Jordt, *Burma's Mass Lay Meditation Movement: Buddhism and the Cultural Construction of Power* (Athens: Ohio University Press, 2007).

41 David Batson, *The Altruism Question: Toward a Social Psychological Answer* (Hillsdale, NJ: Erlbaum, 1991).

42 Davis, *Exchange*, 43.

43 Michaela, Benson and Denise Carter. 'Introduction: Nothing in Return? Distinctions between Gift and Commodity in Contemporary Societies'. *Anthropology in Action* 15, no. 3 (2008): 2.

44 Morny Joy, *Women and the Gift: Beyond the Given and All-Giving*, ed. Morny Joy (Bloomington: Indiana University Press, 2013); *Women, Religion, and the Gift: An Abundance of Riches*, ed. Morny Joy (Basel: Springer, 2017).

45 Such an exchange is described to be conducted in the pretext of incest prohibition described by Levi-Strauss. See Joy in her 'Introduction', 2013, 1–2.

46 Laure Carbonnel, 'On the Ambivalence of Female Monasticism in Theravāda Buddhism: A Contribution to the Study of the Monastic System in Myanmar'. *Asian Ethnology* 68, no. 2 (2009): 267.

47 On their standing of not fitting neatly into a category, see Mary Douglas, *Purity and Danger* (London: Routledge & Kegan Paul, 1966).

48 See Kawanami, *Renunciation and Empowerment of Buddhist Nuns in Myanmar-Burma*.

49 Russell McCutcheon, ed., *The Insider/Outsider Problem in the Study of Religion* (London: Cassell, 1999); Bill Gillham, *Case Study Research Methods* (London: Bloomsbury Academic, 2000); Paloma Gay and Huon Wardle Blasco, *How to Read Ethnography* (London: Routledge, 2007); Alan Bryman, *Social Research Methods* (Oxford: OUP, 2008); Judith Okely, *Anthropological Practice: Fieldwork and the Ethnographic Method* (London: Bloomsbury, 2012).

50 Pamela Baxter and Susan Jack, 'Qualitative Case Study Methodology: Study Design and Implementation for Novice Researchers', *The Qualitative Report* 13, no. 4 (2008): 544–59.

Chapter 1

1 CAF World Giving Index 2017 (Charities Aid Foundation, 2018).

2 John Holt, *Theravada Traditions: Buddhist Ritual Cultures in Contemporary Southeast Asia and Sri Lanka* (Honolulu: University of Hawaii Press, 2017), 190.

3 If an item, for example, a computer was donated to a monastic recipient who did not know how to operate it and did not appreciate receiving it, I was told that it would be *alagà* (a waste), despite the good intention of the lay donor. An ideal donation would have to be appreciated by and suitable for the recipient to produce merit.

4 See Richard Gombrich, *Buddhist Precept and Practice: Traditional Buddhism in the Rural Highlands of Ceylon* (Delhi: Motilal Banarsidass, 1991), 87. *Dānaṃ sīlaṃ ca bhāvanā Patti pattānumodanāVeyyāvacca apacāyan ca Desanā suti ditthiju*.

5 This point was raised by Dr Rita Langer in an email communication on 20 September 2018.

6 The recollection of one's meritorious deeds at the point of death is regarded the most important. It is a common practice in Myanmar for Buddhist family members to remind the dying person about the meritorious deeds done during his/her lifetime. Also see Ananda Guruge and G. D. Bond, 'Generosity and Service in Theravada Buddhism', in *Philanthropy in the Worlds' Traditions*, ed. W. F. Ilchman, N. Katz Stanley and Edward L. Queen II (Bloomington: Indiana University Press, 1998), 86.

7 It is commonly believed in Myanmar that the Buddha visits his mother regularly to teach her Abhidhamma.

8 Diana Paul describes that influential female characters in Mahayana tests are 'inevitably of nuns, married laywomen without children, prostitutes, or young unmarried women, all of whom are freed from the responsibilities and burdens of motherhood while simultaneously defying society's norms'. Diana Paul, *Women in*

Buddhism: Images of the Feminine in the Mahāyāna Tradition (Berkeley: University of California Press, 1985), 61.

9 The term for Wheel of Life is *Bhavachakra* in Sanskrit, a combination of *bhava* (becoming or being) and *chakra* (wheel or cycle).

10 During the *asariya puzaw pwe* held in Sagaing in 2017, 470 retired teachers of local state primary to high schools were invited to the ceremony by former students who wanted to express their gratitude. Their travel expenses, food and accommodation were paid for, and each teacher was given an equivalent in local currency about $1,000 to $1,500 USD from the funds collected in the form of honorarium. This was regarded as a sizable sum in support of former teachers as their meagre state pension was far from sufficient to make a living.

11 The group founded in 2010 had ninety-eight regular members as of 2018, paying regular monthly membership of 2,000 kyats (about $1.5 USD) to support their former teachers. It is run as a voluntary group without any charity status, but administered by the organizer in his early fifties, who is a widely respected popular citizen in the local community.

12 After Burma (Myanmar) was annexed by the British, an instruction was issued in 1903 that local clerks when entering the office of British officials must take off their shoes (and socks) and pay them respect by doing the *kadaw* or *shikoing*, and address them as *phaya* ('my Lord'). This practice was officially brought to an end in 1923. See Wei Yan Aung, 'The End of Shikoing before the British', *The Irrawaddy* (16 August 2019).

13 Khammai Dhammasami, 'Between Idealism and Pragmatism: A Study of Monastic Education in Burma and Thailand from the Seventeenth Century to the Present' (DPhil diss., University of Oxford, 2004), 41.

14 Khin Myo Chit (1915–1999) was one of the most celebrated writers in Myanmar in the twentieth century whose career spanned over four decades. She wrote in many patriotic local papers and served as an editor in the *Working People's Daily*. Khin Myo Chit, *Colourful Burma* (Yangon: Myitta Moe Press, 1984), 41.

15 There is no equivalent to this term in English or in other European languages, pointing to the unique cultural background to this kind of expression.

16 Nevertheless, if the person, however generous, cannot control his or her emotions and is known to be *dosa gyi de* (prone to 'big anger'), for example, he or she will lose respect and cannot be popular in a Buddhist culture.

17 See Hiroko Kawanami, 'Charisma, Power(s), and the Arahant Ideal in Burmese-Myanmar Buddhism', *Asian Ethnology* 68, no. 2 (2009): 223.

18 The significance of public reputation is strongly felt in provincial towns as people talk about past scandals and crimes and also comment on the reputation of important families in town, whether they are trustworthy and generous or not, and place their judgement on such local information when choosing a marriage partner for their children.

19 Manning Nash, *The Golden Road to Modernity: Village Life in Contemporary Burma* (New York: John Wiley & Sons, 1965).

20 Holt, *Theravada Traditions*, 215.

21 See Nicolas Sihlé, 'Towards a Comparative Anthropology of the Buddhist Gift (and Other Transfers)'. *Religion Compass* 9, no. 11 (2015): 369; 371. The type of honorarium offered to monastic members in Myanmar appears different from the kind of remuneration Sihlé mentions from his fieldwork in Tibet. The difference may derive from the different social and religious position of ritual specialists in society.

22 John Ferguson reports that Mahawithudarama Sayadaw 'rejected the donation of newly minted peacock coins as modern substitutes for traditional gifts of food and other necessities', which must have happened around the beginning of the twentieth century. See John Ferguson, 'The Quest for Legitimation by Burmese Monks and Kings: The Case of the Shwegyin Sect (19th–20th Centuries)', in *Religion and Legitimation of Power in Thailand, Laos, and Burma*, ed. Bardwell L. Smith (Chambersburg: Anima Books, 1978), 78.

23 Sihle, 'Towards a Comparative Anthropology of the Buddhist Gift (and Other Transfers)'.

24 In 2018, the going rate for honoraria offered to a Buddhist monk in Yangon was between $30 and $50 USD for a monk, and $100 USD for a prominent scholar or a *dhamma* teacher. The amount of donations offered by donors is listed, printed out and circulated before or after the ceremony.

25 Maurice Bloch and Jonathan Parry, 'Introduction: Money and the Morality of Exchange', in *Money & the Morality of Exchange*, ed. Maurice Bloch and Johnny Parry (Cambridge: Cambridge University Press, 1989), 9.

26 The notion of merit is also invoked to make a person engage in a type of activity that is regarded to be painstaking or potentially degrading, such as cleaning a toilet or engaging in a menial and laborious task. By laying emphasis on the significance of meritorious return, engaging in a difficult task provides the agent with a heightened sense of fulfilment and meritorious gain.

27 Donald Swearer, *Becoming the Buddha: The Ritual of Image Consecration in Thailand* (Princeton: Princeton University Press, 2004), 22–3.

28 Melford Spiro, *Buddhism and Society: A Great Tradition and Its Burmese Vicissitudes* (New York: Harper and Row, 1970), 405.

29 Spiro, *Buddhism and Society*, 107.

30 'The donor may be a terrible person – wicked people attempt to expiate their sins by offering great amounts of *dāna* – but he receives much merit by giving to pious monks', Spiro, *Buddhism and Society*.

31 Dr Alfred Gell, my PhD supervisor, once told me that it was a mistake that he left his pistol to his cook who looked after him during fieldwork. After he presented the gift

and left the field, the cook rose to become an influential 'big man' in the community in PNG, but was eventually killed as others thought he had overstepped his assigned position in the community.

32 Myanmar people offer *dāna* to the monastic community when they encounter life crises: terminal illnesses, accidents, business losses, family problems or any event they consider inauspicious to offset the bad karma by conducting a meritorious deed.

33 On religious days and on special occasions, Myanmar lay Buddhists observe additional three precepts, which include abstention from sex, fasting after midday, and giving up of luxury items and worldly pleasure. The majority of Buddhist nuns in Myanmar observe Eight Precepts as an essential aspect of their religious life.

34 The most commonly chanted and popular *paritta* in Myanmar are *Mangala Sutta* (Discourse on Auspicious Blessing) and *Mettā Sutta* (Discourse on Loving-Kindness).

35 The stance of the Buddha pressing his four fingers of the right hand to the ground is represented as one of his most popular images in Myanmar.

36 Tin Moe Aung, 'Light Festival Inspires Spirit of Selfless Giving', *Myanmar Times* (28 November 2011).

37 Phyoe Wai Kyaw. 'A Chance to Eat Satuditha while Playing Water in Mandalay', *Myanmar Times* (17 April 2018).

Chapter 2

1 Terwiel mentioned that Thai Buddhists believe in the protective power of merit. See B. J. Terwiel, *Monks and Magic: An Analysis of Religious Ceremonies in Central Thailand* (Bangkok: White Lotus, 1994), 112.

2 In Myanmar Buddhism, the term *kutho*, derived from the Pali word *kusala*, meaning 'good deed', is most commonly used to refer to 'merit' rather than the Pali term *puñña*, which is the more common term used for 'merit' in Sri Lanka (*pin*) or Thailand (*boon*).

3 Ingrit Jordt, *Burma's Mass Lay Meditation Movement: Buddhism and the Cultural Construction of Power* (Athens: Ohio University Press, 2007), 98.

4 Melford Spiro, *Buddhism and Society: A Great Tradition and Its Burmese Vicissitudes* (New York: Harper and Row, 1970), 109.

5 Hiroko Kawanami, 'U Nu's Liberal Democracy and Buddhist Communalism in Modern Burma', in *Buddhism and the Political Process*, ed. Hiroko Kawanami (Basingstoke and New York: Palgrave Macmillan, 2016), 50.

6 David Gellner, *Monk, Householder, and Tantric Priest: Newar Buddhism and Its Hierarchy of Ritual* (Cambridge: Cambridge University Press, 1992), 122.

7 If the family already knows an abbot or has some connection with a monastery, organizing a ceremony may be a straightforward affair, but if they decide to offer *dāna* to a popular and well-established monastic institution, a waiting list normally governs when this can take place.

8 Buddhist monks in Myanmar are not vegetarians so they eat whatever is offered. People offer them the most prestigious item of food, which is meat and usually chicken or pork. Although eating beef is not forbidden in Myanmar, most monks do not eat beef, probably due to the close association villagers have with cattle in their daily life.

9 This may be what Jordt meant when she alluded to (intention) as the key factor in driving the 'politics of sincerity'. See Jordt, *Burma's Mass Lay Meditation Movement*, 119–30.

10 One wealthy male donor who owns several clothes factories in Mandalay told me that he had originally spent a few years searching for a suitable nunnery to offer material support as he felt sorry for the nuns. But it just happened by chance one day when he met an elderly abbess who appeared to be very graceful and well educated. He said the first time he visited her nunnery, still at its early stage of development, he knew straightaway that he was going to become her regular supporter.

11 Ordination age is nineteen years and two months old.

12 Jordt, *Burma's Mass Lay Meditation Movement*, 215.

13 Making *dāna* offering to the sangha was once considered to be the 'Burman's insurance policy' for a happy rebirth. See Spiro, *Buddhism and Society*, 271.

14 On 3 November 1985, the government announced the demonetization of 50 and 100 kyats without any warning. It was announced on Friday afternoon that the general public had little time to exchange old notes for new. A few days later, 75 kyat notes were introduced, supposedly to commemorate Ne Win's birthday. In the following August 1986, 15 and 35 kyat notes were introduced. On 5 September 1987, 25, 35 and 75 kyat notes were demonetized, again without any warning, and a few weeks later 45 and 90 kyat notes were issued to replace them. See 'History of Bank Notes', Central Bank of Myanmar, https://www.cbm.gov.mm/content/history-bank-notes, accessed 13 April 2019. The economic upheaval and frustration as a result of these led to many riots and eventually to a huge anti-government uprising in 1988.

15 Spiro, *Buddhism and Society*, 104.

16 Ibid., 105.

17 The attitude of lay donors towards cash offering in other Buddhist countries may be different from that in Myanmar. For instance, in Thailand, Terwiel stated that 'people insist on making cash donations because they believe that there is clear connection between the amount of money offered to the monks and the amount of beneficial *karma* received in return'. However, in order to offer cash without handing it directly to monks, lay donors wrap banknotes in paper or buy a document known as 'declaration

of intention' from shops and offer it to monks, which can be later exchanged into banknotes (1994, 112–13).

18 When I visited a Buddhist monastery in London, the abbot showed me a room full of different types of sofas piled on top of each other filling the place. However, he did not want to complain about them or to his lay donors for fear that they might stop their support especially as he was in an unfamiliar country.

19 An assistant of one prominent abbot told me that his teacher lost his voice after he ate 'cursed' food received from a female donor. The rumour went around saying it was inflicted by a 'witch' who was angry for being rebuffed by the monk, or otherwise, by someone who had grudges against him. As a result, the unsuspecting abbot could no longer preach or even talk. This case shows that a monastic recipient, who cannot choose or reject the food they receive in their alms bowl, is exposed to potential danger in their daily food intake, which can also cause allergy and other types of ailments.

20 Richard Gombrich and Margaret Cone, *The Perfect Generosity of Prince Vessantara* (Oxford: Clarendon Press, 1977).

21 A middle-income family in Yangon may spend more than half a year's wages to conduct a *shinbyu*. A wealthy family spent local currency equivalent to between $5,000 USD and $10,000 USD for a son's *shinbyu* in 2017.

22 A set of a monk's robe costs between 2,000 kyats ($3 USD) and 50,000 kyats ($600 USD) depending on the brand and quality of the material.

23 There are exceptions in some parts of lower country where sending a daughter into the monastic community has been traditionally regarded meritorious for her parents, perceived as remnants of Pyu culture. I have come across several cases of Buddhist parents who 'gave away' their daughter as a son substitute to the monastic community in the hope of making a contribution to the *sāsana*.

24 See Hiroko Kawanami, *Renunciation and Empowerment of Buddhist Nuns in Myanmar-Burma: Building a Community of Female Faithful* (Leiden: Brill, 2013), 75–6.

25 John Holt, *Theravada Traditions: Buddhist Ritual Cultures in Contemporary Southeast Asia and Sri Lanka* (Honolulu: University of Hawaii Press, 2017), 203.

26 Ibid., 199.

27 *Maha Vagga*, two sections.

28 Holt, *Theravada Traditions*, 204.

29 Khin Myo Chit, *Colourful Burma* (Yangon: Myitta Moe Press, 1984), 52.

30 This quote was taken from a sermon tape by the late Mogok Sayadaw whose meditation method focuses on understanding the Dependent Origination and *Cittanupassana*. There are currently over 300 meditation centres that instruct the Mogok method and it is one of the most popular methods in Myanmar today.

31 Soumhya Venkatesan, 'Giving and Taking without Reciprocity', *Social Analysis* 60, no. 3 (2016): 36–56.

32 Spiro, *Buddhism and Society*, 107.

33 The four stages to sainthood in Buddhism are: *Sotāpanna, Sakadāgāmi, Anāgāmī* and *Arahant*. See Ananda Guruge and George Bond, 'Generosity and Service in Theravada Buddhism', in *Philanthropy in the World's Traditions*, ed. Warren F. Ilchman et al. (Bloomington: Indiana University Press, 1998), 84.

34 In Tambiah's list of merit-making ranking in northern Thailand, people listed *dāna* as high up in the ranking chart of what they regarded as 'meritorious'. See Stanley Tambiah, *Buddhism and Spirit Cults in Northeast Thailand* (Cambridge: Cambridge University Press, 1970), 146–7. In my recent interview (2017) with twenty regular donors from Mandalay, offering *dāna* still weighed heavily as a top priority in their notion of merit-making.

35 Spiro, *Buddhism and Society*, 99.

36 Ibid., 12.

37 Ibid., 104–5.

38 Ibid., 103.

Chapter 3

1 Hiroko Kawanami, 'Sangha and Society', in *Wiley-Blackwell Companion to Religion and Social Justice*, ed. Michael D. Palmer and Stanley M. Burgess (Oxford: Wiley-Blackwell, 2012), 281.

2 The Letpadaung copper mine dispute in Salingyi township near Monywa, fought during 2012–2015 between local villagers and Wanbao, a Chinese mining company with connections to the Myanmar military government, is still new in our memory. It is reported that 2,500 villagers were displaced and 8,000 acres of farmland were polluted by chemicals from the mine. Villagers defending their ancestral land refused to relocate; although many suffering from ill health, they contested insufficient compensation. It was the Buddhist monks from Ledi monastery in Monywa who rose to support the anti-mining protests. During the demonstrations in November 2012, they were fired upon by incendiary devices, and more than 100 monks were injured, who were in the frontline praying for a peaceful solution. They were badly burned and maimed, apparently with white phosphorus, and many are still suffering from the aftermath of those terrible injuries. See Lawyers Network and Justice Trust, 'Submission of Evidence to Myanmar Government's Letpadaung Investigation Commission', 5 February 2013.

3 Hannah Beech, 'The Face of Buddhist Terror', *Times* Magazine, 21 June 2013.

4 U Wirathu is one of the monk leaders of the '969' movement, which instructed Buddhist shop owners to signpost its faith by putting '969' on the shopfront and Buddhists were encouraged to buy exclusively from these shops. Some saw the use of symbolic digits of '969' by Wirathu and his sympathizers to have instigated a Burman-Buddhist nationalist movement. The nationalistic sentiments in Myanmar had already been heightened by Daw Aung San Suu Kyi and NLD, her party, winning the by-elections in April 2012, with forty-three representatives being elected to the parliament. Freed from decades of oppression, the ideology exemplified in '969' touched the sentiments of the majority population, triggering mass hysteria that spread erratically without a specific organizer or an organization. Meanwhile, many prominent monks spoke out against the '969' campaign, appalled that the Buddhist symbolics were misused to create divisions between people of different faiths.

5 This seems to be a misconception of a Buddhist monk, which is widely disseminated by Weber's description of a monk as a reclusive living an 'inner-worldly life'. Max Weber, *The Religion of India: The Sociology of Hinduism and Buddhism*, trans. and ed. Hans H. Gerth and Don Martindale (Glencoe: The Free Press, 1958), 329–43.

6 In the case of male novices circulating teashops and asking for money, Myanmar people normally refuse to transact with them by saying *gadaw ba paya*, 'excuse me venerable (but I cannot offer you anything)'.

7 See Hiroko Kawanami, 'Charisma, Power(s), and the Arahant Ideal in Burmese-Myanmar Buddhism', *Asian Ethnology* 68, no. 2 (2009): 211–37.

8 See Erica Bornstein, *Disquieting Gifts: Humanitarianism in New Delhi* (Stanford: Stanford University Press, 2012), 13. In comparison to American people, she points out that Asian people normally do not say 'thank you' or show appreciation for receiving gifts.

9 I have had regular conversations on these topics with at least eight monks I have known for over three decades.

10 John Ferguson, 'The Quest for Legitimation by Burmese Monks and Kings: The Case of the Shwegyin Sect (19th–20th Centuries)', in *Religion and Legitimation of Power in Thailand, Laos, and Burma*, ed. Bardwell L. Smith (Chambersburg: Anima Books, 1978), 75.

11 Keiko Tosa, 'The Cult of Thamanya Sayadaw: The Social Dynamism of Formulating Pilgrimage Site', *Asian Ethnology* 68, no. 2 (2009): 244.

12 Daw Aung San Suu Kyi was also one of his devout supporters during the 1990s.

13 Tosa, 'The Cult of Thamanya Sayadaw', 245.

14 Guillaume Rozenberg, *Renunciation and Power: The Quest for Sainthood in Contemporary Burma*, trans. Jessica Hackett (New Haven: Yale University Southeast Asia Studies, 2010), 97.

15 Foreign visitors are often invited to receive blessings from the monk personally as they are seen to bring him special credentials and, just like children, the lack of deference towards him by those who are unaware of his holy impact is probably more appreciated by the monk himself.

16 Rozenberg, *Renunciation and Power*, 97; Tosa, 'The Cult of Thamanya Sayadaw', 245.

17 Even after the passing of an *arahant* or a *weikza*, his spirit is believed to linger around the place where he once resided. His lay devotees keep spiritual connection with the deceased monk and celebrate his birthday annually by offering commemorative feasts to local monks. His personal items such as robes and glasses are retained, and his bedroom called *dat-kan* (power room) is kept in a supreme condition as if he was still alive. Mummified bodies of deceased *arahants* are on display in many parts of Myanmar; for instance, the body of Shinbyushinla Sayadaw in the Sagaing Hill and the three successive abbots in Gwenkau town in the Ayeyarwady region. Their dried-up bodies are placed in raised glass coffins, and pilgrims continue to visit them, marvelling at the un-decomposed state of their bodies. It is well known that the body of the late Thamanya Sayadaw was stolen soon after his passing and was never found. Devotees continue to worship him almost as if he was still alive and find solace in his spiritual presence.

18 The thirty-one floors within the Buddha statue are said to represent the thirty-one abodes of existence advocated in the Theravada tradition.

19 Kawanami, 'Charisma, Power(s), and the Arahant Ideal in Burmese-Myanmar Buddhism', 218–19.

20 Ma Ha Na is an abbreviation for Naingandaw Thangha Maha Nayaka Ahpwe, translated as the 'National Committee of Supreme Sangha Council'.

21 This Buddhist university was established in Yangon in December 1998 under the auspices of the Ministry of Religious Affairs to train international Buddhist missionaries.

22 Pa-chok Sayadaw, Bamaw Sayadaw of Ma Ha Na and Sitagu Sayadaw were the three senior Buddhist monks invited to address the nation and they gave *ovada* on Independence Day, 4 January 2019, Yangon. Their sermons were attended by 30,000 followers in a convocation hall and the half-day event is said to have collected $10 million USD in donation.

23 Khammai Dhammasami, 'Between Idealism and Pragmatism: A Study of Monastic Education in Burma and Thailand from the Seventeenth Century to the Present' (DPhil diss., University of Oxford, 2004), 301.

24 Tipitakadhara Tipitakakovida Selection Examination has been held by the Ministry of Religious Affairs since 1949. The whole examination process, in both oral and written, takes thirty-three days, and the candidates have to recite from 8,026 pages of Tipitaka, and from its commentaries and sub-commentaries. In the last seventy years, fourteen monks were granted the title of Tipitakadhara and currently only ten monks hold the title in Myanmar.

25 Spiro referred to this trait as the 'emotional timidity' of monks; ibid., 348.

26 Stanley Tambiah, *Buddhism and Spirit Cults in Northeast Thailand* (Cambridge: Cambridge University Press, 1970), 470.

27 Even leftover cooked rice is dried and given away to those who cannot afford to buy rice grains.

28 John Holt, *Theravada Traditions: Buddhist Ritual Cultures in Contemporary Southeast Asia and Sri Lanka* (Honolulu: University of Hawaii Press, 2017), 202.

29 Stanley Tambiah, *The Buddhist Saints of the Forest and the Cult of Amulets: A Study in Charisma, Hagiography, Sectarianism, and Millennial Buddhism* (Cambridge: Cambridge University Press, 1984), 195–298.

30 Terwiel describes that the monk's ability to generate protective power is regarded to be much more effective and stronger than the layman's, but a monk cannot lower himself to directly address and supplicate the unseen powers. See B. J. Terwiel, *Monks and Magic: An Analysis of Religious Ceremonies in Central Thailand* (Bangkok: White Lotus, 1994), 244.

31 Justin McDaniel, *The Lovelorn Ghost and the Magical Monk: Practicing Buddhism in Modern Thailand* (New York: Columbia University Press, 2011), 208–9.

32 Kawanami, 'Charisma, Power(s), and the Arahant Ideal in Burmese-Myanmar Buddhism', 225–6.

33 Ibid., 229.

34 Rozenberg, *Renunciation and Power*, 88.

35 Rozenberg described how his many devotees prepared for the event for several months: collecting funds, building temporary accommodations for guests and cooking for the thousands of visitors expected to turn up.

36 Ibid., 98–9.

37 Senior Buddhist nuns also celebrate their birthdays and use them as occasions to show gratitude and return the favours they have received from their lay supporters. For instance, Pwa Mii, a popular nun-teacher, marked her eighty-first birthday in 2017 by giving each of the eighty-one monks who had been invited with the equivalent of $100 USD in local currency and a lacquerware tray inscribed with her name. She also provided lunch to all the invited monks and nuns, as well as her lay donors and guests.

38 Even U Wirathu has solid academic credentials as *dhamma* teacher being affiliated with Masoein Kyaung monastery, a prominent Buddhist seminary in Mandalay, where his former teacher was the late abbot U Kowida, a staunch opponent of the previous military regime who was imprisoned during the early democratic uprising in the late 1980s.

39 Bénédicte Brac de la Perrière, 'A Generation of Monks in the Democratic Transition', in *Metamorphosis: Studies in Social and Political Change in Myanmar*, ed. Renaud

Egreteau and François Robinne (Singapore: National University of Singapore Press, 2016), 329–31.

40 This has also resulted in the large number of male novices disrobing, adding to a new sense of crisis within the monastic community.

41 Expectations by the international community for Myanmar to implement a democratic mode of governance and political reforms in a short span of time have brought relentless scrutiny, expecting religious tolerance and inclusion to be an integral part of her democratic transition. However, Myanmar has not been given much time to adjust to the new liberal environment despite the fact that democratization process has taken centuries in many countries in the West. 'Religion and Democracy Go Hand in Hand', by Nehginpao Kipgen, *Myanmar Times*, 1 July 2013.

42 In January 2014, Ma Ba Tha was endorsed at a conference attended by more than 1,500 monks from the whole of Myanmar and established a central committee of forty-five monks, including both scholarly monks and political monks, to oversee the operation. The official name of the Association was Sāsana Vamsa Pāla, literally meaning 'Protector of the Race and Sāsana'. Insein Ywama Sayadaw U Tiloka-bhivamsa was elected as the chairman and three vice-chairmen monks were chosen. *Tharkithwe Journal*, 6 August 2013, 45, achatpo, B–C.

43 Matthew Walton, Melyn McKay and Khin Mar Mar Kyi, 'Women and Myanmar's "Religious Protection Laws"', *The Review of Faith & International Affairs: Special Issue on Religion, Law, and Society in Myanmar* 13, no. 4 (2015): 36–49.

44 See 'Its Aims and Objectives; *Tharkithwe Journal*; ibid., achatpo D.

45 Melyn McKay and Khin Chit Win, 'Myanmar's Gender Paradox', *Anthropology Today* 34, no. 1 (February 2018): 1–2.

46 National and international media have often equated monk Wirathu with Ma Ba Tha, but he was never accepted into Ma Ba Tha as an official member nor had any role in it, and it is also equally wrong to suggest that Ma Ba Tha was born out of the '969' campaign.

47 A total of 2,558 monks from the nine Buddhist orders attended the fifth All Orders Sangha Conference at Kabar Aye Pagoda held during 11–13 May 2014. See Aung Kyaw Min, 'Ma Ba Tha Monks Declare Political Independence', *Myanmar Times*, 27 June 2014.

48 Cherry Thein and Aung Kyaw Min, 'Sangha Reforms Planned to Improve Discipline, Cooperation', *Myanmar Times*, 16 May 2014.

49 Several *Tipitakadara* monks were also included in the executive committee of Ma Ba Tha.

50 Insein Ywama Sayadaw played a vital role when the State Pariyatti Sasana University (SPSU) was established in 1986, where he was the Pro-Rector and Professor of Abhidhamma Studies for four years. He was also a member of the State Sangha Maha Nayaka Committee (Ma Ha Na) between 2003 and 2010, during which time, he acted

as the Vinayadhara in the First Multi-Sects Sangha Association of the States and Divisions.

51 See Ingrit Jordt, *Burma's Mass Lay Meditation Movement: Buddhism and the Cultural Construction of Power* (Athens: Ohio University Press, 2007), 11. She uses the term 'a shared social field' rather than a 'moral field'.

Chapter 4

1 To understand the ambiguity of the nuns' religious standing, see Hiroko Kawanami, 'The Religious Standing of Burmese Buddhist Nuns (*Thila-shin*): The Ten Precepts and Religious Respect Words', *Journal of the International Association of Buddhist Studies* 13, no. 1 (1990): 17–39. For the ambivalent position they occupy in relation to monks and the laity, see Laure Carbonnel, 'On the Ambivalence of Female Monasticism in Theravāda Buddhism: A Contribution to the Study of the Monastic System in Myanmar', *Asian Ethnology* 68, no. 2 (2009): 265–82.

2 U Aung Than Sein is a fish trader and breeder, originally from the Delta region in the Ayeyarwady region. I had a short conversation with him on 6 January 2018.

3 Melford Spiro, *Buddhism and Society: A Great Tradition and Its Burmese Vicissitudes* (New York: Harper and Row, 1970), 107.

4 In May 1987.

5 Some of these chants have been passed down from nun-teachers to students and thus can be studied to identify particular scholarly lineages of nuns. However, liturgies and prayer sequences are not static and change over time; Buddhist nuns incorporate new *gāthā*s into their existing compilation, for instance, when starting a nunnery or on a special auspicious occasion.

6 It is commonplace to offer a set of robes to the nuns just as it is common to offer monastic robes to the monks, although the nuns have no set time or any special ritual for the robe offering.

7 In a traditional nunnery as of 2018, each unit on the premises comprising three to five nuns, spent about $50–$80 USD a month to pay for its utility expenses.

8 In a large nunnery school run on a communal system, with about 200 resident students, the monthly cost of running and feeding them cost a minimum of $2,000 USD; but senior nuns and teachers normally have a number of regular donors who help with the expenditure.

9 Jonathan Parry, 'The Gift, the Indian Gift and the "Indian Gift"', *Man, N. S* 21, no. 3 (1986): 468.

10 To sustain her religious position as a Ten Precept observer, however, a nun will need a lay helper or a personal assistant who would handle cash on her behalf and see to her daily needs.

11 Spiro, *Buddhism and Society*, 109.

12 *Dictionary of the Social Sciences*, ed. Craig Calhoun (Oxford: Oxford University Press, 2002). The concept of 'symbolic capital' was developed by Pierre Bourdieu as an extension of Max Weber's analysis of 'status'. See Bourdieu, *Distinction: A Social Critique of the Judgement of Taste* (Cambridge: Harvard University Press, 1984).

13 Myanmar nuns are known for their care and hospitality. Their generosity is not only directed towards the monks and male novices, but also towards any layperson who visits the nunnery. For example, if a female pilgrim arrives late, she would most probably be accommodated for the night and even offered food.

14 See Chapter 2, f. n. 3 on the Ten Ways to acquire merit.

15 Kirsch pointed out that Buddhist women sought out menial roles and services in the secular domain because they generally needed more merit. See Thomas Kirsch, 'Buddhism, Sex-Roles and the Thai Economy', in *Women of Southeast Asia*, ed. Penny Van Esterik (Dekalb: Center for Southeast Asian Studies, 1996), 13–32.

16 There is a section on the biography of Daw Dhammasari. See Hiroko Kawanami, *Renunciation and Empowerment of Buddhist Nuns in Myanmar-Burma: Building A Community of Female Faithful* (Leiden: Brill, 2013), 186–7.

17 Ibid., 187.

18 Tambiah said that daily chores and merit-making activities were a 'function of women rather than men'. Stanley Tambiah, *The Buddhist Saints of the Forest and the Cult of Amulets* (Cambridge: Cambridge University Press, 1984), 144.

19 In 2013, there were fifty-six *baka kyaung* (monastery schools for children from disadvantaged backgrounds) in the Yangon region and eleven were in operation in the Ayeyarwady region. Although *baka kyaung* may suggest that these schools are administered by the monks as the term *baka* suggests, many of these institutions are often administered by nuns who look after the children.

20 Thomas Kirsch, 'Text and Context: Buddhist Sex Roles/Culture of Gender Revisited', *American Ethnologist* 12, no. 2 (1985): 303.

21 Joanna Cook, 'Alms, Money and Reciprocity: Buddhist Nuns as Mediators of Generalised Exchange in Thailand', *Anthropology in Action* 15, no. 3 (2008): 19.

22 In Thailand, large monasteries and meditation centres are run by lay administration staff who are paid salaries and deal with accounts and bookkeeping, but in many

monastic institutions, *mae chee* are also active in overseeing the operation. See Cook, 'Alms, Money and Reciprocity', 17.

23 See Kirsch, 'Buddhism, Sex-Roles and the Thai Economy', 21.

24 Monica Lindberg Falk, and Hiroko Kawanami, 'Monastic Discipline and Communal Rules for Buddhist Nuns in Myanmar and Thailand', *Journal of Buddhism, Law & Society* 3 (2017–2018): 79–108.

25 If the offence involves sexual transgression, social norms in the nuns' community dictate that the nun-perpetrator is asked to move out or even disrobe immediately. Less serious cases, such as land disputes or succession issues, may be referred to the Nuns' Township Council where a nun representative negotiates between the parties involved to find a quick solution. See Falk and Kawanami, 'Monastic Discipline and Communal Rules for Buddhist Nuns in Myanmar and Thailand', 90.

26 Insein Ywama Sayadaw; one of the most respected *dhamma* teachers in Myanmar, has more than 5,000 students in his scholarly lineage, but his most trusted disciples are Buddhist nuns who always accompany him on his foreign tours.

27 I have come across an abbess who kept every item of donated goods to herself, locking up the garage so that the car could not be used by others, and kept the telephone line to herself (in the 1980s), which were donated for the use of all resident nuns.

28 There are several cases of senior nuns caring for their mother in the nunnery, but if the nun-daughter is of a junior rank, she will normally return home as she does not have the resources or influence in the nunnery to take her mother in. I have also come across nun-students looking after the elderly mother of their monk-teacher at their nunnery.

29 This is one of the major causes of property disputes in Myanmar nunneries. There are many old nunneries left in a run-down state when there is no one to claim ownership or take responsibility for their upkeep. See Kawanami, *Renunciation and Empowerment of Buddhist Nuns in Myanmar*-Burma, 202.

30 Ibid., 214–20.

31 *The Path of Purity (Visuddhimagga)*, trans. Pe Maung Tin (London: Pali Text Society, 1975), 252.

32 The building I lived in with a few nuns on the premises of an old nunnery was in desperate need of renovation. I offered to pay for the expenses to fix the roof and help the resident nuns on many occasions, but the nuns could not do anything until they were given permission by the relatives of the original couple who donated the building; already deceased for more than twenty years. When the roofs started leaking and needed urgent repair, the original donor's relatives did not have the funds for it and yet, would not let anyone else to enter their 'merit field', which they saw as their inherited entitlement. What this meant was that old nuns who lived there continued to suffer from the poor living conditions.

33 Sahlins listed three forms of reciprocity: balanced reciprocity (market trade), generalized reciprocity (everyone in this social context accepts the unwritten rule for a return gift) and negative reciprocity (fraud or theft). See Marshall Sahlins, *Stone Age Economics* (Chicago: Chicago University Press, 1974), 193–6.

Chapter 5

1 The term *mithazu* literally means 'the mother and children coming together' (but there is no mention of the father in the term). The concept of the Myanmar family is extended to those who are related through marriage or adoption, and at times even to close friends who are not related by blood.

2 Donald Swearer, *Becoming the Buddha: The Ritual of Image Consecration in Thailand* (Princeton, NJ: Princeton University Press, 2004), 60–1.

3 Myint Win Maung (AZ), *Post-Modern hnit Ponnya Kriya (kyiya) Wut-tu Se-ba* (Yangon: Zin Yatana Sapei, 2009), 26. Commonly known as AZ, he is an award-winning writer in Myanmar.

4 John Holt, *Theravada Traditions: Buddhist Ritual Cultures in Contemporary Southeast Asia and Sri Lanka* (Honolulu: University of Hawai'i Press, 2017), 202.

5 Ibid., 202.

6 As of February 2019, Sagaing had a population of 78,739. Currently, there are only two cities in Myanmar with a population of over 1 million people: Yangon with over 4 million and Mandalay 1.2 million in 2018. Twenty cities have between 100,000 and 1 million; forty-four cities between 1,000 and 100,000 people. http://worldpopulationreview.com, accessed 30 March 2019.

7 These pagodas are: Kaungmudaw, Maha Bodhi, Ngadat-gyi, Shinbyushinhla, Shwe Mohtaw, Sun U Ponyashin, Legyunman Aung, Tilawkaguru, Umin Thonse, Yadanar Zedi Sinmyar Shin and Zeitila.

8 Spiro spoke about the village 'bachelors' association, which appears to have a similar function to these; ibid., 469.

9 Alicia Turner, *Saving Buddhism: The Impermanence of Religion in Colonial Burma* (Honolulu: University of Hawai'i Press, 2014), 76.

10 During my sixteen months' stay as a Buddhist nun in the Sagaing Hill during 1986–87, I received two big bags of rice twice a year from the Malun Association.

11 Khammai Dhammasami, 'Between Idealism and Pragmatism: A Study of Monastic Education in Burma and Thailand from the Seventeenth Century to the Present' (DPhil diss., University of Oxford, 2004), 147. He described that 'the colonial

authorities wanted to encourage the monks to teach not only their traditional faith-based curriculum but also the curriculum prepared by the Department of Public Instruction, which was secular in nature'.

12 Turner, *Saving Buddhism*, 35.

13 Khammai Dhammasami, 'Between Idealism and Pragmatism', 136–37.

14 For a detailed description of how U Tun became a 'consummate organizer' and led this group to support Buddhist scholarship, see Turner, *Saving Buddhism*, 16–18.

15 Khammai Dhammasami, 'Between Idealism and Pragmatism', 139.

16 The first Sakyasiha was conducted in 1902 in the Sakyasiha Pagoda premises in Mandalay, and thus its exams came to be known in this name. See Khammai Dhammasami, 'Between Idealism and Pragmatism', 138.

17 In the past decade, several more lay Buddhist associations have begun to hold private examinations for male novices and for Buddhist nuns under the age of twenty-three. These *Samane-pwe* examinations are conducted in Pakkoku, Yangon and Thaton, usually a few months prior to the annual *Pathamapyan*. They are meant to encourage scriptural learning, especially among young monastic students, and passing them has been particularly beneficial to Buddhist nuns, providing them with a new channel for upward mobility and recognition of their academic potential.

18 Turner, *Saving Buddhism*, 79.

19 Ingrit Jordt, *Mass Lay Meditation and State-Society Relations in Post Independence Burma*. PhD diss., Harvard University, Cambridge, 2001, 318. Jordt came up with this term by observing how lay donors formed close *dāna* offering groups, based on trust and piety, and a mutually shared interest in supporting the *sāsana*. See also Ingrit Jordt, *Burma's Mass Lay Meditation Movement: Buddhism and the Cultural Construction of Power* (Athens: Ohio University Press, 2007), 106.

20 Jordt, *Burma's Mass Lay Meditation Movement*, 107.

21 Ibid., 120–1.

22 Ibid., 103.

23 Juliane Schober, 'Buddhist Just Rule and Burmese National Culture: State Patronage of Chinese Tooth Relic in Myanma', *History of Religions* 36, no. 3 (1997): 242.

24 Jason Carbine, *Sons of the Buddha: Continuities and Ruptures in a Buddhist Monastic Tradition* (Berlin: Walter de Gruyter, 2011), 26.

25 Jordt, *Burma's Mass Lay Meditation Movement*, 104; 133.

26 Donald Seekins, *State and Society in Modern Rangoon* (London: Routledge, 2011), 180–1.

27 Wai Moe, 'A Monk's Tale', *The Irrawaddy* 16, no. 4 (April 2008).

28 Juliane Schober, *Modern Buddhist Conjunctures in Myanmar: Cultural Narratives, Colonial Legacies, and Civil Society* (Honolulu: University of Hawai'i Press, 2011), 107–8.

29 Ibid., 134.

30 Spiro, from his fieldwork, mentioned that villagers would not engage in voluntary, collective activities unless they were religious in nature and conducted for merit-making purposes; ibid., 470.

31 http://www.ffssyangon.org/, accessed 21 February 2019.

32 Ibid.

33 May Sandy, 'Celebrities Make Charity a New Tradition', *Myanmar Times*, 11–17 July 2011.

34 Interview with U Dhammapiya at Thukhakari, Sagaing, 20 December 2015.

35 Hiroko Kawanami, *Renunciation and Empowerment of Buddhist Nuns in Myanmar-Burma: Building a Community of Female Faithful* (Leiden: Brill, 2013), 49.

36 Ibid., 49–50.

37 Anthony Ware, *Context-Sensitive Development: How International NGOs Operate in Myanmar* (Sterling: Kumarian Press, 2012), 7.

38 Ibid., 64.

39 Ibid., 61–2.

40 Bornstein provides specific cases of those engaged in humanitarian work in India and explores the role of empathy in such work. Erica Bornstein, *Disquieting Gifts: Humanitarianism in New Delhi* (Stanford: Stanford University Press, 2012), 83.

41 Ware, *Context-Sensitive Development*, 5.

42 Jaquet and Walton stated that the public response to the aftermath of Cyclone Nargis was a catalyst in changing donation practices for Myanmar Buddhists. They also warned that the participation of monks in relief work and the expansion of monastic influence beyond the traditional religious duties of monks could become a threat to the government. See Carine Jaquet and Matthew Walton, 'Buddhism and Relief in Myanmar: Reflections on Relief as a Practice of Dāna', in *Buddhism, International Relief Work, and Civil Society*, ed. Hiroko Kawanami and Geoffrey Samuel (Basingstoke and New York: Palgrave Macmillan, 2013), 53.

43 Jaquet and Walton, 'Buddhism and Relief in Myanmar', 57.

44 Ibid., 57.

45 Ibid., 52.

46 Ibid., 67.

Towards a society of interdependence

1. https://www.collinsdictionary.com/dictionary/english/interdependence
2. *The Principle of Dependent Origination in Buddhism* by Barbara O'Brien https://www.learnreligions.com/dependent-origination-meaning-449723, accessed 26 June 2019
3. Stephen Batchelor, *The Awakening of the West: The Encounter of Buddhism and Western Culture* (London: Aquarian, 1994), 361.

Bibliography

References

Dictionary of the Social Sciences, edited by Craig Calhoun. Oxford: Oxford University Press, 2002.
Myanmar-English Dictionary. Yangon: Ministry of Education, Union of Myanmar, 1994.
Pali-English Dictionary, edited by T. W. Rhys Davids and W. Stede. Oxford: Pali Text Society, [1925] 1999.
The Path of Purity (Visuddhimagga), translated by Pe Maung Tin. London: Pali Text Society, 1975.

Sources in Myanmar-Burmese

Myint Win Maung (AZ). *Post-Modern hnit Ponnya Kriya (kyiya) Wut-tu Se-ba*. Yangon: Zin Yatana Sapei, 2009.

Sources in English

Ames, Michael, M. 'Magical-Animism and Buddhism: A Structural Analysis of the Sinhalese Religious System'. *Journal of Asian Studies* 23 (1964): 21–52.
Appadurai, Arjun. *The Social Life of Things: Commodities in Cultural Perspective*. Cambridge: Cambridge University Press, 1986.
Batchelor, Stephen. *The Awakening of the West: The Encounter of Buddhism and Western Culture*. London: Aquarian, 1994.
Batson, Daniel, C. *The Altruism Question: Toward a Social-Psychological Answer*. Hillsdale, NJ: Erlbaum, 1991.
Baxter, Pamela, and Susan Jack. 'Qualitative Case Study Methodology: Study Design and Implementation for Novice Researchers'. *The Qualitative Report* 13, no. 4 (2008): 544–59.
Benson, Michaela, and Denise Carter. 'Introduction: Nothing in Return? Distinctions between Gift and Commodity in Contemporary Societies'. *Anthropology in Action* 15, no. 3 (2008): 1–7.

Blackburn, Anne, M. *Locations of Buddhism: Colonialism and Modernity in Sri Lanka*. Chicago: University of Chicago Press, 2010.
Bloch, Maurice, and Jonathan Parry. 'Introduction: Money and the Morality of Exchange'. In *Money & the Morality of Exchange*, edited by Maurice Bloch and Johnny Parry, 1–32. Cambridge: Cambridge University Press, 1989.
Bornstein, Erica. *Disquieting Gifts: Humanitarianism in New Delhi*. Stanford: Stanford University Press, 2012.
Bourdieu, Pierre. *Outline of a Theory of Practice*, translated by Richard Nice. Cambridge: Cambridge University Press, 1977.
Bourdieu, Pierre. *Distinction: A Social Critique of the Judgement of Taste*. Cambridge: Harvard University Press, 1984.
Brac de la Perrière, Bénédicte. 'Religious Donations, Ritual Offerings, and Humanitarian Aid: Fields of Practice According to Forms of Giving in Burma'. *Religion Compass* 9, no. 11 (2015): 386–403.
Brac de la Perrière, Bénédicte. 'A Generation of Monks in the Democratic Transition'. In *Metamorphosis: Studies in Social and Political Change in Myanmar*, edited by Renaud Egreteau and François Robinne, 320–44. Singapore: National University of Singapore Press, 2016.
Braun, Erik. *The Birth of Insight: Meditation, Modern Buddhism, and the Burmese Monk Ledi Sayadaw*. Chicago: University of Chicago Press, 2013.
Brook, Timothy. 'Institution'. In *Critical Terms for the Study of Buddhism*, edited by Donald S. Lopez, 143–61. Chicago: University of Chicago Press, 2005.
Bryman, Alan. *Social Research Methods*. Oxford: Oxford University Press, 2008.
Bunnag, Jane. *Buddhist Monks, Buddhist Layman: A Study of Urban Monastic Organization in Central Thailand*. Cambridge: Cambridge University Press, 1973.
Byles, Marie. *Journey into Burmese Silence*. London: Allen & Unwin, 1962.
Caple, Jane. 'Faith, Generosity, Knowledge and the Buddhist Gift: Moral Discourses on Chinese Patronage of Tibetan Buddhist Monasteries'. *Religion Compass* 9, no. 11 (2015): 462–82.
Carbine, Jason, A. *Sons of the Buddha: Continuities and Ruptures in a Buddhist Monastic Tradition*. Berlin: Walter de Gruyter, 2011.
Carbonnel, Laure. 'On the Ambivalence of Female Monasticism in Theravāda Buddhism: A Contribution to the Study of the Monastic System in Myanmar'. *Asian Ethnology* 68, no. 2 (2009): 265–82.
Carrier, James, G. 'Gifts, Commodities, and Social Relations: A Maussian View of Exchange'. *Sociological Forum* 6, no. 1 (1991): 119–36.
Carrithers, Michael. *The Forest Monks of Sri Lanka: An Anthropological and Historical Study*. New Delhi: Oxford University Press, 1983.
Carrithers, Michael. 'The Domestication of the Sangha'. *Man, N. S.* 19 (1984): 321–2.
Chiu, Tzu-Lung. 'Contemporary Buddhist Nunneries in Taiwan and Mainland China: A Study of Vinaya Practices'. PhD diss., Universiteit Gent, Gent, 2016.
Cone, Margaret, and Richard Gombrich. *The Perfect Generosity of Prince Vessantara*. Oxford: Clarendon Press, 1977.
Cook, Joanna. 'Alms, Money and Reciprocity: Buddhist Nuns as Mediators of Generalised Exchange in Thailand'. *Anthropology in Action* 15, no. 3 (2008): 8–21.

Davis, John. *Exchange*. Buckingham: Open University Press, 1992.
Douglas, Mary. *Purity and Danger*. London: Routledge & Kegan Paul, 1966.
Evers, Hans-Deiter. '"Monastic Landlordhism" in Ceylon: A Traditional System in a Modern Setting'. *Journal of Asian Studies* 24, no. 4 (1969): 685-92.
Falk, Monica Lindberg. 'Women in Between: Becoming Religious Persons in Thailand'. In *Women's Buddhism Buddhism's Women: Tradition, Revision, Renewal*, edited by Ellison B. Findly, 37-57. Boston: Wisdom Publications, 2000.
Falk, Monica Lindberg. *Making Fields of Merit: Buddhist Female Ascetics and Gendered Orders in Thailand*. Copenhagen: NIAS, 2007.
Falk, Monica Lindberg, and Hiroko Kawanami. 'Monastic Discipline and Communal Rules for Buddhist Nuns in Myanmar and Thailand'. *Journal of Buddhism, Law & Society* 3 (2017-2018): 79-108.
Ferguson, John, P. 'The Quest for Legitimation by Burmese Monks and Kings: The Case of the Shwegyin Sect (19th-20th Centuries)'. In *Religion and Legitimation of Power in Thailand, Laos, and Burma*, edited by Bardwell L. Smith, 66-86. Chambersburg: Anima Books, 1978.
Gay, Paloma, and Huon Wardle Blasco. *How to Read Ethnography*. London: Routledge, 2007.
Gellner, David, N. *Monk, Householder, and Tantric Priest: Newar Buddhism and Its Hierarchy of Ritual*. Cambridge: Cambridge University Press, 1992.
Gillham, Bill. *Case Study Research Methods*. London: Bloomsbury Academic, 2000.
Godelier, Maurice. *The Enigma of the Gift*, translated by Nora Scott. Chicago: University of Chicago Press, 1999.
Gombrich, Richard, F. *Buddhist Precept and Practice: Traditional Buddhism in the Rural Highlands of Ceylon*. Delhi: Motilal Banarsidass, [1971] 1991.
Gombrich, Richard, F. '"Merit Transference" in Sinhalese Buddhism: A Case Study of the Interaction between Doctrine and Behavior'. *History of Religions* 11 (1971): 203-19.
Gombrich, Richard, F., and Gananath Obeyesekere. *Buddhism Transformed: Religious Change in Sri Lanka*. Princeton, NJ: Princeton University Press, 1988.
Graeber, David. *The Debt: The First 5000 Years*. New York: Melville House, 2011.
Gregory, Chris, A. *Gifts and Commodities*. London: Academic Press, 1982.
Gudeman, Stephen. *Economics as Culture: Models and Metaphors of Livelihood*. London: Routledge & Kegan Paul, 1986.
Guruge, Ananda, W. P., and George D. Bond. 'Generosity and Service in Theravāda Buddhism'. In *Philanthropy in the World's Traditions*, edited by Warren F. Ilchman et al., 79-96. Bloomington: Indiana University Press, 1998.
Heim, Maria. *Theories of the Gift in South Asia: Hindu, Buddhist, and Jain Reflections on Dāna*. New York: Routledge, 2004.
Holt, John Clifford. *Theravada Traditions: Buddhist Ritual Cultures in Contemporary Southeast Asia and Sri Lanka*. Honolulu: University of Hawai'i Press, 2017.
Houtman, Gustaaf. *Mental Cultural in Burmese Crisis Politics*. Tokyo: Institute for the Study of Language and Culture of Asia & Africa, Tokyo University of Foreign Studies, 1999.
Jackson, Peter, A. *Buddhism, Legitimation and Conflict: The Political Functions of Urban Thai Buddhism*. Singapore: Institute of Southeast Asian Studies, 1990.

Jaquet, Carine, and Matthew J. Walton. 'Buddhism and Relief in Myanmar: Reflections on Relief as a Practice of Dāna'. In *Buddhism, International Relief Work, and Civil Society*, edited by Hiroko Kawanami and Geoffrey Samuel, 51–73. Basingstoke and New York: Palgrave Macmillan, 2013.

Jordt, Ingrit. 'Mass Lay Meditation and State-Society Relations in Post-Independence Burma'. PhD diss., Harvard University, Cambridge, 2001.

Jordt, Ingrid. *Burma's Mass Lay Meditation Movement: Buddhism and the Cultural Construction of Power*. Athens: Ohio University Press, 2007.

Joy, Morny, ed. *Women and the Gift: Beyond the Given and All-Giving*. Bloomington: Indiana University Press, 2013.

Kawanami, Hiroko. 'The Religious Standing of Burmese Buddhist Nuns (*Thila-shin*): The Ten Precepts and Religious Respect Words'. *Journal of the International Association of Buddhist Studies* 13, no. 1 (1990): 17–39.

Kawanami, Hiroko. 'Charisma, Power(s), and the Arahant Ideal in Burmese-Myanmar Buddhism'. *Asian Ethnology* 68, no. 2 (2009): 211–37.

Kawanami, Hiroko. 'Sangha and Society'. In *Wiley-Blackwell Companion to Religion and Social Justice*, edited by Michael D. Palmer and Stanley M. Burgess, 280–91. Oxford: Wiley-Blackwell, 2012.

Kawanami, Hiroko. *Renunciation and Empowerment of Buddhist Nuns in Myanmar-Burma: Building a Community of Female Faithful*. Leiden: Brill, 2013.

Kawanami, Hiroko. 'U Nu's Liberal Democracy and Buddhist Communalism in Modern Burma'. In *Buddhism and the Political Process*, edited by Hiroko Kawanami, 11–30. Basingstoke and New York: Palgrave Macmillan, 2016.

Keyes, Charles. 'Mother or Mistress but Never a Monk: Buddhist Notions of Female Gender in Rural Thailand'. *American Ethnologist* 11, no. 2 (1984): 223–41.

Khammai Dhammasami. 'Between Idealism and Pragmatism: A Study of Monastic Education in Burma and Thailand from the Seventeenth Century to the Present'. DPhil diss., University of Oxford, Oxford, 2004.

Khin Myo Chit. *Colourful Burma*. Yangon: Myitta Moe Press, 1984.

Kirsch, A. Thomas. 'Text and Context: Buddhist Sex Roles/Culture of Gender Revisited'. *American Ethnologist* 12, no. 2 (1985): 302–20.

Kirsch, A. Thomas. 'Buddhism, Sex-Roles and the Thai Economy'. In *Women of Southeast Asia*, edited by Penny Van Esterik, 13–32. Dekalb: Center for Southeast Asian Studies, 1996.

Laidlaw, James. 'A Free Gift Makes No Friends'. *Journal of the Royal Anthropological Institute* 6, no. 4 (2000): 617–34.

Langer, Rita. *Buddhist Rituals of Death and Rebirth: Contemporary Sri Lankan Practice and Its Origins*. London and New York: Routledge, 2007.

Lévi-Strauss, Claude. *The Elementary Structure of Kinship*. Boston: Beacon Press, [1949] 1969.

MacCormack, Geoffrey. 'Reciprocity'. *Man, N. S.* 11, no. 1 (1976): 89–103.

Malalasekera, G. P. '"Transference of merit" in Ceylonese Buddhism'. *Philosophy East and West* 17 (1967): 85–90.

Mauss, Marcell. *The Gift: The Form and Reason for Exchange in Archaic Societies*, translated by W. D. Halls. London: Routledge, [1925] 1990.

McCutcheon, Russell, ed. *The Insider/Outsider Problem in the Study of Religion*. London: Cassell, 1999.
McDaniel, Justin, T. *The Lovelorn Ghost and the Magical Monk: Practicing Buddhism in Modern Thailand*. New York: Columbia University Press, 2011.
McMahan, David, L., ed. *Buddhism in the Modern World*. London: Routledge Curzon, 2011.
Mendelson, Michael, E. *State and Sangha in Burma: A Study of Monastic Sectarianism and Leadership*, edited by John Ferguson. Ithaca: Cornell University Press, 1975.
Michaels, Axel. 'Gift and Return Gift, Greeting and Return Greeting in India: On a Consequential Footnote by Marcel Mauss'. *Numen* 44, no. 3 (1997): 242–69.
Nārada, Ven. *The Buddha and His Teachings*. Kuala Lumpur: Buddhist Missionary Society, 1988.
Nash, Manning. *The Golden Road to Modernity: Village Life in Contemporary Burma*. New York: John Wiley & Sons, 1965.
Ohnuma, Reiko. 'Gift'. In *Critical Terms for the Study of Buddhism*, edited by Donald S. Lopez, 103–23. Chicago: University of Chicago Press, 2005.
Okell, John. *Burmese (Myanmar): An Introduction to the Script*. DeKalb: Northern Illinois University, Center for Southeast Asian Studies, 1994.
Okely, Judith. *Anthropological Practice: Fieldwork and the Ethnographic Method*. London: 2012.
Parry, Jonathan. 'Ghosts, Greed and Sin: The Occupational Identity of the Benares Funeral Priests'. *Man*, N. S. 15, no. 1 (1980): 88–111.
Parry, Jonathan. 'The Gift, the Indian Gift and the "Indian Gift"'. *Man*, N. S. 21, no. 3 (1986): 453–73.
Parry, Jonathan. 'On the Moral Perils of Exchange'. In *Money & the Morality of Exchange*, edited by Jonathan Parry and Maurice Bloch, 64–93. Cambridge: Cambridge University Press, 1989.
Paul, Diana, Y. *Women in Buddhism: Images of the Feminine in the Mahāyāna Tradition*. Berkeley: University of California Press, [1979] 1985.
Pyyhtinen, Olli. *The Gift and Its Paradoxes: Beyond Mauss*. Farnham: Ashgate, 2014.
Raheja, Gloria Goodwin. *The Poison in the Gift: Ritual, Prestation, and the Dominant Caste in a North Indian Village*. Chicago: University of Chicago Press, 1988.
Rozenberg, Guillaume. *Renunciation and Power: The Quest for Sainthood in Contemporary Burma*, translated by Jessica Hackett. New Haven: Yale University Southeast Asia Studies, 2010.
Sahlins, Marshall, D. *Stone Age Economics*. Chicago: Chicago University Press, 1974.
Salgado, Nirmala, S. 'Teaching Lineages and Land: Renunciation and Domestication among Buddhist Nuns in Sri Lanka'. In *Women's Buddhism Buddhism's Women: Tradition, Revision, Renewal*, edited by Ellison B. Findly, 175–200. Boston: Wisdom Publications, 2000.
Salgado, Nirmala, S. *Buddhist Nuns and Gendered Practice: In Search of the Female Renunciant*. New York: Oxford University Press, 2013.
Schober, Juliane. 'Buddhist Just Rule and Burmese National Culture: State Patronage of Chinese Tooth Relic in Myanma'. *History of Religions* 36, no. 3 (1997): 218–43.

Schober, Juliane. *Modern Buddhist Conjunctures in Myanmar: Cultural Narratives, Colonial Legacies, and Civil Society*. Honolulu: University of Hawai'i Press, 2011.

Schopen, Gregory. *Buddhist Monks and Business Matters: Still More Papers on Monastic Buddhism in India*. Honolulu: University of Hawai'i Press, 2004.

Scott, Rachelle. *Nirvana for Sale? Buddhism, Wealth, and the Dhammakāya Temple in Contemporary Thailand*. Albany: State University of New York Press, 2009.

Seekins, Donald. *State and Society in Modern Rangoon*. London: Routledge, 2011.

Sihlé, Nicolas. 'Introduction: The Comparative Anthropology of the Buddhist Gift'. *Religion Compass* 9, no. 11 (2015): 347–51.

Sihlé, Nicolas. 'Towards a Comparative Anthropology of the Buddhist Gift (and Other Transfers)'. *Religion Compass* 9, no. 11 (2015): 352–85.

Spiro, Melford E. *Buddhism and Society: A Great Tradition and Its Burmese Vicissitudes*. New York: Harper and Row, 1970.

Strathern, Marilyn. *The Gender of the Gift: Problems with Women and Problems with Society in Melanesia*. Berkeley: University of California Press, 1988.

Strenski, Ian. 'On Generalized Exchange and the Domestication of the Sangha'. *Man*, N. S. 18, no. 3 (1983): 463–77.

Strong, John, S. 'The Transforming Gift: An Analysis of Devotional Acts of Offering in Buddhist *Avadāna* Literature'. *History of Religions* 18, no. 3 (1979): 221–37.

Swearer, Donald, K. *The Buddhist World of Southeast Asia*. Albany: State University of New York Press, 1995.

Swearer, Donald, K. *Becoming the Buddha: The Ritual of Image Consecration in Thailand*. *The Buddhist World of Southeast Asia*. Princeton: Princeton University Press, 2004.

Tambiah, Stanley, J. *Buddhism and Spirit Cults in Northeast Thailand*. Cambridge: Cambridge University Press, 1970.

Tambiah, Stanley, J. *The Buddhist Saints of the Forest and the Cult of Amulets*. Cambridge: Cambridge University Press, 1984.

Terwiel, B. J. *Monks and Magic: An Analysis of Religious Ceremonies in Central Thailand*. Bangkok: White Lotus, 1994.

Testart, Alain. 'Uncertainties of the "Obligation to Reciprocate": A Critique of Mauss'. In *Marcel Mauss: A Centenary Tribute*, edited by Wendy James and N. J. Allen, 97–110. New York: Berghahn Books, 1998.

Testart, Alain. 'What Is a Gift?' *Hau: Journal of Ethnographic Theory* 3, no. 1 (2013): 249–61.

Tosa, Keiko. 'The Cult of Thamanya Sayadaw: The Social Dynamism of Formulating Pilgrimage Site'. *Asian Ethnology* 68, no. 2 (2009): 239–64.

Trainor, Kevin. *Relics, Ritual and Representation in Buddhism*. Cambridge: Cambridge University Press, 1997.

Trautmann, Thomas, R. *Dravidian Kinship*. Cambridge: Cambridge University Press, 1981.

Turner, Alicia. *Saving Buddhism: The Impermanence of Religion in Colonial Burma*. Honolulu: University of Hawai'i Press, 2014.

Venkatesan, Soumhya. 'Giving and Taking without Reciprocity: Conversations in South India and the Anthropology of Ethics'. *Social Analysis* 60, no. 3 (2016): 36–56.

Walton, Matthew, J. *Buddhism, Politics and Political Thought in Myanmar*. Cambridge: Cambridge University Press, 2016.

Walton, Matthew, J., and Susan Hayward. *Contesting Buddhist Narratives: Democratization, Nationalism, and Communal Violence in Myanmar*. Honolulu: East-West Center, 2014.

Walton, Matthew, J., Melyn McKay and Khin Mar Mar Kyi. 'Women and Myanmar's "Religious Protection Laws"'. *The Review of Faith & International Affairs: Special Issue on Religion, Law, and Society in Myanmar* 13, no. 4 (2015): 36–49.

Ware, Anthony. *Context-Sensitive Development: How International NGOs Operate in Myanmar*. Sterling: Kumarian Press, 2012.

Weber, Max. *The Religion of India: The Sociology of Hinduism and Buddhism*, translated and edited by Hans H. Gerth and Don Martindale. Glencoe: The Free Press, 1958.

Wijayaratna, Mohan. *Buddhist Monastic Life: According to the Texts of the Theravada Tradition*, translated by Claude Grangier and Steven Collins. Cambridge: Cambridge University Press, 1990.

Newspaper and magazine articles and reports

Aung Kyaw Min. 'Ma Ba Tha Monks Declare Political Independence'. *Myanmar Times*, 27 June 2014.

Beech, Hannah. 'The Face of Buddhist Terror'. *Times Magazine*, 20 June 2013 (cover).

CAF World Giving Index 2017: Charities Aid Foundation, 2018.

Central Bank of Myanmar. 'History of Bank Notes'. https://cbm.gov.mm/content/history-bank-notes, accessed 11 November 2018.

Cherry Thein and Aung Kyaw Min. 'Sangha Reforms Planned to Improve Discipline, cooperation'. *Myanmar Times*, 16 May 2014.

Free Funeral Social Services. http://ffssyangon.org/, accessed 21 February 2019.

Kipgen, Nehginpao. 'Religion and Democracy Go Hand in Hand'. *Myanmar Times*, 1 July 2013.

Lawyers Network and Justice Trust. 'Submission of Evidence to Myanmar Government's Letpadaung Investigation Commission'. 5 February 2013, http://burmalibrary.org/docs15/Letpadaung-Lawyers_report-en-red.pdf, accessed 2 March 2018.

McKay, Melyn, and Khin Chit Win. 'Myanmar's Gender Paradox'. *Anthropolgy Today* 34, no. 1 (February 2018): 1–3.

Phyoe Wai Kyaw. 'A Chance to Eat Satuditha While Playing Water in Mandalay'. *Myanmar Times*, 17 April 2018.

Sandy, May. 'Celebrities Make Charity a New Tradition'. *Myanmar Times*, 11–17 July 2011.

Tin Moe Aung. 'Light Festival Inspires Spirit of Selfless Giving'. *Myanmar Times*, 28 November 2011.

'*Tharkithwe Journal*'. achatpo. B–C, D, 6 August 2013.

Wai Moe, 'A Monk's Tale'. *The Irrawaddy* 16, no. 4 (April 2008).

Wei Yan Aung. 'The End of Shikoing before the British'. *The Irrawaddy*, 16 August 2019.

Index

Abhidhamma 92, 127, 155, 165
accountability
    corporate model of 120, 140
agency 12, 50
alchemy 78, 85
    daloun 78
alms bowl 55, 72, 159
    upturning of 39, 137
alms collecting 8, 45
    of nuns 99
altruism 13
    altruistic services 37, 106
amulets 85
arahant 73, 85, 162
    spiritual power of 85
    See saintly monks
Aung San Suu Kyi, Daw 92, 161

beggar 38, 58, 65
    state of, 38, 65
benefactor 10, 15, 20, 40, 43, 46, 58, 73, 82, 87, 101–3, 133, 135, 145
    monastic member acting as 83–6
    See patron
beneficiary 101, 145
    monastic 15, 47, 54, 58, 74, 85, 96, 101–5, 132
birthday celebrations 23, 43, 84, 121–2
    of monks 86–8, 92–3, 163
    of nuns 164
bodhi tree 37, 78
Bornstein, Erica 141, 171
Buddhism 6, 8, 13, 27, 81, 91, 132, 145–6
    decline of 40, 63, 129
    dissemination 38, 127
    See sāsana
    engaged Buddhism 66
    in relation to state power 136
    Myanmar Buddhism 15, 90, 93, 100, 157
    Theravada Buddhism 4, 19, 21, 103
    Tibetan Buddhism 9
    See also cosmology
Buddhist monks
    as benefactor 83–6
    as recipient 73–5
    former (ex) monks 127, 129
    idealized prototype 9, 74
    preachers 34, 73, 79–80, 126
    transactions with 71–5
    See celebrity monks
    See charismatic monks
    See saintly monks
    See scholarly monks
    See also Sayadaws for prominent monks
Buddhist nuns
    ambiguous position 16, 117–18
    as carers 54
    as nurturers 15
    as recipients 3, 10, 15, 59, 102–4
    bridging roles 19, 23, 40, 95
    relationships with monks 106–11
    relationship with other nuns 111–14
    relationship with their families 115–17
    transactions with 61, 95, 98–102
Buddhist scriptures 55, 65, 70, 81, 127, 130, 142
    examinations 10, 13, 80, 129–30, 163, 170
    See Pathamapyan
    study group 113, 127

celebrity monks 34–5, 79–80, 132
celibacy 61, 73, 98
　See deprivation
chants 72, 99, 127, 166
　blessing 9, 16, 23
　protective 71, 85
charisma 32, 52, 95, 134
charismatic monks 11, 13, 76–7, 81, 85
charities 119, 140
civil society 20, 90, 139–40, 142–3
communal cohesion 106, 112
communication technology 19, 89
　See social media
congregation 23, 28–9, 40–1, 43, 63, 70, 77, 99, 109, 127
　activities of monks 142
cosmology 50, 134
credentials 80, 95, 104, 141, 163–4

dāna 6–9, 11–5, 18–9, 23–4, 35–9, 45–9, 55–6, 59, 63–5, 71, 75, 82–4, 92, 95–9, 102, 106, 115–17, 120–5, 129, 132, 135, 142–3, 153, 158–9
dāna cliques 131–3, 135
daughter 61, 109, 114–15, 132, 160
　as carer for parents 114, 168
demonetization 56, 159
Department of Religious Affairs of Religious Ministry 70, 129
dependency 102, 146
　parasitic 2, 10
deprivation 97–8
detachment 73, 75, 77, 79
　See non-reciprocity
devotion 76, 87–8, 112
dhamma 23–4, 28–9, 83
　hall 37
　learning groups 127
　talks 37, 80–1, 91
　teachers 11, 81, 91, 100, 112, 157, 164, 168
Dhammasari, Daw (Tipitaka Medaw) 108
discipline 65, 74, 76, 105, 131
　monastic 20, 38, 61, 72, 143
disputes 71, 90

monastic property 113, 115, 168
donations 2–3, 5, 13, 18, 20–4, 34, 39–40, 46–8, 51, 53, 55, 57, 73, 76, 87, 95, 97, 99–102, 113, 118, 125, 129–31, 135–43, 155, 171
　in cash 20, 35, 37, 56–7, 100, 157, 159, 163
　inappropriate 58–9
　See dāna
donors
　regular donors 11, 16, 46–7. 49–50, 58, 73, 83, 88, 92, 96, 98–102, 105, 117, 135, 161, 166
　See patron
donor groups 19, 119–27, 132–4, 137–9
　See dāna cliques
doubt 13, 39, 42
Durkheim, Émile 13, 40, 44

economy 33, 54, 110, 147
　monastic, 110
education 34, 100
　monastic (Buddhist) 34, 79, 82, 112, 129
　secular 130, 143
Eight Requisites 55, 62
emotions 10, 75, 98–9, 156
empathy 96, 98, 171
ethnic autonomous zones 70
　Karen 77
　Shan 80

family 1, 14–5, 18, 25, 30–1, 49–57, 61, 65–6, 72–5, 87, 101, 116, 120, 139, 155, 158–60, 169
　as a unit of offering 4, 41, 48, 89, 120–3, 136
　Buddhist 27, 55, 59, 71, 97, 155
　of monastic members 51, 100, 114–15, 117–18
　pseudo-family relationship 81, 101, 106
fear 7, 42, 81, 89, 160
feasts 23, 55, 67, 71, 75, 87, 123–4, 131, 163
　ahlu 32, 40, 75
Ferguson, John 76, 157

forgiveness 28–29, 112
    confession ritual 29
funeral 35, 66, 71, 108, 138–9

gambling 50, 54
gāthā 41, 99, 166
generosity 3, 6, 15–6, 22, 35–6, 39–40, 43, 46, 63, 65, 75, 87, 89, 97, 99, 103–4, 114, 124, 133–4, 145, 147, 167
    global list 19, 21
    misdirected 39, 64
gift 9, 11, 14, 22–3, 30, 35, 39, 101
    debates 3–6
    gendered 15–6, 101
    'pure' 2, 7, 10, 13, 88
    reverse (return) 10, 85–6, 88, 93
    social 1–2, 34, 138, 143, 152
    token 23, 26, 86, 88, 112
    un-reciprocated 7, 103
    See offering
giver 1–4, 12, 15, 32, 38–39, 45, 58–59, 64, 83–85, 95, 125, 145, 147–48
    See receiver
gratitude 2, 5, 9, 22–3, 25–8, 32, 74, 83, 85–9, 99–101, 156, 164
greeting phrases in Myanmar 29–30

hierarchy 28, 39, 65, 112
    monastic 3, 11, 13, 45, 83, 91, 111
    moral 23–5
Holt, John 21, 34, 61–2, 84, 123
honoraria to monastic members 35, 157
    renumeration 35, 157
honorifics 47, 109
humanitarian work 20, 140–1, 120, 171
humility 28, 49, 97, 103

identity 33, 73
    religious (Buddhist) 71, 106, 117, 141
impulse 14, 43, 49, 73
INGO 119, 141
interdependence 22, 24, 27, 54, 70, 89, 103, 137, 145–8
international community 120, 140, 165

Jaquet and Walton 142–3, 171
Jordt, Ingrit 46, 52, 131–2, 137, 159, 170

karma 14, 32, 36, 38, 49–50, 88, 146, 158–9
kathina 24, 61–3, 123, 125, 132
Khin Myo Chit 29, 63, 156
Konbaung dynasty 76, 124
Kyaw Thu, U 138–9

laity 3, 9, 12, 19, 22, 27, 41, 45, 58, 63, 71, 74–5, 81, 89, 91, 95–6, 99, 103, 105, 110–11, 166
    lay-monastic relationship, 10–11, 45
Langer, Rita 23, 155
Levi-Strauss, Claude 5, 9, 15, 154
lineage 134
    higher lineage of monks 130
    monastic 4, 83
    scholarly 18, 112–13, 165, 168

Ma Ba Tha ('Amyotha-batha Thathana Saungshauk-yei Apwe', Association for the Protection of Race and Religion) 70, 89–92, 165
Maha Myamuni Pagoda 125–6
Ma Ha Na ('Naingandaw Thangha Maha Nayaka Ahpwe', National Committee of Supreme Sangha Council) 80, 90–2, 163, 165
Mahasi Thathana Yeitha (Mahasi Meditation Centre) 130–2
Malun Sanhlu Athin Association (Malun rice-offering Association) 128, 169
Mandalay 33, 51, 56, 124–5. 128–30, 139, 159, 161, 164, 169
Mara 41–2
materialism 19, 34
Mauss, Marcel 3, 5–6, 15, 45
    The Gift, 3, 151
meditation 23, 65–6, 78
    centres 52, 110, 119, 127, 131–2, 160, 167
    groups 127

mentor 26, 81, 113
  See preceptor
merit 2, 5–9, 14, 23–4, 32, 34, 36–9, 52, 56–8, 42, 45–6, 63, 65–6, 67, 88, 104, 119, 121–5, 137, 147, 157–8
  collective 12, 14
  demerit 37, 39, 65
  'economy of merit' 137
  field of 9, 115–16, 118, 134, 142, 147, 168
  kutho 38, 46, 158
  akutho 39
merit-making 21, 24, 37, 45, 56, 64–5, 67, 86, 103, 119–23, 131, 133, 136–8, 161, 167, 171
  as a collective act 12, 14, 120–3, 131, 137–8
  ranking 161
meritorious deeds 6, 8, 19–20, 23–5, 32, 36–7, 40–3, 50, 53–8, 75, 82, 89, 127, 135, 143, 155, 158, 160
  occasions 59–63
  returns 4, 14, 36, 70, 84, 106
military regime(s) 16, 134–5, 137, 164
misfortune 29, 37, 45, 54
monastery 4, 8, 14, 31, 46, 48, 51–2, 83–5, 88, 105, 108, 116, 122–3, 132, 136–7, 142, 159–61
  finances, 110
  schools, 34, 52, 82–3, 119, 124, 132, 164, 167
Monywa 77–8, 85, 161
moral community 28, 45, 66, 71, 75, 77, 84, 119, 136
moral instruction 112
  ovada 112, 163
morality 23, 63, 71, 76, 91–2, 127
  sīla 23
moral purity 76–7, 79, 96
motherhood 25–6, 155
  honorary mother 106, 108
mother's day ceremony 25–6
motives 2, 9, 19, 63, 67
  religious 37
  to offer donations 2, 63, 96

Muslim communities 75
  anti-Muslim sentiments 90–1
  threat to Buddhism 12
Myanmar Diaspora 139, 142

Nargis, Cyclone (2008) 20, 89, 110, 120, 139–40, 143, 171
natural disasters 71, 83, 98, 120, 138
Ne Win, General 97, 125, 159
NLD (National League for Democracy) 92, 136, 162
969 movement 162, 165
Nu, U, Prime Minister of Myanmar 47, 131
nunnery 18, 46, 49–50, 54, 97, 99–100, 105, 114, 159, 166–8
  As an autonomous unit 112–13
  ownership 115–18
  reputation 95, 104–5
nurturer 75, 95, 108

offerings 2–4, 6–9, 11–6, 18–9, 22–3, 31, 35–40, 45, 47–8, 54–9, 63–4, 72, 74–7, 82–5, 87, 89, 92, 104, 116, 119–25, 128, 132–3, 135–7, 141–2, 154, 170
  gift 31, 87, 102
  cash 27, 35, 37, 56–7, 100, 159
  to Buddhist nuns 95–9, 102–3
  See dāna
ordination of monks 40, 46, 51, 73, 108, 117, 159
  repeat ordination 51–2

paritta 41, 127
  Mangala Sutta 41, 158
  Mettā Sutta 41, 158
  Ratana Sutta 85
Parry, Jonathan 4, 7
Pathamapyan 104–5, 129–30, 170
patron 46–7, 51–4, 65, 116, 128–9
  of monk's ordination 46, 51, 108
  patron–client relationship 52, 121
patronage 12, 31, 35, 52, 124, 133, 136
Patthāna 50, 127

pilgrimage 85, 124
  pilgrimage groups, 127
poverty 81, 143
preceptor 51, 81, 112–13
precepts 41, 65–6
  Eight Precepts 16, 41, 96, 110–11, 127, 158
  Ten Precepts 96, 104
prestige 11, 47, 105, 130, 132
protection 86, 90
  from misfortune 29, 45, 100
  legal protection 118
  prayers for 41
  See paritta
protective power 85–6, 158, 164

receiver / recipient 2–3, 5, 7, 9–10, 12, 15, 23, 28, 31–2, 39–40, 64, 83, 86, 93, 103, 142–3, 145, 147
  appropriateness of 38–9, 46, 65
  monastic recipient 4–6, 8–12, 14, 35–9, 45–59, 64, 71, 103–4, 133, 137, 140, 147, 155, 160
  monk as receiver 37, 73, 75, 84–5, 104, 115, 154
  nun as receiver 19, 95, 101–4, 115–16
receiving 1–3, 5, 15, 22–3, 27, 34, 40–1, 74, 84, 87, 103, 120, 137, 142, 145, 148, 162
  danger of 35
  problem of 3, 31, 58, 102, 105, 110
reciprocity 2–3, 5–6, 8, 11, 19, 21, 27, 30–1, 33–4, 40, 84, 95, 102, 104, 118, 146. 148, 152
  non-reciprocity 4–5, 77, 137
redistribution 84, 114
religious investment 35, 105, 116
religious transactions 2, 8–11, 14–5, 18, 20–1, 36, 95, 102, 137
ritual 9, 14, 17, 22–6, 28–9, 61, 108, 112, 116, 123
  Buddhist 35, 40–3, 127
  consecration of the Buddha 37, 122
  specialist 157
  See shinbyu

robe-offering 24, 61–2, 100, 123–4
  See kathina
Rozenburg, Guillaume 76–7, 87, 164
  'cumulative process of sanctification' 76–7

Saffron Revolution 39, 70, 136
Sagaing 27, 34, 66, 77, 85, 105, 125–6, 129, 139, 156, 169
Sagaing Hill 110, 116, 124, 129, 163, 169
sainthood 65
  four stages towards 161
saintly monks 76–7, 85–8
  miracle stories of 86
  weikza 77, 85, 163
saṃsāra 25, 42, 65
sangha 3–4, 9, 12, 15–6, 19, 24, 37, 40, 47, 55, 57, 59, 61–2, 65–6, 69–71, 73, 83, 89–91, 95–6, 104, 106, 108–10, 115, 117, 125, 129, 135–6, 154, 159
sāsana 12, 24, 38, 40, 47, 61, 69, 91–2, 115, 129–30, 134, 160, 170
Sayadaws (prominent monks in Myanmar Buddhism)
  Anisakhan Sayadaw U Pandita 79
  Bamaw Sayadaw 80, 163
  Bodhi Ta-htaung Sayadaw, U Narada 77–9, 85
  Dhammaduta Sayadaw U Sekeinda 81
  Insein Ywama Sayadaw, U Tiloka-bhivamsa 88, 92, 165, 168
  Khammai Dhammasami, U Oxford Sayadaw 80
  Konlon Sayadaw, U Tezaniya 85
  Ledi Sayadaw 70
  Mahasi Sayadaw, U Sobhana 70, 130
  Mingun Tipitaka Sayadaw, U Vicittasara-bhivamsa 70, 108
  Mogok Sayadaw, U Vimala 63, 160
  Oak Gyaung Sayada, U Dhammapiya 139, 171
  Oxford Sayadaw, Dr Khammai Dhammasami 80
  Pa-chok Sayadaw, U Nandamala-bhivamsa 80, 163

Shinbyushinla Sayadaw 163
Shwe Parami Sayadaw, U Sandadhika 80
Shwegyin Sayadaw, Ashin Jāgara 76
Sitagu Sayadaw, U Nyanissara 79, 91, 141–2, 163
Sunlun Sayadaw 70
Taungphila Sayadaw 70, 85
Thamanya Sayadaw, U Vinaya 76–7, 87, 163
scholarly monks 80–3
seniority 97, 111, 127
sermons 23–4, 41, 49, 71, 79–81, 91–2, 124, 126, 163
services 1–2, 56, 66, 71, 76, 84, 143, 167
  religious 22, 56, 77, 106, 109, 125–7, 148
  social 23, 25, 101, 109, 138
shinbyu 59–61
Shwedagon pagoda 62, 125, 133
Shwegyin sect 76, 157
Sihlé, Nicolas 5–7, 10, 35, 157
SLORC (State Law and Order Restoration Council) 134–5
social media 19, 27, 34, 62, 77, 79, 89, 113, 133–4, 143
social-welfare activities 20, 66, 71, 84, 138–41, 143, 148
South Asia 7–8
Southeast Asia 7–8, 110
spectrum 2, 58, 79
  of giving 10–11
Spiro, Melford 9, 38, 57, 65, 81, 98, 164, 169, 171
  Kammatic and Nibbanic Buddhism 65
Sri Lanka 4, 23, 80, 127, 158
suffering 41, 57, 63, 71, 76, 98, 142, 146, 161
  dukkha 146

symbolic capital 35, 73, 104–5
  Bourdieu, Pierre 167

Tambiah, Stanley 9, 83, 161, 167
Terwiel, B. J. 9, 158–9, 164
Testart, Alain 5–6, 152
Thingyan 24–5, 43
Tipitakadhara 80, 91, 108, 163, 165
Township Council of *Thilashin* 113, 168
Triple Gem 24, 28–9, 37–8, 41, 48, 62, 99
Turner, Alicia 128, 130

Vinaya 5, 71, 75, 92, 109, 117–18
  Vinayadhara, 166
vipassana 63, 131
  samatha 78
volunteers 66–7, 133, 138, 142

Weber, Max 167
  perception of reclusive monks 70, 162
Wheel of Life 25, 156
Wirathu, U, (the Buddhist Face of Terror) 69, 91, 162, 164–5
  See 969 movement
wish-fulfilling tree 62–63, 124–5
women 15, 95, 105–6, 110, 114, 118, 124–5, 131, 133
  as donors, 98
  in relation to monks 75, 109
  unmarried single women 27, 71, 101, 155
  women's rights 90
  See motherhood
Yangon 11, 33–4, 51, 57, 62, 88, 97, 125, 130–3, 157, 160, 163, 167, 169–70

www.ingramcontent.com/pod-product-compliance
Lightning Source LLC
Chambersburg PA
CBHW070639300426
44111CB00013B/2176

'The result of extensive experience in the field, a strong network of relationships and a deep love for the communities she engages with, *The Culture of Giving in Myanmar* is a wonderful contribution that highlights the interdependent reciprocity that is at the heart of so many transactions in Myanmar's Buddhist life.'
Vanessa Sasson, Marianopolis College, Canada

'Hiroko Kawanami is undeniably one of the most important contributors to the evolving understanding of Buddhism in Myanmar. This intriguing book, based on Kawanami's decades of anthropological research, is a captivating account of the dynamics of generosity both inside and outside of religious contexts.'
Monica Lindberg Falk, Lund University, Sweden

How can people living in one of the poorest countries in the world be among the most charitable?

In this book, Hiroko Kawanami examines the culture of giving in Myanmar, and explores the pivotal role that Buddhist monastic members occupy in creating a platform for civil society. Despite having at one time been listed as one of the poorest countries in the world in GNP terms, Myanmar has topped a global generosity list for the past four years with more than 90 per cent of the population engaged in 'giving' activities.

This book explores the close relationship that Buddhists share with the monastic community in Myanmar, extending observations of this relationship into an understanding of wider Buddhist cultures. It then examines how deeply the reciprocal transactions of giving and receiving in society – or interdependent living – are implicated in the Buddhist faith.

The Culture of Giving in Myanmar fills a gap in research on Buddhist offerings in Myanmar, and is an important contribution to the growing field of Myanmar studies and anthropology of Buddhism.

Hiroko Kawanami is Senior Lecturer at the Department of Politics, Philosophy and Religion, Lancaster University, UK. She has extensive experience of working with the Buddhist community in Myanmar and is editor of *Buddhism and the Political Process* (2016), author of *Renunciation and Empowerment of Buddhist Nuns in Myanmar-Burma* (2013), and co-editor of *Buddhism, International Relief Work, and Civil Society*, and *Religions in the Modern World*, 3rd edition (2013).

RELIGIOUS STUDIES

BLOOMSBURY ACADEMIC

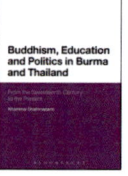
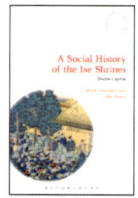

Also available from
Bloomsbury Academic
www.bloomsbury.com

ISBN 978-1-350-26730-5

www.ingramcontent.com/pod-product-compliance
Lightning Source LLC
Chambersburg PA
CBHW070638300426
44111CB00013B/2153